Medieval Andhra

Medieval Andhra
A Socio-Historical Perspective

ALPANA PANDEY

PARTRIDGE
A Penguin Random House Company

To order additional copies of this book, contact
Partridge India
000 800 10062 62
orders.india@partridgepublishing.com

www.partridgepublishing.com/india

FOR THE AWARD OF THE DEGREE OF

Doctor Of Philosophy

IN HISTORY

July 1998

DEDICATED TO MY PARENTS.

ACKNOWLEDGMENTS

I owe a debt of gratitude to several individuals and institutions for their help and encouragement in the completion of this thesis. In the first place, I will forever remain deeply to Prof. R. Soma Reddy, Department of History, Osmania University, under whose supervision I have completed the thesis. In spite of many engagements, he spared his precious time and gave scholarly guidance at every stage in the preparation of the thesis. His abiding interest in my work and concern for my well being were an invaluable source of strength and inspiration to me.

I wish to express my deep sense of gratitude to Prof. Bhanumathi Ranga Rao, Head, Department of History, Osmamia University, who has all along been helpful and encouraging.

I take this opportunity to express my heartfelt thanks for the inspirations that I received from my husband, Shri M. K. Mishra and my brother Shri Devender Kumar. I am especially grateful to my husband for providing me technical guidance while typing the thesis. I am also appreciative of my daughter, Shreya who showed immense patience and understanding during my research work.

I am greatly obliged to the University Grant Commission for awarding me the Junior & Senior Research Fellowship, which enabled me to complete the thesis.

I am obliged to the Osmania University Library, State Archives, Govt. of Andhra Pradesh, District Gazetteer Office, Govt. of Andhra Pradesh, Oriental Manuscript Library, Govt. of Andhra Pradesh, Salarjung Museum Library, Telugu University Library and the Govt. Public Library, Afzalgunj, for extending their Library facilities to me for the study.

I also thank Shri. Safdar Shafiq who translated the Persian records for my research work.

Finally, I express a deep sense of indebtedness to all the Scholars whose published works and opinions in the field have benefited me immensely.

CONTENTS

ABBREVIATIONS

A.R
: Annual Report on Indian Epigraphy.

Abbe Carre
: The Travels of Abbe Carre in India and the Near East, 1672-1674, Tr. Lady Fawcett, ed. Charles Fawcett, New Delhi, 1990.

Edgar Thurston
: Castes and Tribes of South India, vols. 7, New Delhi, 1975.

Francois Martin
: India in the 17th century-Memories of Francois Martin, 1670-1674. Tr. Lotika Varadrajan.

Gordon Mackenzie
: Kistna District Manual, Madras, 1883.

H. V.
: Hamsa Vimshati: Ayyalaraju Narayanmatya.

I.R. Hemingway
: Godavary Gazetteer, Madras, 1907.

Johan A. C. Boswell
: Nellore Manual, Madras, 1873.

Johan Fryer
: A New Account of East India and Persia, being 9 years Travels, 1672-1681, ed. William Crooke, Hakluyt Society, London, 1909.

Mc. Ms.	Mackenzie Manuscripts.
Narahari Gopalakistamha Chetty	Kurnool Manual, Madras, 1886.
Relations	Relations of Golconda in the Early 17th century: ed. W. H. Moreland.
S. S	Suka Saptati: Palavekari Kadiripati.
S. I. I.	South Indian Inscriptions.
Samuel Purchas	Purchas, His Pilgrims, Hakluyt Society, London, 1905.
Tavernier	Tavernier's Travels in India, ed. V. Ball, London,1889.
Thevenot	The Travels of Thevenot and Carreri, ed. S. N. Sen, New Delhi, 1949.
Thomas Bowrey	A Geographical Account of the Countries Around the Bay of Bengal, 1669-1679, ed. R. C. Temple, Hakluyt Society, London. 1905.
W. Francis	Gazetteer of the Anantpur District, Madras, 1905.

****

Chapter I

INTRODUCTION

I

Society means a community of persons living together and having common aims and interests. Society is a place where the custom and organization of civilized nation exist. The changes taking place in a society are termed as social changes. Social Changes can be defined as; "the significant alteration of social structure including consequences and manifestations of such structure embodied in norms, values, and cultural products and symbols."[1] Social change, rapid in some cases, slow in other, has characterized all societies,

---

[1]   Wilbert E. Moore, <u>Order and Changes</u>, New York, 1967, p.3

whether pre-historic, historic or modern. The causes for the social changes may be many and varied. Increase in the size of the group, alteration or diversification of economy, shift from nomadic to settled way of life, modification of the social structure, new emphasis in religious beliefs and practices, new philosophies, war and famine are among the phenomena associated with such changes. Frequently the political structure of a society has altered in the course of history.

The social changes in India grew in two stages, first through orthogenetic or indigenous evolution, and second, through heterogenetic encounters or contacts with other cultures or civilizations. The Indian society has microstructures and macro-structures existing within it. While the range of microstructure is limited to sub-caste, caste and village community, the range of macro-structure of the society is concerned with inter-regional and pan-Indian spread of relational networks.[2]

As far as the Andhra Desa of the 17th and the 18th century is concerned, both the internal and the external factors have played key roles in the changes in the social structure and in the final evolution of the culture of modern Andhra Pradesh. In this work an attempt has been made to visualize the changes brought in the microstructure of the Andhra society as a result of the orthogenetic and hetrogenetic factors. The

---

[2]   Yogendra Singh, <u>Modernization of Indian Tradition</u>, Jaipur, 1986, p.194.

arrival of the foreigners, both Muslims and Europeans, the subsequent defeat of the local rulers and the ascendancy of the foreigners in the political field of the region brought about alterations in almost all-social spheres of life.

The consequences of the global colonization by the Europeans, there arose a large demand for slaves. The slaves were required to work in their newly acquired colonies. This global change had its effect even on the population of Andhra Desa. During famines and wars, a large number of people were either voluntarily sold or captured by the Europeans, from the region, and taken away to far lands like Batavia, Pegu, and to the other south east Asian countries to work on farmlands.

Considerable work has been done on the various aspects of the history of Andhra Desa of the seventeenth and eighteenth century. There are some independent works done on the different aspects of the society of that period. While some works have dealt with the political and dynastic histories of the period, they contain only a few chapters of the contemporary society. However, no exhaustive work has been done on the society and the changes witnessed therein, during both the 17th and 18th centuries. The book dealing with the history of the Vijaynagar Empire, The Aravidu Dynasty of Vijayanagar written by Henry Heras, has only a few chapters on the prevailing social condition of the times and only signifies the dynastic history of the last rulers of the Empire. Similarly, the book of Prof. H.

K. Sherwani, The History of the Qutb Shahs, is basically a book on the political conditions of Andhra Desa under the Qutb Shahs. He has only lightly touched upon the society of those times. The First Nizam of Yusuf Hussain Khan, The Nizam by H. P. McAulliffe, and Eighteenth Century Deccan by P. Setu Madhav also fall into the same category. There are also some works on administration of this period. The work of J. F. Richards Mughal Administration in Golconda is an important work on Mughal administration in Andhra Desa. The book, Administration of Justice under the Nizam, 1724-1948, of Prof. M. A. Muttalib, and Misrule of the Nizam by D. Raghavendra Rao likewise give us some vital information on the administration of the Asaf Jahis. The Nizam: His History and Relation with the British Government by Henry George Briggs, and Nizam – British Relations deal with the ascendancy of the English in the political sphere of Andhra Desa. The work of Karen B. Leonard The Kayasthas of Hyderabad is mainly concerned with the social history of a particular immigrating caste, the Kayasthas, during the Asaf Jahi dynasty. It does not even mention the names of the other castes and communities. Though some of these books give us some information about the society of period, they do not say much about the common man and his lifestyle. The French in India, 1736-1816, by S. P. Sen and The Dutch Factories in India, 1617-1623, are books related to the economic and maritime activities of the foreign trading companies which cover the social history of the period though partially. However, there are a few articles like <u>Early History of the Dutch Factors of Masulipatnam and Petapoli</u> of T. I. Poonen, Masulipatnam and the North Coromandel region during the 18th century of I. P. Gupta, <u>Social Awakening among certain oppressed communities in Andhra during the Vijaynagar Period</u> of R. Soma Reddy provide some useful information regarding the social structure of the contemporary period.

But no comprehensive and systematic account of the society of the Telugu country, during the two centuries from AD 1600 to 1800, has so far been attempted. The impact of the consolidation of power by the Muslims and the presence of the Europeans, resulting in widespread changes in the social fabric of the region has been left untouched. The society of the Andhra Desa saw the emergence of new castes and communities and the decline of the traditionally strong upper castes and the rise of the lower castes. The new religions like Islam and Christianity contributed in the decline of the Hindu religious sects like Vaishnavism and Saivism that were flourishing hitherto. But the influences of the local village Gods and Goddesses and various other minor cults on the general masses continued to be the same. There were some positive and negative trends witnessed in the position of the women. The material conditions of the people witnessed changes. The intermingling of different cultures and traditions was the most visual impact of all the changes. The lack of research in the social field of the

17th and the 18th centuries, has prompted me to take up this study under the title **'Social Changes in 17th and 18th Century Andhra'** for my Ph.D. thesis.

The period under study, AD 1600-1800 constitutes a distinctive epoch in the history of Andhra Desa. The beginning and the closing years of this period and also the intervening period are characterized by momentous political, social and cultural changes. The decline of the Vijayanagara Empire, rise of the Nayakas, the expansion and disappearance of the Qutub Shahi kingdom of Golconda in 1688 AD, the subsequent short Mughal rule and the emergence of the Asaf Jahi Kingdom in 1724 A. D., its wars with the Marathas, Mysore, and its deep involvement with the British East India company, and the consequent secession of the Northern Sarkars in 1766 AD, and the Ceded Districts in1800AD to the British, left its scar on the society in the Andhra country.[3] By the mid seventeenth century, the boundaries of Golconda closely co-incided with the Telugu linguistic and cultural region which has found political expression today in the state of Andhra Pradesh.[4] The Qutb Shahi dominions in the times of Abdullah Qutb Shah included practically the whole of present Andhra

---

[3]   Sarojini Regani, The Shataka Literature, Source Material for "A Study Of The Social History of Andhra Pradesh, 15th-19th Century", in Itihaas, 1990, p.40.

[4]   J. F. Richards, Mughal Administration in Golconda, Oxford, 1975.

Pradesh. However, the Telugu-speaking district of Kurnul still remained under the Adilshahi sway.[5]

The local people had subsequently, started identifying themselves with the ruling dynasty. The Muslim population had also successfully assimilated itself in the local society. The society had almost become one with the Hindus accepting and celebrating the Muslim festivals and vice versa. Again, the centuries also saw the arrival of Europeans on the soil of Andhra for trading purposes. It culminated in substantial growth in trade and commerce of the region, with the exports touching an all time high record. Not only the urbanites but also the village community become prosperous. The economic prosperity along with the other causes resulted in the rise of the social consciousness amongst the masses. The social reform movements of Vemana and Swami Veerabrahmam, in the Andhra Desa, occurred during this period. On the other hand the eighteenth century saw the decline in the trading fortunes of the region. The economic prosperity of the seventeenth century was very short and the region saw the de-industrialization of the native industries in the very next hundred years.

Similarly, the end of the 18th century AD where the study closes is also characterized by notable political and cultural changes. It marks the end of the Muslim predominance and the consolidation of the English hegemony in Andhra. The

5   J. F. Richards, <u>Mughal Administration in Golconda</u>, Oxford, 1975.

closing years of the eighteenth century is equally important because it saw the exit of all the European trading companies except the English East India Company form the soil of the Andhra country. It was by the year 1800 AD that the English trading company came to establish its rule over the Ceded Districts and the Northern Circars of Andhra Desa.

II

<u>SCOPE:</u>

The scope of my thesis is confined to the Telugu speaking areas only. The terms Telugu country and Telugu Desa have also been used as synonyms of Andhra Desa. From the 17th to the 18th century the eastern Deccan region comprising of the state of Andhra Pradesh saw the disappearance of the old order on the social and political fronts. The emergence of new elements like the Zamindars or landlords and new castes with different values of life.[6] The unsettled condition during the decades of the 17th century after the disappearance of the Qutubshahi power, and the subsequent attempts of the Mughals in the early 18th century to restore order were the order of the day[7]. In the 18th century, the Mughal power had declined and the British were trying to administer

---

[6]   Sarojini Regani, p.41.
[7]   Bhalla Perakavi, <u>Bhadragiri Shataka</u>.

the country through the permanent revenue system and through the Zamindars on the East Coast.[8]

The scope of my work is to highlight the changes that took place in the social set up of Andhra Desa as a result of the establishment of the Muslim rule and the arrival of the European traders on the soil of Andha Desa in the 17th and 18th centuries. There was a tremendous alteration witnessed in the social, economic and religious fields of the Telugu speaking areas. The social hierarchy was troubled and the ancient religious order had been replaced by new and bold sects. There was also the entry of two international religions in Andhra Desa, which had positive & negative impacts on the people of the region.

III

<u>SOURCES:</u>

The Primary sources available for this thesis are principally epigraphic and literary. Of these, again, the contemporary literay works constitute the major portion of the sources available. However, these sources available are not uniform either region wise or period wise. As such only in some cases generalization has been made. Sometimes, the sources belonging to the period under study are not available. Hence, the sources belonging to the preceding

---

[8]   Adidamu Surakavi, <u>Ramalingeshwar Shatakam.</u>

and the succeeding period had to be utilized in view of the continuity of the changes indicated.

LITERARY SOURCES:

The contemporary literature is an important source of information. It throws considerable light upon the history of the society and the changes witnessed therein. It can be divided into five sub-categories:

i)   The Telugu literature
ii) The Muslim chronicles in different languages like Persian, Arabic, Urdu, etc., and the Royal Farmans.
iii) The Kaifiyats.
iv) The Travelers' Accounts.
v)   The administrative papers of the Dutch and the English East India Companies.

THE TELUGU LITERATURE

There is no history proper of the Kings, of the period under study, in the contemporary Telugu literature. However, there are poetical works in Telugu, which deal with the religious and social aspects of the kingdom. They are a significant source of information regarding the changes witnessed in the contemporary society as a result of the political and economic changes. They are a direct source of information about the life of the general public as they are not eulogical works but the work of a poet troubled by the ongoing changes in the Andhra society.

a) <u>HAMSA VIMSHATI:</u> This is a Telugu treatise written by Ayyalaraju Narayanamatya. It consists of stories told by a Hamsa or a swan to the mistress of the house. The swan protects the integrity of the house by narrating stories, total twenty in number, to the mistress of the house. The husband was out on a business trip and in the meantime the wife comes under the influence of the King who wants her to come to him. The lady is willing to leave but the swan succeeds in keeping her in the house by narrating interesting stories to her for twenty days. The husband returns in the meantime and the lady is saved from disgrace. The book is of special significance as it provides a large list of people who belonged to different castes and communities of Andhra Desa during the seventeenth century. In the various stories, the author mentions the four traditional castes and their various sub castes that existed in the nation under study. He refers to about one hundred and eleven castes and communities. The list of castes mentioned in Hamsavimshati includes agricultural communities, artisan and industrial communities, mercantile and trading communities, pastoral communities, dependent communities, entertainers, forest tribes, religious and foreign communities. However, some of the important castes in the society are omitted. Besides these, many other interesting details of social life are also given in the book.

b) <u>SUKA SAPTATI:</u> This book in Telugu was written by Palavekari Kadiripati. This book gives the information that is not found in the Hamsa Vimshati. Suka Saptati tells us about the agricultural communities and the other dependent communities. It also gives us informations about the Pariah caste or the untouchables and about their dependent castes. The various aspects of the society like the celebration of festivals, the superstitious practices, the different types of food eaten and the dresses of the people are described in great details.

c) <u>YAYATICHARITRA:</u> The writer of this book was Ponnaganti Telanganarya. It is a mythological poem consisting of the story of Yayati who was said to have descended from Moon, and his descendents were called Chandravamshis. It is a story of the Prince Yayati and his queens Devayani and Sharmistha. It is a poem in Atsa or pure Telugu without any Tatsam Sanskrit word, and is dedicated to the Zamindar Amin Khan of Patancheru. The author gives a fairly long account of Amin Khan's family, its position in field of diplomacy and public service and the general set up of the village society. The marriage customs, the dress and the ornaments of the bride and the other daily routine of the village life is beautifully described.

d) <u>SHATAKA LITERATURE</u>: The Shatakas are poetical works. They occupy a unique place in the social life and literature of the telugu speaking people. They normally comprise of hundred verses or a Shataka! Sometimes, it could be a little less or even more than a hundred verses. It seemed to have originated in the 11th century A. D.[9] Majority of the Shatakas are devotional, while quite a few are philosophical in their content. However, there are Shatakas that are either historical biographies or deal with historical events that took place during the lifetime of the poet. The Shatakas of the 17th and the 18th centuries have highlighted the changing pattern of the society due to the external changes. They lament the absence of the Hindu political authority to enforce the Varna Ashrama Dharma. Their absence was creating havoc in the Hindu society. There was anarchy everywhere and each caste was trying to outclass the other. The Sudras and the untouchables were being patronized and the learned men were living in poverty. They attributed all changes to Kali Dosham. The changes taking place in the Andhra Desa during the 17th and the 18th centuries are vividly reflected in the Shatakas of the contemporary period.

  i)   The <u>Shatakas of Chowdappa</u>, AD 1600-1630, relates to us the prevalence of the custom of child marriage and its resultant demerits. He has emphasized the

---

[9]   Diwakarla Venkatavadhani, <u>Andhra Vangmaya Charitra</u>.

importance enjoyed by the dancing girls and the loose morals amongst the Brahmanical priests. He was a Niyogi Brahmin and a Brahmin Karnam belonging to the Cuddapah district. Being a Niyogi and a Brahmin he boasts in his work that however clever and intelligent a ruler might be, he cannot carry on the administration without the help of the Niyogi Karnams. This emphasizes the dominance of the Niyogi Brahmins in the contemporary society, though on a much lesser scale.

ii) The <u>Kukkuteshwara Shataka</u> of Kuchimanchi Timmanna, AD 1690-1760, gives us an insight into the various aspects of the contemporary society. The poet belonged to Pittapur. He has described the chaos created by the chieftains in the coastal regions of the region and has criticised them. He has portrayed the attempt made by the Sudra community to rise in the social hierarchy.

iii) <u>The Ramalingeshwar Shataka</u> of Adidamu Surakavi, AD 1720-1785, narrates the difficulties faced by the priestly class due to the lack of the patronizing authority. This source gives us the information regarding the decline of the position of the forward castes. He was a contemporary of Kuchimanchi Timmanna and has written about the depredations of the Zamindars on the East Coast. The lawlessness on the coast can be assumed from his poem.

iv) The <u>Venugopala Shataka</u> gives us information regarding the material condition of the people. From it we also come to know that the administration was completely Mughalised and Persianised by the beginning of the 18th century.

v) The other important Shatakas of the period are the Bhalla Perakavi's <u>Bhadragiri Shatakamu</u>, the <u>Shatrusamhara Venkatachala Vihara Shatakamu</u> of Vaddikasula Venkanna Kavi, <u>Chandrasekhara Shatakamu</u> by Chandrasekhara, and <u>Simhadri Narasimha Satakamu</u> by G. Kurmanadhudu. All of the above mentioned poems deal with the contemporary events and highlight the changing social system of Andhra Desa.

vi) The <u>Vemana Shatakamu</u> of the social reformer, Vemana, also reflects the conditions of the contemporary society. Though his verses are mainly moralistic in nature, they reflect the evils present in the social system of the Andhra country. I have mainly referred to the English translation of his verses by C. P. Brown and have been published under the title "<u>Verses of Vemana</u>".

THE MUSLIM CHRONICLES

The books written by the contemporary Muslim writers are also an important source of information about the society of the 17th and 18th centuries. As such books are written by foreign immigrants to Andhra Desa, the language differs from person to person. While some have written in Persian, others have written the contemporary history in Arabic or in the local language Deccani-Urdu. As most of these works were written at the instance of the King or his nobles, the works are more or less eulogies. They praise their patrons and generally deal with only him or his period of rule. Hence one has to be very careful while utilizing their material as a source. The Hadiqatus Salatin, A.D. 1614-1644, by Mirza Nizamuddin Ahmed Saidi, Tarikh-i-Sultan Muhammad Qutbshah, popularly known as Tarikh-e-Qutbshahi by the Anonymous historian, Shahi Shadi by the Kayastha immigrant from north of India, Raja Girdhari Prasad, Tarikhe Zafrah, AD 1771-1772, by Girdharilal Ahqar are some of the Persian manuscripts that were followed by me while writing my thesis. Though they deal mainly with the political history of the Muslim dynasties of the period, they also contain some information, which is useful for the subject. They refer to the policy followed by the Muslim rulers towards the Hindus and the position of different religions in Andhra Desa. They furnish information about the building of the mosques. The lifestyles of the Muslim saints and their teachings can be gleamed from these works. The social history is also referred to in the Hadiqatus Salatin and the Shahi Shadi. The former book was written during the rule of Abdullah Qutb Shah, the Qutb Shahi King of

Golconda, at the instance of the well-known Peshwa of the kingdom, Shaikh Muhammad ibn Khatun. It gives us a fairly correct picture of the social life of the people, their superstitions, their rites and ceremonies, and the cordial relations that existed between the different sections of the population, chiefly the Hindus and the Muslim. It also gives us information about the foreign immigrants and the envoys to the Golconda kingdom. The traditional rituals and rites connected with the Muslim marriages are discussed in details in the Shahi Shadi of Lala Girdhari Prasad. Though it was written in commemoration of a royal wedding, it describes the ceremonies that the Muslim population generally followed in Andhra Desa.

The Urdu books like <u>Kulliyat</u> of Muhammad Quli Qutb Shah, the Urdu Mathnawis of Mullah Wajhi, namely, <u>Sabras</u> and <u>Behram and Gulandan</u> and <u>Mah wo Paikar</u> of A. Junaidi, and also the Hayathe Mahalaqa belonging to the year AD 1909 and written by Ghulam Samdani Khan Gauhar, were also referred to. These works are a storehouse of information regarding the social fabric of the region during the period under study. Though the Mathnawis are of a fictious nature, they do help in understanding the various customs and practices of the Muslim society of the 17th and 18th centuries.

FARMANS

The Farmans are another important source of information for the subject. A Farman is a mandate or an order issued by a Muslim monarch. They record various types of grants made to individuals, religious institutions, and the functionaries of those institutions. The Farmans and other documents of the Sultans of the Deccan are very rare. They are either lost to the ravages of time or are lying in the private hands. The Farmans of this period generally contain, a religious superscription, the seal or the sign manual of the monarch, the name of the administrative authorities entrusted with the execution of the Farman, a brief history of the case or the reason what necessitated the issue of Farman, the date and the Parwanagi officers under whose Parawanagi the Farmans were issued. The Farmans issued by the kings were often bi-lingual. The orders were written in Persian and also in Telugu, for the local population.

The study of these Farmans reveal that there was a genuine spirit of tolerance in the administration of the Suatans. The non-Muslims shared higher posts and they were honoured with titles and grants. Sometimes they were issued in more than two languages also. Some of such Farmans have the Marathi language too inscribed on them. They also show us the prevailing calligraphic work. I have consulted the English translations of the Qutb Shahi Farmans of the years 1406-1687 AD, and also the Waqai of the years 1660-1671 AD in the State Archives, Hyderabad. Similarly, the Newsletters in-between the years AD 1767 and 1799 provide us with vital information regarding the religious tolerance that existed during the rule of the Asaf Jahis.

THE KAIFIYATS

These are also known as the Mackenzie Manuscripts. They are infact a mass of village accounts that were kept by the village Karnam or the revenue officer. They are the digests of the village registers or Dandakaviles and the inscriptions, which were recorded and binded together. They contain information about the political, religious, social and economic conditions of the village, including the report on the contemporary events. The Kaviles that are literally hundreds in number were collected at the instance of Colonel Colon Mackenzie, an engineer in the East India Company battalion and hence these manuscripts are also known as the Mackenzie Collections or Manuscripts. However, these manuscript are more useful for the construction of the history of the Rayalseema area and to some extent the coastal areas. They are silent as far as the history of Telangana area is concerned. One has to be very careful while utilizing the material from the Kaifiyats as sometimes they are full of legends than real events. Some of the important Kaifiyats relevant to the period under study are the Srisailam Kaifiyat, the Kaifiyat of <u>Srikakulam Jilla</u>, <u>Kaifiyat of the Nidadavolu village</u> and <u>the Kaifiyat of the Amberpet village</u>, of the West Godavari District, the <u>Kaifiyat of Ganim</u> and the <u>Kaifiyat of Nivartisangam</u>, both from the Kurnool Taluq, the <u>Tadaparthi Kaifiyat,</u> the <u>Kaifiyat of the Ceded Districts or of Chantipalle, Bammayapalle, and Nekanampeta</u> and the <u>Kaifiyat of the Dasari Chenchus</u>. These Kaifiyats are from the A. P. Archives and also the Telugu University library. All of them give us the information on the religious conditions of the coastal regions of the Andhra Desa. The last Kaifiyat gives details about the change in the religious beliefs of the Chenchu tribe. Another important Kaifiyat is the <u>Guntur district Kaifiyat</u> that gives us the information regarding the fanaticism of the French company towards the Hindu religion.

THE TRAVELLERS' ACCOUNTS

The accounts of the Europeans, who visited the Telugu country during the period under study, also contain some basic information, regarding the subject under study. The different travelogues are an interesting source of social history as the Europeans have written down the day to day events. As every single incident was new and interesting to them, they have recorded all the happenings that they witnessed. However, some of the men have left behind accounts based only on heresy and had not cared to corroborate the facts.

Furthermore, they were not conversant in the local tongue and customs, and must have taken down things without going into the facts. Hence, it becomes very essential that one should take utmost precaution while dealing with the written accounts left behind by them. The Accounts of the three men that have been grouped under the title Relations are very useful for writing the history of Andhra Desa of the 17th and the18[th] century. An Englishman William Methwold, the Dutch official Antony Schoerer wrote the accounts, and the writer of the third account was most probably another Dutch official who has not written down his name. All the three men lived in the region in-between the years 1608 AD and 1622 AD Their accounts are published under the title "Relations of Golconda in the Early Seventeenth Century, A. D. 1608-1622" edited by W. H. Moreland published in the year 1931 in London. The social set-up of the kingdom, the religions conditions, the produce of the kingdom, the currency and the weights and measures have been described. Methwold is explicit about the social and religious condition of the population and gives an account of the clothes the people at work, the workers' emoluments, the rites observed at time of marriage and death and also other matters, which are both interesting and instructive.

The work of the two Frenchmen Jean Baptiste Tavernier and Jean de Thevenot have also proved to be good source for the structuring of the social history of the Telugu speaking regions. "Travels in India of Tavernier" is edited by V. Ball and was published in London in the year 1889 AD. Tavernier made several trips to the Qutb Shahi Kingdom. He visited Golconda thrice i.e. in 1638-1639 AD, 1657-58 AD, and the last one in the year 1662-63 AD. He is a very good source for knowing the life of the contemporary people in general. However, his enunciation of the events is sometimes faulty and incorrect. "The Travels of Thevenot and Carreri, 1666-1667" was edited by Surendranath Sen in the year 1949 and was published in New Delhi. The two travellers noted down the things that they saw. They write about the army, the rites and ceremonies observed by the people and their economic conditions. Similarly, "The Travels of Abbe Carre in India and the Near East, AD 1668-1671", edited by Charles Fawcett and published by the Hakluyt Society of London in the year 1903, gives us information about the local women and the Christian and Hindu religions of Golconda. He is very explicit when he writes that Catholics enjoy complete religious freedom in the capital city of the kingdom i.e. Haidrabad. The Abbe was a French missionary and he has written about the freedom of religious conditions in Golconda that goes on to speak volumes about the attitude of religious tolerance of the Golconda monarchy.

The book of Thomas Bowrey called "A Geographical Account of the Countries Around the Bay of Bengal, 1669-1679", edited by Richard Temple and published in the year 1905 by the Hakluyt Society at London, and the book of John Fryer named "A New East India and Persia, 1672-1681" which was edited by William Crooke and published by the Hakluyt Society, in-between the years 1909-1915 AD, give us information about the prevailing social conditions in the Andhra country. Bowrey in his account has narrated the social customs like early marriage and widowhood of the Hindu women and the Sati system. Fryer has written about the living styles of the immigrants like the Persians and the English who stayed on the coasts of Andhra Desa. He also gives us vital information about the Hindu and the Muslim women. The information regarding the different sects of Christianity followed by the Europeans has also been left to us by Fryer.

"The Diaries of Streynsham Master, 1675-1680, and other Contemporary Papers Relating Thereof", vols. I & II edited by Richard Temple, and published by the Hakluyt Society, London in 1911, is a very useful book that gives us precise information. Streynsham Master was the Governor of the English East India Company and hence the observations made by him and the points noted down by him are accurate to a great extent. His writings are mainly concerned with the economic conditions of the various European companies. However, at some instance he does describe the local conditions also. The account of another Frenchman, by name Francois Martin, is also very relevant in framing the history of Andhra Desa of Andhra Desa of the 17th century. It is called as "India in the 17th century-Memoirs of Francois Martin, 1670-1694".

Lotika Varadarajan has translated the book from French to English. The book of Abbe J. A. Dubois named "<u>Hindu Manners, Customs, and Ceremonies</u>" was edited by Henry K. Beauchamp and published in the year 1897 AD from Oxford. He was a French missionary who remained in India and roamed about the different parts of the country in-between the years 1792-1823 A. D. He described the marriage system of the Hindus and the absurdities of the widowhood. He also mentions the migrations of the Telugu speaking population to the Tamil lands and to Mysore.

RECORDS OF THE DUTCH AND THE ENGLISH EAST INDIA COMPANIES

These include the communications of the Dutch and the English trading companies, settled on the soil of Andhra Desa, with their headquarters in their motherlands. It also includes the correspondence that the various settlements had with each other in the Indian sub continent and also with their trading centers situated on the other foreign lands. The Dutch had their center at Batavia or modern Jakarta and the English centered primarily at Surat on the west coast of India. As such there is a lot of correspondence that is available to us. When the English established their head quarters at Fort St. George or the modern Madras, then the correspondence ceased in its intensity with Surat and increased with Fort St. George.

Though they are all basically administrative communiqués and not proper history, yet they throw considerable light on the different aspects of the trade and commerce of the region where they were located and had their factories built. They also deal to some extent with the different aspects of life led by the local people and also visualize the cordial relationship that exited within the different sections of the population. We derive information regarding the condition of the roads and the means of transport in the kingdom. They also deal with the nature and some important state official and their jurisdiction, the control they exercised on the trade of the different European Companies and the underhand manner by which they were able to get special privileges from the concerned governments. On the international plane they deal with the relation between Mughal power, the Deccan Sultanates, and the rising power of the Marathas.

The papers consulted by me include the District Records such as the <u>Godavari District Records</u> of the years in-between AD 1770 and 1835, the <u>Masulipatnam District Records</u>, dealing with the years in-between AD 1757and 1857 and are numbered as vols. 2891, 2892, 2893 and 2951. The vols. Numbered 3116, 3117 and 3119 of the <u>Nellore District Records</u>, and the volumes numbered 24521 and 3997 of the <u>Kurnool District Records</u> were also consulted by me. Besides these I also consulted the <u>Guides to the Vizag, Cuddapah and the Guntur District Records</u>. These District

Records give us information about the tribes, famines and the consequent migrations of people, the condition of women and also the religious conditions. The Godavari District Record gives us the vital information regarding the prohibition of the practice of Sati Sahagamana. The volumes of the <u>English Factories in India</u> edited by William Foster, in-between the years, AD 1618-1621, 1622-1623, 1630-1633, 1634-1636, 1637-1641, and 1655-1660 formed a very important source of information for my work. <u>The Letters to and from Fort St. George</u>, from the Records of Fort St. George, of the years 1684-1685, 1688, and1693-1694, and the <u>Calender of the Madras Dispatches, 1744-1755</u>, edited by Henry Dodwell and the <u>Press List of Ancient Records in Fort St. George</u> of the years AD 1765-1769, 1782, 1793 and 1795 give us insight into the life of the English officers and the rules and regulations passed to control their morality. They also tell us about some of the professional castes like the washermen, the merchants, the Dubashis and their relationship with their European masters. The high handedness of the English while dealing with the Telugu subordinates is very clearly sighted. I also consulted the English translation of the Duch papers. All of the papers mentioned above, were consulted by me in the library of the A.P. State Archives, Hyderabad.

EPIGRAPHIC SOURCES

During the period under study the epigraphic sources are very limited in nature. Unlike the local Hindu Rajas, the Muslim Kings were more interested in issuing Farmans than recording their orders and gifts on stone plaques or on pillars. However, whenever, the boundary of a village was defined or on order of gift made to the eminent people, it was done though the issue of inscriptions. One such grant was written down on copper and was issued during the rule of Muhammad Qutb Shah of Golconda. The script is Telugu and the inscription fixes the boundary of the Gunupundi village in the Bhimavaram district and contains inscriptions on both sides. It was dated Kalayukti Samvat Sravana 14, i.e. on a Sunday, in 1617-1618 AD. Some of the inscriptions were also issued whenever common people as made donations to the temples or to the Brahmins. The donees got them inscribed mostly on rocks.

Some inscriptions denoting the encouragement offered by the Qutb Shahi government official to the people to come and populate a village have been found. An inscription of the year 1691 AD from Pulivendhula, Cuddapah District, records the terms offered by the order of Muhammad Jafar to the merchants and the oil pressers to come and settle down in that village had been discovered. The terms include the exemption of taxes on certain articles of the village.[10] Another epigraph of the same district records the foundation ceremony of a village. According to this epigraph, when one Subbadasari at the instance of a local Qutbshahi officer established the village of Kottalapalle, a small fortress was built for the village. The area was cleared of the bushes, boundaries were fixed, the Ayagars or the village officials and the servants were appointed. On this ocassion he-buffaloes and sheep were sacrificed at the site.[11]

IV

CHAPTERISATION:

This thesis has six chapters. The first chapter is **INTRODUCTION**. It introduces the subject and contains its definition, scope, methodology and the evaluation of the sources.

In the second chapter **SOCIETY** the prevailing social conditions of region has discussed. The diverse society of Andhra Desa was divided into a number of segments. The two major components of the contemporary society were the followers of Hindu religion and the followers of Islam. The Europeans had entered the region but were very few in numbers. It deals with the various castes and sub-castes that were present in the Hindu society. The growth of new

---

[10]   S. I. I., vol.X, No. 770, p.404.
[11]   N. Venkataramanayya, Cuddapah Inscription, p.108.

sub-castes, the rise in the social consciousness of the lower castes, their subsequent disregard for the caste system and the degradation of the position of the upper castes has been pointed out. The attempts made by these various sub sects to come up in the social ladder have specially been highlighted. The impact of the new communities like Muslims and the Europeans on the Hindus and vice versa has been discussed. The increase in immigrants to Andhra and the flow of migrants also forms a part of this chapter. The changes that took place in the region, due to the diverse population, were of a considerable nature. There was birth of new castes due to the intermingling of the different peoples.

The third describes the **RELIGIOUS LIFE** that was prevailing in the Telugu speaking area. In this chapter the different religious followed by the people and the changes occurring due to the intermingling of Hinduism, Islam and Christianity, who were several have been discussed. The conversions of the Hindus to Islam and Christianity and the impact have also been shown. The relative positions of each religion and the importance of each had been described.

The fourth chapter is the **POSITION OF WOMEN**. The women constituted an important part of the society. However, the women were in no better condition. The evils like child marriage, dowry, Sati, divorce, Parda, polygamy, and lack of education was the cell of the day. Even the contemporary social reformers did not pay much attention to their lot. The changes in the life of the Hindu widows as a result of the steps taken by the Muslim authorities, for their upliftment, have been visualized.

The fifth chapter is discussed under the sub heading the **MATERIAL CONDITIONS**. The chapter has different sub heading like Housing, Furniture, Food, Dress, Ornaments and Cosmetics. The changes as a result of the interaction of three cultures have shown on all of them. The changes in the lifestyle of the natives due to the effect of foreign culture and style have been described.

The sixth chapter, **EDUCATION, RECREATION AND MEDICINE**, describes the changes that crept into these three fields and their positive impact on the Telugu people. Under the last chapter the different education system followed by the different sections of society is discussed. The entertainment enjoyed by the people has been highlighted. The arrival of the Muslim in the region brought in the Unani medicine. The existing Ayurveda of the Hindu and the Unani medicines benefited the population a lot. The English and the other Europeans brought in the modern medicinal benefits. The region enjoyed the benefits of all the three types of medicines.

Finally the major finding and the conclusions of the study are given at the end.

Chapter II

SOCIETY

The society of Andhra Desa witnessed wide-ranging changes in its system. While there was growth of the caste system into its mature form and the proliferation of Sudra caste into innumerable sub-groups, the region also witnessed the arrival of a number of immigrants who further increased the number of the sub castes. The caste the system which is a form of social differentiation is intimately connected with changes in material life and thereby the study of the growth of the caste system, can be made with the social processes and social changes. In this chapter the rise in the economic status and thereby the rise in the social consciousness of the various sub sects of the Sudra caste is dealt with. The decline of the upper castes in social hierarchy and the social reform movements questioning the supremacy of the upper caste is also discussed. The movement of immigration and migration, which was remarkable, has also been covered.

The society of 17th and 18th centuries Andhra consisted of two main sections namely the Hindu and the Muslims. The Hindus, being the original inhabitants of the region constituted the bulk of the population. The Muslims, though a minority in numbers, constituted the ruling elite. They held the reins of power in their hands. The Europeans came to Andhra Desa in the 17th century and formed the third important section. They never claimed to be a native of this region and continued to stay here as outsiders. They were very few in numbers but by mid eighteenth century, they came to acquire power over the region and became an important constituent of the local population. With the passage of time, while the Muslim started calling the region as their motherland, the Europeans never forgot the countries that they came from. They took pride in calling themselves as British, French, Danes etc.

SOCIAL STRATIFICATION:

The social stratification of the time was that the Hindus were divided amongst themselves on caste lines while the Muslims were divided on racial lines. There was no Hindu unity within the divisions of these two main religious.

While the lower Hindu castes were becoming socially more conscious and were trying to climb up in the social ladder, the Muslims were busy in claiming the superiority of one Islamic race over the other. However, there was no hostility between the two major sections of society i.e. the Hindus and the Muslims. The Hindus had finally accepted inferior position in the society and the Muslims thought of themselves as the superior partner who had to rile over the 'infidels'. Later on, in mid eighteenth century the European nations, especially the British and the French, came and took over the responsibility of riling over both the Hindus and the Muslims, with the defeat of the French, only the Britishers remained on the soil of Andhra.

Castes were groups with a well developed life of their own, the membership whereof unlike that of voluntary associations and of classes, was determined not by selection but by birth. The status of a person depended not on his wealth as in the classes of modern Europe, but in the traditional importance of the caste in which he had the luck of begin born.[12] The castes were ranked in accordance with their social status. The Brahmins occupied the highest position in the caste system. The rest of the castes came behind them. The Kshatriyas, the Vaishyas and the Sudras with their several sub castes followed them in the hierarchy. The untouchable castes, the Mala and Madiga, being the

---

[12]   G. S. Ghurye, Caste and Race in India, London. P.1.

pariahs of Telugu country occupied the lowest rank.[13] During the period under study. The age-old division of the Hindu caste system into four major castes came to be multiplied into hundreds of sub-castes.

The Europeans, who came to Andhra basically for commercial purpose, have mentioned some of these castes and subcastes of the Hindu society. They were foreigners, and hence, could not fully understand the Hindu social division. As such, different writers have given different numbers of the castes that were prevalent in the Andhra society of the seventeenth and eighteenth century. William Methwold, the English official, has written that the Hindus were divided into 44 sects.[14] The mention of 18 castes by the Dutch writer of the same period finds credulence with the mention of "Ashtadasa Varnalavaru" in the contemporary epigraphs.[15] Fourteen of these castes are mentioned in a copper grant of later Vijayanagara period. They include, Vyavaharikas, Panchalas or the five sects of the smiths, Kunbalikas or potters, Tantuvahins or weavers, Vastrabedakas or the cloth dyers, Tilaghatakas or the millers, Kurantakas or the shoe makers, Vastrarakshas or tailors, Devangas or the weavers, Perikalettevaru or the keepers of the Pack bulls, Gorakshakas or the cowherds, Kiratas or the hunters, Rajakas or the

---

[13] Madras Census Report, 1901, pp. 136-137.
[14] William Methowold, Relations of Golconda in the early 17th century, ed. W.H. Moreland, London, p.14.
[15] <u>Anonymous Relationd</u>, p. 70 and A. R., 1918, p.174.

washermen, and Ksavarkas or the barbers.[16] Probably the Vyavaharkas included farmers, priests, traders to make up the total number 18. Similarly, According to Mackenzie and Brackenbury, there were 30 castes and sub castes present in every village of Andhra Desa.[17] The contemporary books mention some of the castes and sub castes of the Telugu country but do not give us the whole picture of the society. They lack of an uniform view regarding the total number of castes makes it very difficult to mention all the castes and their subdivisions. The other problem is that the number of sub castes kept on growing into several new ones. However, the four major castes, of the period were same as mentioned in the ancient texts. The Brahmins, the Khstraiyas, the Vaisyas and the Sudras. These formed the four major castes of the period under study.

The hierarchy of the caste system was very rigid.[18] The economic prosperity of a man did not help in the upliftment of his caste. A poor Brahmin always came before a rich Komati in the hierarchical system. The caste of a man was decided by his birth into it and not by his prosperity or by any other thing. It was almost impossible to improve upon the caste one had been born in. One could only demand certain privileges of ones' caste. But it was seldom that it

---

[16]   A.R., 1918, p.174.

[17]   Mackenzie Manuscripts, vol.III.7 and C. F. Brackinbury, Cuddapah District Gazeteer, Madras, 1915.

[18]   William Methowold, Relations of Golconda in the early 17th century, ed. W.H. Moreland, London, p.14.

was accepted by the higher castes. This only resulted in caste conflicts.

However, social mobility was witnessed in the caste system with the rise in the social consciousness of the lower caste people. The time had definitely changed and several high castes' people had to work under the Sudra chief of the village. There are references stating that the Brahmins were taking to agriculture and to keeping accounts for the sake of subsistence. These were considered to be the profession of the Sudras, and the Brahmins had been forced to give up their ancient profession of teaching and priesthood. As the social position of the upper castes dwindled, that of the Sudra and the untouchables saw an upliftment. They took to new profession of learning and gaining knowledge.

BRAHMINS:

Of all the castes the Brahmins took the highest social position. The Telugu Brahmins were also called Andhras. They were divided into two great classes –Dravida and Gauda.[19] On the basis of the religious sects followed by them, they were subdivided into Vaishnavites and Smartas. The Vaishnavites were the followers of the Lord Viashnu and the Samartas the followers of Lord Shiva. They were further

---

[19] I. R. Hemmingway, <u>Madras District Gazetteers, Godavari</u>. Vol. I. p.51.

divided into Niyogi Brahmins and Vaidiki Brahmins. This division was based on the profession that each followed.

The Vaidiki Brahmins dedicated themselves to their religious duties, specializing in the Vedic lore and living peaceful lives, unmoved by external pulls and pressures. It was they, who were the custodians of the Vedic religion. Their daily routine started with the sunrise when they took oblation on the river chanting the hymns of god, collected fruits, grass, flowers and wood required for performing various Vratas and Yajnas. The study of Vedas was considered to be of utmost importance by them and the performance of sacrifices was equivalent to serving God.

The Barhmins remained a bachelor till they completed their studies. The student or the Barhmachari as they were called were dressed in Kulai or shirt and Panchelu or Dhoti. They carried books written on the palm leaves or Talapatra in a bag alone with them.[20] Methwold, while describing a Brahmins has written that they always wore a sacred thread over one shoulder and under the other arm. They always had a religious mark on their forehead and a few corns of rice dyed yellow in turmericke was stuck on it.

The Vaideki Brahmins mostly acted as priests in the temples, and performed the daily Pujas. Some of them even maintained the Homadundams in their own houses for the doing the daily worship. They usually led simple and peaceful lives, and strictly obeyed the rules of caste system.

---

[20] Ayyalaraju Narayanamatya, <u>Hamsa Vimahati</u>, p.152.

They were honest, reserved, pious and worked for the welfare of all. They were highly intelligent and experts in Vedas and Puranas. It can be said of them that they were the upholders of the Hindu religion. Their adherence to the religious duties always received appreciation from the Hindu kings. The kings always took it upon themselves to help the Brahmins. In 1601 AD, the Vijayanagara king Venkata I, granted a "Vilavaka" to the Brahmins. It says that the king was engaged in establishing Mahadevas i.e. Lingas of Siva, and Mahadevas i.e the Braqhmins.[21] However, some were also engaged in dubious methods for earning money. They befooled them, by drawing certain lines and writing the holy words on the floor and drawing the face of the woman to be called.

Some of them were well to do. They were the reservoir of knowledge or Gyana. The Vaideki Brahmins were well versed in the art of reading and writing, they knew the sacred text by heart. They guarded their knowledge very jealously and did not allow the other castes to even hear the recitation of the Holy texts. They were famous astrologers and palmists who predicted the "Sakunam" or the bad omen.[22] The Muslim and the Europeans were quite impressed with their knowledge of astronomy. The Brahmins were called and always consulted whenever the Muslim were going to doing something auspicious.

---

[21]   <u>Epigraphia Indica</u>, vol. I, No.39,p.272.
[22]   Methwold Relations, p.15, and <u>H.V.</u>

On the other hand, some of the Vaideki Bragmins were suffering from acute poverty. They had to undertake several jobs meet their household needs. They read 'Panchang', performed 'Puja' at homes, begged alms at the pilgrimage centers, sold the sacred thread, lifted the corpses and also accepted the left overs off the dead etc. Hari Varma, a Brahmin was so poor that he had to beg at the houses of the Kapus also.[23] Because of their poverty, they had to suffer problem at the domestic front. Their homes were always not peaceful due to the luck of basic necessities. Over a period of time, the Brahmins had become defunct in the knowledge of the scriptures though some maintained the hereditary occupation of gaining knowledge and defeating their opponents in the debates. They had lost the zeal to acquire 'Gyana'. [24]

The Niyogi Brahmins were those who had turned professionals and took interest in material activities like military, trade and agriculture. The compelling necessity to eke out livelihood, consequent to the changed political atmosphere may have forced them to take up secular activities. This section was known as Niyogi Brahmins. These people had taken up secular activities as their profession. A majority of them had names ending with words Raju, Arasu, and Preggada indicating their following other occupations, originally meant for other castes. These surnames were

---

[23] Ayyalaraju Narayanamatya, <u>H. V.</u> II, p.152.
[24] Palavekari Kadaripati, <u>Suka Saptati.</u>

adopted by the people of the priestly class who indulged in activities such as, landholders, ministers, poets, generals, accountants etc. The Niyogis had been very successful in their professional filed. They became Prime Ministers, Karnams, judges etc. under the Muslims and the English. Tirambak Rao was the Brahmin Bakshi of Golconda during Mir Jumla. He was a military officer also and latter was on given the title of Raja.[25] There was also Brahmin merchant named 'Pispott Ancata' in the court of the Golconda king who had a ship at Narsapore. [26]

Madanna and Akkanna were the two very famous and efficient prime ministers of king abdul Hasan, of the Qutabshahi dynasty. The appointment of these two Brahmins to the highest post of authority which was next to only that of the king's, speak volumes about their administrative brilliance. The seculer outlook of these two persons and their unflinching loyalty would have prompted the Muslim king to appoint them as his prime Ministers. Similarly, Kasi Viranna, a Brahmin, was said to be a very powerful and the richest merchant in the country. "He had in his hands all the English trade on the coast and neighbouring in the countries". [27]Viranna has been described

---

[25] Alexander Hamilton, <u>A new Account of the East India's, 1690-93</u>, London, 1811.

[26] <u>Records of Fort St. George, Letter to Fort St. George, 1684-85</u>, vol.III, Madras, p.191,

[27] <u>The Travels of the Abbe Carre in India and the Near East, 1672-1674</u>, ed. Charles Fawcett vol.III, p.361.

as the most powerful man in the country "who was now living at Madras". A Brahmin, Soma Sharma, by name, has been described as having gardens of betel nuts betel leaves and sold the products in the market. He had a number of cows, buffaloes, sheep etc. in his cattle shed. He also got the juice of the sugar cane taken out for the manufacture of sugar and jaggery.[28]

Many of them came to be employed as 'Karnams' under the new political regime of the East India Company. The Karnams got a special mention in the Telugu literary works of the time. In the Andhra sub division, while the Niyogi Brahmins were dominating as the Karnams, in the Telangana areas of the Golkonda kingdom, the Vyapari Brahmins were the Karnams.[29] Their appearance was so majestic that by looking at them one could understand that he was the Karnam. They were always dressed in silk robes, put a turban on the head, had a bag around his waist which had his stamp and was also used to store the money collected as taxes. The Brahmin Karnam loved to smoke a 'Chutta' or a cheroot.[30] He was the most unpopular man in the village. He was both feared and hated. The murders of accountants, though infrequent, are not unkown.[31] the Niyogi Brahmins had become so invincible that a rular could not do without

---

[28] <u>S. S.</u>
[29] <u>Andhra Sahityamu Sanghika Jeevana Pratifalamu</u>, p.318.
[30] H. V.
[31] Thurston and Rangachari, <u>Castes and Tribes of South India</u>, vol. IV.

them. However, clever a ruler might be, he held to take the help of these Niyogi in the administration of the region.[32]

The Brahmins had also been clever enough to work their way into favour with the great European power. They occupied the highest and most lucrative posts in the different administrative boards and Government offices, as well as in the judicial courts of the various districts. Infact there was no branch of public administration in which they had not made themselves indispensable. Thus it was nearly Brahmins who held the posts of sub-collectors, of revenue writers, copyists, translators, treasurers, of bookkeepers etc. it was especially difficult to do without their assistance in all matters connected with accounts, as they had a remarkable talent for arithmetic. "I have seen some men in the course of a few minutes work out, to the last fraction, long and complicated calculations, hich would have taken the best accountants in Europe hours to get through."[33] At Viravasaram, the Governor was a Brahmin named Surrena in between 1637-41.[34]

However, an important aspect of the Brahmin community was that there was no unity among the various divisions. The Niyogis were proud and aggressive and they resented any attempts on the part of the Vaidiki tocome

---

[32] Chowdappa's Shatakas.

[33] Abbe J. A. Dubois, <u>Hindu Manners, Customs and Ceremonies</u>, ed. Henry K. Beauchamp. P.276.

[34] William Foster, <u>The English factories in India</u>, 1637-41, p.68-69.

into the limelight.[35] The sectarian differences the Niyogi Brahmins, who were generally karnams, poets and some times ministers, and the Vaidiki Brahmins, who were generally priests or purohit and teachers, had become acute in the eighteenth century. The contemporary poets have also ridiculed any attempt of the Vaidiki Brahmin to their administration as ministers.[36]

KSHATRIYAS:

The Razus stood high in the social scale. They claimed that they were Kshatriyas. They used to wear the sacred thread, and had Brahmanical Gotras. They kept their womenfolk under seclusion or Gosha. The women were made to remain behind Parda very strictly. They never came outdoors. The Kshatriyas declined to eat with the other non-Brahmin castes. They were divided into the three clans of Surya or sun, Chandra or moon, and Machi or fish.[37] During the period under study, the Razus were chiefly employed in cultivation. They had given up their traditional occupation of fighting the enemies and ruling over the areas. Though some of them still held small principalities under them and also waged successful wars. However, most of them had lost the valour for which their ancestors were famous. An

---

[35] Adidamu Surakavi. <u>Ramalingeshwar Shatakam</u>.
[36] Koochi Manchi Timmanna, <u>Kukkuteshwara Shataka</u>.
[37] I. R. Hemmingaway, p.51.

inscription of 1605 AD refers to the achievements of the Matli chiefs' Ellamaraja and his son Anantaraja against the onslaught of the Muslim invaders.[38] They belonged to the Kshatriya clan and were under the Vijayanagara King, Venkataraja, who had the Golconda King and driven them out of Ahobilam. However, the contemporary writers spoke contemporary of them. The Venugopala Shataka refers to them as Rachavaru and laugh at them saying that though these people call themselves as Kshatriyas they are incapable of facing the enemy in the battlefield. They wasted their time surrounded by their companions who also belonged to the same caste. They acted as their advisor and often misdirected the prince by giving him wrong advice.[39] The European acconts are silent as far this community is concerned which shows their lack of any important position in the society.

VAISHYAS:

The Vaisyas were the third division of the caste system. The main profession followed by them was trade and commerce. In Andhra Desa, the Komatis claimed that they were from the Vaishya caste. The sub sects of the Sudra caste who had taken to trade and commerce as their occupation also started claiming Vaishyahood. During the period, under Study, the Vaishyas had accumulated vast wealth and

---

[38] Inscriptions of Andhra Pradesh, Cuddpah, vol. II, p.244.
[39] Anonymous, Venugopala Shataka,

were enjoyed greater privileges and respectability. In order to immortalize their name and win divine grace, they made huge donations to temples. An inscription dated 1609 AD, records a gift of seven gold pinnacles or Kalasa for the big Gopura of the Viranarasimha temple at Diguva-Tirupati, and of two fly-whisks, and an umbrella of white silk with a gift Kalasa over it, made by some merchants of Aravid, for the merit of 150 headman or Nagarasvamins of their community.[40] An inscription of the seventeenth century gives us the names of the various Gods of the Vaisyas. They were Gauresvara, Nagaresvaradeva and Kanyaka Parameshwari.[41]

They also become rich with trade transaction with the European merchants. Many of the poor Vaishyas accoumulated great wealth as a result of this. They were also very hard working and were very shrewd in their business. The English records describes them as "being poore and beggarly fellowes, have in shorte time raysed themselves to great wealth and riches."[42]

The foreign travelers, who visited Andhra, portrayed the nature and character of Vaisyas in their works. Tavernier, the French visitor did not seem to have had a good impression on them. He says, "these Banians are in business a thousand times worse than Jews, and more cunning than they in all

---

[40] <u>South Indian Inscription, vol.X</u>, No.495, and A.R.No.387, 1926

[41] <u>Annual Reports on Indian Epigraphy</u>, 1918-21, No. 1172, 1918, p.174.

[42] William Foster, <u>E. I. C. 1630-33</u>, p.16.

kinds of dodge and in malice when they wish for revenge".[43] They were very shrewd in their profession. It was seldom that they had a bad bargain from a business deal. They were also very miserly, when it came to spending money and were hard taskmasters.

The Komatis were the great trading and money-lending caste of the Telugu country, and were not popular. They called themselves Vaisyas. They wore the sacred thread and claimed to have 102 'Gotras'. In the late 18th century, some of them adopted Vedic rites at their marriages and funerals in place of the Puranic rites, which were traditional with them. But on the other hand their Gotras were not Brahmanical and they followed the Dravidian rule of Menarikam in their marriages. They were subdivided into the Gavaras, Kalingas, and Traivarnikas. These sections neither intermarried nor dined together and the last of whom differed from the other as they followed the Brahmanical doctrines very strictly.[44] The Gavaras were in majority.

The Europeans have mentioned them as 'Comits' or 'Commity'.[45] Some were "shopkeepers selling all sorts of grain, vegetables, spices, butter, oil, and other similar articles." It was only the lower ranking Komatis who kept shops; the rich ones did big business with the European companies. The Hamsa Vimshti mentions the prevalence of

---

[43] Tavernier, <u>Tavernier's Travels in India</u>, Vol.I, p.111.

[44] I. R. Hemmingway, op.cit.,pp.54.

[45] Abbe Carre, op.cit., p595.

Vaishyas in Andhra Desa. They had good houses, cattle, and servants to serve them.[46] Some of them were also engaged in the carpet trade. They, on their own or through their servants, collected the different types of clothes from the weavers by going around the kingdom. Some were also engaged in the money transaction and gave loans on gold pieces. They had a very sound knowledge of ascertaining good quality of metal and no body could fool them. The common man took the advice of Komatis while purchasing gold.

The Komatis did not take the meat of any animals and ate the diet similar to the Brahmins.[47] They were all vegetarians. They also copied the ceremony of washing themselves before taking their food.

SUDRAS:

This was the fourth caste of the Hindu caste system. They formed the majority of the people residing in the Telugu-speaking region. The general profession of the Sudras was tilling of the land. However, they were a highly divided caste. Each of these sub-castes specialized in a particular occupation. There was a continuous friction between them regarding the superiority of one over another. Some of the caste and the sub castes have been mentioned in the

---

[46] S. S.
[47] Methwold, op.cit., p.16.

contemporary Telugu book called 'Hamsa Vimshati'. The following castes are some of those that have been mentioned in it.

1. Agriculture Castes:	Kapu or Reddy, Velama, abd Kamma
2. Pastoral Communities :	Golla or Gopalaka i.e. the shepherds, Jalagari, Besta or the fisherman and Boya or the Palanquin bearer.
3. Artisan Communities :	Panchanamvaru, which included Kammara, Vadrangi, and Kasevaru or Vadasale, Gamadla, Pinjari, Kancharas, Kummaras, Upparas, Agalasa, Tellakoka-battulu, Chitrakara, Jogata-weaver, Jandra-acertain tribe of weaver, Vane-Banian caste, Vannegattu- engaged in painting, Satuni-who wove sack cloth.
4. Service Communities:	Rajaks, Kshauraka, Katika, Katipapalu, Medara, Idige, Talari,Bheri, Mashti, Jetti, Chipe-tailor, Chatra. Charmakarmulu.

5. Trading Communities:	Telika,Balija, Komati, Kamchi Kavallavaru, Perika, Ganugula, or oil pressers.
6. Priestly Communities:	Jangalu, Teranatakapu, Janagalu, Talakrimdu, Ramagovindulu, Gorada, Jogulu, Pairagulu, Jatadharulu, Avadhutalu, Paramahamsalu, Sannyasulu, Valandulu, Ekadamdulu, Ekangulu, Tridamdulu Vanaprasthulu, Digambarulu Gomukhulu, Niyamasthulu Urdhvabahulu Satani Sivasttulu Tambala, Yogulu, Jaina, Viramushti, Kali, Mailari, Parasalu.
7. Dependent Communities:	Pinchukuntulu, Bavinis, Runjalu,Pambalas, Budbudke Vaitalika, Vamdimagadhulu, Bhattu, Chandala, Matangulu-of Mala caste, Mamdapichchulu, Kommuri Dasallu, Taviru Dasallu, Suddulu, Kamallu.

8.	Entertainers:	Parihasakulu, Suta Nataka, Bogamvaru, Dommari, Bommalatavaru, Vipravinodinulu, Palanativirulu, Indrajalika, mahendrajalika Hastalaghava, Konanguluo-buffoon, Bhaliya.
9.	Miscellaneous:	Nasidavaka, Malneri, Piddemvaru, Chatiki, Srugalaka, Jatikarta, Domini, Sevaparulu, Padigevaru, Valagamda.
10.	Foreigners:	Parangulu, Ingilisulu, parasulu, Turaka, Odde, Ghurjsra, Gauda Misra, Parasulu,
11.	Untouchables:	Malas, Madigas
12.	Tribes:	Chenchu, Boya, Gonda, Yanadis, Savaras, Kolis, Erukalas, Venkari-a gypsy tribe, Patra-akin to Boyas

Some of the important Sudra castes have been discussed below.

Kapus:

The Kapus or Reddis, were landowners by occupation. They were among the most respected of the non-Brahmin bodies. The Kapus had totemiatic subdivisions.[48] The different sub-sects of the Kapus were Panta, Motati, Pedakamti, Are, Kammas, Velama, Konda, Adi, Gona, and Konide.[49] They were a prosperous caste. They dressed up nicely, employed servants and other domestic help in their household. Their wives enjoyed considerable freedom. Most of them were landowners. Some also worked as workers on the fields, as planters, builders of dams, diggers of wells etc. However, the life of the poor farmers was not always gay and carefree. The agricultural practices were very backward and stereotyped. Whenever the rains failed crops were destroyed over large areas. They were forced to leave their homes behind and move in search of better areas. During these bad days, the land owning families were forced to turn into labourers on the land of other for subsistence. They would suffer from deficiency, diseases and malnutrition during those days.[50]

Velamas:

The Velamas were said to have migrated from North but in course of time they got accustomed to the local customs

---

[48] I. R. Hemmingway, p.55.
[49] H.V., Canto, IV, V.136, p.237.
[50] Sir Thomas Munro, <u>Summary of the Ceded Districts</u>, pp.10-11.

and adopted them. Though in earlier days they were a part of the Kapu clan, later on they developed into a separate sub caste of the Sudra caste. In the 'Rangaraya Charitra' we find mention of the Velamas. It describes the Bobbili war

between the French and the Velamas. The latter lost the war and massacred their ladies and the name of adherence to honour. This ancient practice of the Velama chief is said to have French soldiers.[51] By this time there were many Velama principalities whose were called the Nayakas. Some of the famous Velama Nayakas of the time were those of the Kalahasti, Bellamakonda, jataprolu, bobbili, Velugodu principalities.

Kammas:

The Kammas were a cultivating caste. Like Velamas they too become a separate land holding caste of the Sudra clan. Some of them claimed that they were originally Kshatriyas. They were subdivided into the Kavitis, Eredis, Gampas or Gudas, Uggams and Rachas, who would eat in each other's houses and inter-marry. They kept their women strictly under Gosha or in seclusion. They were a proud race and never allowed their women to come out of the compound.

---

[51] Dittakavi Narayana Kavi, Rangaraya Charitra.

They practiced strict exclusiveness and the women remained always indoors.[52]

PANCHANAMVARU:

They were the five smith class who claimed to have originated from the God Vishwakarma and his five sons.[53] Their guild called variously as Panchanamvaru or Panchadulu might have continued during the period under study. Besides attending to the general public, they also helped in the construction and repair of temples, chariots, making and repairing the temple ornaments, supply of vessels, and in the making of images. They had, during the Vijayanagar Kings, asserted for themselves certain temples honours and privileges, especially on occasion of temple car festival. They got such privileges as coming in front of chariots and offering puja by mounting on the chariots, in their traditional dress, etc.[54]

They had become economically prosperous and to come up in the social ladder they donated various items to several temples. In 1619 AD, a man from the Vishwakarma Kula donated land for the upkeep of a perpetual lamp in the

---

[52] Thueston & Rangachary, Castes and Tribes of South India, vol.III.

[53] A. R. E., No. 804,1919.

[54] Dr. R. Soma Reddy, Social Awakening Among Certain Oppressed Communities in Andhra during the Vijayanagar Period, South Indian History Congress, Quilon, 1988, p.75-80.

temple of Chennakesava of Mahadevicherala.[55] They were becoming popular as belonging to the Vishwakaramakula or Vishwabrahmins sect. In 1581 Venkatayya of Dommaragidda grama, and of the Vishwakaramakula got a gift of land in return for the construction of a tank and the image of God Hanumantha.[56]

Methwold, the English official during the seventeenth century has called them as the 'mechanic trades', and says that "the carpenters masons, turners, founders, goldsmiths, and black- smith are all one tribe".[57] The Agsala or the Gold-smith constituted the most important sub-division of the Panchanam community. They were one of the twelve village Ayagars. Locally theywere also knows as the Kamsalis. The Kasevaru or the Silpi, an important sub-division of the Panchanam community, were another important caste that rose to prominence during this period. Their main profession was stone cutting. The Kammaras or the black smith was the caste that took up the profession of making tools, implements and wares of iron. It constituted the prime sub-caste of the Panchanam community. The Perusomula Kaifiyat for instance, says that the Kammaras were considered superior to the other four sub-division of the Panchanam community.[58] The Kancharas or the Brass-workers also formed a part of the Panchanam community.

---

55 <u>S. I.I</u> X, No. 756 and A. R. No. 579, 1909.
56 <u>Annual Reports on Indian Epigraphy</u>, No. 133 of 82.
57 Methwold, op.cit., p.19.
58 Mackezie Manuscripts, <u>Perusomula Kaifiyat</u>, V.99.

The Kancharas seem to have prepared their wares and sold them during the festivals and fairs. That their services were significant to the society is revealed by the fact that they were at times given tax-remissions. An inscription of 1645 AD, says that chief Venkatapatinayaningaru of Madala Gotra remitted all taxes and tolls payable by metal-dealers (Kanchara) that sold their wares in Srigiri during festivals and other days.[59] The Vadrangi or the carpenter formed the last but not the least important sub sect of the Panchanamavaru community. With the increase in the building of houses and in the use of furniture, as a result of the Anglican influence their importance, increased manifolds in the eighteenth century.

Kummaras or Potters:

The Kummaras or the potters were the other sub caste of artisans during this period.[60] As a caste, they made items required by all the inhabitants of the village. They made the pots and other articles needed by the people to store water, grain for cooking, etc. As the manufacturing of the most important requirements, they must have enjoyed considerable respect and a better position in the society. At times they were for their services, through land grants. They took their post and other items to the fairs or 'Santa' during

---

[59] V. Rangacharya, <u>Topographical List Instruction From the Madras Presidency</u>, No. 482, II 46 of 1915, p.958.
[60] Mackenzie Mss., <u>Perusomula Kaiiyat</u>.

Sankranti festivals. In the three days fair their products are sold so fast that they regret for having brought very less quantity of the pottery items.[61] In the other Telugu work, their art of making the pot is described.[62] The potter was also one of the twelve Ayagars of the village.

Upparas:

The Upparas were the diggers of well and also constructed the houses. They were also involved in the manufacturing in the manufacture of earth salt.[63] They also lifted the silt from the rivers made it viable for shipping once again.

Salevaru:

They were the weavers' caste, which prospered a lot during the period under study, because of the trade connections with the European countries. This period witnessed the division of Sales into various sub-sects like Devangas, Togata-Kulas, besides Padmasale, Pattusale, Swakulasale, Kurni-sale and Kanchu-sale. While the Padmasale specialized in coarse weaving, the Pattusales confined their activities to silk weaving and superfine cloth weaving. The Devangas produced pure cotton cloth, the Jandras specialized in

[61] S. S
[62] H. V
[63] C. F. Brackenbury, Cuddapah District Gazetteer, 1915, p.82.

weaving long cloths. The Goddess Yellamma was the chief deity of the Padmasales. Goddness Renuka was prayed by all the sub-sects. There was professional rivalry between the various sub sects and we find the Devangas standing up against the Sale caste weavers regarding the paying of alms to the Viramushtivallus.[64] Their art of making thread is described in the <u>Hamsa Vimshati</u>. They paid tax on the weaving loom that was called as Maggari.

Chippe:

Another name of this clan was Mera. They were the tailors and have been mentioned in the Hamsa Vimshati. They were in great demand by the Europeans who needed clothes to be stitched. They also resided in the factories. Sometimes, as many as five or six were kept in employment by them. they have been said to their clothes for wearing under their own supervision and has been made of their stitching the pillow covers also.[65]

Mangals:

They were the barber caste. Their main job was the shaving work. They also played music and the Mangala Vadiyam in temples and during marriages. Their association

---

[64] Godavari District Records. 946/B, pp.617-19.
[65] William Foster, ed. E. I. C. 1630-33, p.231.

with the marriage along with Brahmins and the gold smith gave them certain amount of respect. They claimed equality with Brahmins and called themselves as Nai Brahmins.

Their women acted as midwives during child delivery. They were generally ignorant women and employed barbarous method while acting as midwives.[66] The men of the Mangala caste also acted as surgeons and performed some operations on the patients. The expertise of the Hindu barber in surgery had reached even the shores of England. In a letter dated 20th Feb.1663, the Court of Directors of England wrote to the officials at the Fort St. George requesting them to send few "Gentue Barbers" to the islands of St. Helena.[67]

Gollas:

They were also known as the Yadavas. They were herdsmen.[68] As they were handling cattle, some of them also acted as Pujaris in temples where animal sacrifices were performed. There existed sub-divisions within the Golla community. They were Yakari Gollalu, Narra Gollalu, Patte Gollalu, Pedapotu Vandlu and Patra Gollalu.[69] Some of the sub-sects like Erragollalu and Beerannalu specialized in the recitation of Golla Suddulu or story of the medical period.

---

[66] Thurston and Rangachari, op.cit, vol.IV

[67] Thomas Bowrey, p.9.

[68] C. F. Brakenbury, op. cit., p.80.

[69] I. R. Hemmingway, op. cit.,.

The shepherds roamed from one place to another in search of green pastures for their sheep and goats. To escape from the heat the Gollas used heavy rugs while taking their cattle out to graze.[70] Some of the Gollas could read and write. They entertained the people by reading from the Katamraju's stories and by dancing and singing on the Sri Krishnaleela songs. They performed the 'Roopachitrama' and performed on 'Tabla', and on the musical instruments made of leather and flutes made of bullocks' horns,etc. During Sankranti festival the villagers organized fairs where the different artisans came and sold their produce. The Gollas too went to the fairs and their goats and sheep. These animals were in great demand then as the people who wanted to appease her with their offerings sacrificed them to the Goddess during the festivities.[71]

Kurumas:

Kurumas were another important pastoral caste, who were shepherds, goat herders and blanket-weavers. They traced their descent from the tribal God Mallana.[72]

---

[70] H. V., op. cit.
[71] S. S.
[72] Sirajul Hasan, Castes and Tribes in Nizam's Dominions, p.362.

Balijas:

Their main profession was and commerce. They added "Settis" to their names, which showed their supremacy over other castes in trade. The sub-sects of the Balijas indicate the professions pursued by them. some prominent sub-division were Gajula Balija, Gandhamvallu, Kavarai, etc. They proved a much tough competitor to the Vaishyas in trade and commerce. They had their own guilds to protect their interests. They even became a political force in the Vijaynagar empire. However, in the 17th & 18th century they lost their hegemony in trade as a result of the mercantile activities of the British. As such they had to give up their caste professions of trading in Kumkum, Sandal, Bangles etc. They were forced to take to agriculture but faced tough competition from the Kapus and Velamas on the agricultural lands.

Chakali:

They have been mentioned in the Hamsa Vimshati as taking the clothes from the Kapus housewife for washing.[73] The European merchants realized the importance of washermen and when they established their factories at different places on the coast of the Golconda kingdom, they made it a point to have a 'dhobi' in each of their factories. The

---

[73] H.V.

'washers' were allowed to stay in the areas of the Europeans. The foreigners built houses for the dhobhis and their family in the precincts of the company. They were very much in demand as they washed the clothes after dyeing which were being shipped to Europe. Sometimes, these people played cunning and while washing added 'Chunam' to whiten the clothes. This was bad for the clothes and spoilt them. This was disallowed by the Governor of Masulipatnam and fearing him they fled from Masulipatnam.[74] They were in great demand among the competing European settlements. They were offered inducement for their permanent service. The washers or the 'dhobhis' could not be induced to go to Petapoli from this palce i.e Masulipatnam "through the great employment they receave heer from the Dutch, Danes and Moores."[75] They were also very useful in determining the quality of the cloth. They got up early in the morning, had their food and took the clothes to river banks or to same water spot to wash and clean them.

Perikas:

The Perikas were a small cultivating caste. The name means a gunny bag, and the caste were originally gunny-bag weavers. Their social position is similar to that of the Kapus

---

[74] Records of Fort St. George, Letters to Fort St. George, 1684-1685, vol. III, Madras, 1917, p.5.
[75] William Foster, op. cit., p.a235.

and Kammas, whom they resemble generally in character and customs. It is noted in the Census Report of 1891, that "the Perikes claim to be a separate caste, but they seem to be in reality a sub-division, and not a very exalted sub-division, of Balijas, being infact identical with Uppu Balijas".[76]Their hereditary occupation was carrying salt, grain etc., on bullocks and donkeys in Perikes or packs.

Telikis:

The Telikis were the oil-mongers. They are summed up in the Madras Census Report, 1901, as "Telugu oil-persser caste". They were also known as Ganiga or Gandlavaru. It was basically an industrial community. They had to pay a tax on oil collection. It was called Gangari.

Idigas:

The Idigas or Indras were the Telugu toddy-drawing caste.[77] They were largely employed in toddy drawing, though some were cultivators. They occupy a low position in the social scale. The Idiga's special god was Kattumai. They must have been in a prosperous position during the period under study. The toddy was regarded as a whole some drink in those days. It was taken by all and sundry. Tavernier, the

---

[76] Thurston, op.cit., vol.VI, pp. 191-2.
[77] I. R. Hemmingway, op. cit, p.57.

contemporary French traveler, has written that the demand for Toddy was very high and several donkeys carrying the drink from the outskirts of the Hyderabad city, daily, could be seen. Even the Europeans found its effect to be cool in the hot summer month.

Gamallas:

The Gamallas were originally supposed to be Idigas. As they bettered themselves they separated from that caste. The wealthier of them are toddy and arrack shop-keepers, but the poorer members of the caste drew toddy like the Idigas. Some of them also acted as servants to the Kapus.

UNTOUCHABLES:

These were the 'Pariah' caste of the Andhra Desa. They were the fifth group in the Hindu caste system and they were a world in themselves as they were divided into a number of sub castes. They stayed outside the village and any person touching them by mistake washed his body immediately. They did not have any contact with the villagers and mostly lived by themselves in their separate quarters. They made the shoes worn by the Muslims and the sandals for the Hindus. They removed the skin from the dead body of the animals and utilized it for various purposes.

Malas:

The Malas were the great agricultural labourer class.[78] They were split into endogamous sub division, the Kantes, the Boyas or Sadur Boyas, the Payikis and the Mala Dasaris and Jangams. The Mala Dasaris were the caste priests of the followers of the Vaishnava sect while the Mala Jangam offered priestly services to the saivite Malas. The payikis were sweepers by occupation. The Malas ate beef and were consequently, almost at the bottom of the social scale. They were not allowed to enter the Hindu temple; and no other caste, not even excluding the Madigas would eat in their houses.

They polluted all Sudra castes by touching them or entering their houses, and a Brahmin by even approaching him. The ordinary barbers would not work for them. the ordinary washermen did not wash their clothes. But if the clothes have first been given a preliminary soaking them they accepted to wash their clothes. They wove coarse while cotton fabrics, which was usually worn by men. While their women spun the thread from the local cotton, the men did the weaving. The Kapus provided the cotton for the clothes that was women for other castes. They employed the Mala women for spinning the thread at regular wage and also the men for weaving it into cloth. At some temples of Andhra Desa like at Vanavolu, in the Hindupur taluk of

[78] ibid., p.58.

the Anantpur District, the Malas acted as the Pujaris. At the temple of Rangaswami, the 'Pujari' or the priest was a mala. The temple was frequented by the upper castes also but the Puja was done by them while the Mala Pujari stood aside for the time.[79]

Madigas:

The Madigas' traditional occupations were tanning and shoe making.[80] They were the leather working caste of the Telugu country. They were subdivide into the occupational classes of Madiga Dasaris who acted as priests, Madiga Payikis who acted as sweepers, the Kommalas who blew horns and the ordinary Madigas who followed the profession of tanning and shop-making. These sub castes did not dine together or intermarry. The Madigas were much despised by other castes because they were leather workers and ate beef and even carrion. They occupied the same low social position as the Malas.

Bavanilu or Paninindlu or bainedu are the Madiga musicians performing the rituals to the Goddess. [81] Some of them known as Pambalavar used to play music on a musical instrument called Pamba praising and singing abot play music to the goddess. They would sing the dofferent

---

[79] W. Francis, <u>Gazetteer of the Anantpur District.</u>
[80] I. R. Hemmingay, op. cit., p.60.
[81] ibid.

stories of encomiums of their goddess, Ankalamma, the origin of the Mata, etc. Anthore subsect of the Madigas was Kommuvaru, who used to king Katamaraju Kathalu and Ganga Kathalu while going around the village. Mala Dasaris used to narrate the stories of the Pandavas and entertain the public of different villages.[82]

TRIBES:

A large number of tribes existes in the forests of Andhra Desa. They had their own dialects and social customs and traditions. Some of them like the Chenchues had started to take an important part in the village life whereas the Koyas had still not got accustomed to the settled life of the village and to the life style of the prinicipal castes of region. This class of men formed the sixth group of people in the Andhra Desa.

Koyas: The Koyas were tribals founds in the numerous parts of the country. Their language was called Koya. Most of the men, however, could speak Telugu, though the women knew little but their own vernacular. The_Koyas were looked upon with a respect by the Hindus of the plains, but are held to pollute a Brahmin by touch and the other non-Brahmin upper castes by entering their kitchens. But the Koyas, like other hill tribes, had no respect at all for Brahmins or Hindus merely on account of their caste. The

---

[82]   S. S., Canto V, 414 & 415, pp.209-210.

Koysa were chifly engaged in agriculture. Some of them reared silk worms and sold it to the manufactures of carpets. They excited admiration by their truthfulness. Tattooing was common. It was considered very important for the soul in the next world that the body should have been adequately tattooed.

Hill Reddis:

The hill reddis or Konda Reddis were a caste of jungle men, who resembled the Koyas in some of life. They talked a rough Telugu. They lived by shifting or Podu cultivation. Professed to be both Saivites and Vaishnavites. They employed Brahmin priests at their funerals.[83]

Chenchus:

The chenchus were a semi wild, innocent, inoffensive hill tribe living on roots honey, wild fruits and game.[84] They were subdivided into various groups like the Golla-Chenchus, Yanadi-Chenchus and Dasari-Chenchus. They were further divided into four endogamous groups. Their main occupation was hunting, begin and robbing the pilgrims. Some of them were also cultivators. They worshipped the Hindu gods. However, their main deity

---

[83] Godavary Manual.
[84] ibid.

was Chenchu Mallana, a tribal God. The head of the Chenchu tribe was called as 'Nayaka'. They lived in very unhygienic conditions. They did not bathe regularly and did not even wash their clothes. The description of a Chenchu is given in the local literary works of the period. They always had a peacoxk feather in their head and a sticky Bottu on the foreheads.[85] they wore green leaved on the waist and decorated their hair with red flowers. They had big mustachios but small hands.

Gonds:

The Gonds were mainly of a warrior class. They originally inhabited the wild forests of Adilabad and carved out small kingdoms. Thus established, they continued their rule for five centuries from 1240 AD to 1750 AD

Boyas:

they were also known as Mudirajus. The main profession of the Boyas was hunting. They also worked as palanquin bearers. They always wanted to be paid in advance before the start of a journey.[86] Some of them had also become Polegars or rulers, and ruled over small principalities of Andhra Desa.

---

[85] Telangana Arya, Yayaticharitra.

[86] Chowdappa's Shatakamu in Sarojini Regani's, The Shataka Literature, Source Material for A study of social History of Andhra Pradesh, 15th -19th Century, p.42.

Yanadis:

The main occupation of Yanadis was hunting. However, some of them also lived by robbing the travelers. They were great experts in the preparation and use of medicinal herbs. They lived in forests by putting on temporary huts. Their food consisted of rice, salt, peacocks, tubers, millets, bajra etc. they also ate the flesh of various animals. Their weapons were bows and arrows, spears, daggers, sharp-knives, and guns.

Erukala:

The Erukala were another important tribe whose main profession was robbery. They were notorious for their criminal activities. While thus most of them indulged in anti-social activities some of them also pursued peaceful avocations like baskets and mat-making. The people who lived by making baskets were called as Dabbala Yerukulas and the others who made Kunchulu or the brushes for the weavers were known as the Kunchugattu Yerukulas.[87] The Erukula Sani was the tribal woman who performed in the Yakshaganas and she was an important character in it. The Erukala women were famous as fortune-tellers and tatooers. Some of these women were also the ladies.they dressed up in

---

[87] Cuddapah District Gazeteer, p. 83

bright coloured attires.[88] They had stared staying in village and had given up their nomadic habits during the period under study.

Lambadas:

They were known by different names, such as, Sugali, Banjaras or Labhan. They first came to Andhra along with the army of Shah jahan, the Mughal Emperor.[89] They have been said to come with the armies of Asaf Jah, the Vazir of Shah Jahan.[90] They were basically traders who supplied the armies with the ration and other necessary items during the war. They also traded in the cotton and food stuffs from the inland to the coastal areas and from the costal region they brought the much demanded salt to the Telangana region.[91] They originally hailed from Rajasthan. They stayed outside the village, in Tandas and their chief was called the Nayak. Their women tattooed themselves elaborately on the backs of the hands and tattooed a dot on the left side of their nose. Their Gods were Seva Bhaya, Hathi Ram, Lalya Saad etc. the Hindu Gods like Balaji of Tirupati Krishna, Gddess Durga etc. were also prayed by them. They performed

---

[88]   H.V.
[89]   D.R. Pratap, Festivals of Banjaras, p.2-3.
[90]   Siraj ul Hassan, The castes and Tribes of H.E.H. the Nizam's Dominions, p.20.
[91]   Joseph J.brenning, Textile Producers and Producation in late 17th century, in Sanjay Subramaryam ed. Merchants, Markers and the State in Early Moder India, pp.67-68.

human sacrifices earlier, but from the eighteenth century onwards they have limited themselves to the animal scarifies only. They were divided into a number of a sub-sects, all of whom were no-vegetarians except the Badavath clan who are strictly vegetarians.[92] The men as well as women were heavy drunkards.

Dependent Communities:

One of the interesting features of the caste system prevalent in the Andhra society was that the different castes had beggar communities attached particular to themselves. In some cases these dependent communities were said to consist of the illegitimate descendants of their main castes. They mostly led a semi nomadic life and roamed different villages in order to collect their alms. These beggar castes sought alms only from their main communities and subsisted only on it. These begging communities laid a claim on these supporting castes, and if the rules were not adhered to, then a fight was sure to break out. The dependent castes as they were also called did not take refusals lying low.

These dependent communities maintained an account of the history their main communities. They could also be described as groups of entertainers as every summer, they

---

[92] G. Bhadru, <u>Role of the Lambads in Telangana Armed Struggle in Janagaon Taluk</u>, 1945-1951, M.Phil. Dessertation, Kakatiya Universty.

sang and praised the history and the Prasasti about the main sub caste. They wold sit under a tree and sing the Oggu Katha or the Koyal Oggulu and ebtertained them. they played an important role in the maintenance of the history of the mains castes. In return, they received some contributions from their benefactor for their living.

Attached to the caste of the Brahmins was the beggar community called the Vipravinodis. They were the amusers of the Brahmins. The Vipravinodis were professional sorcerers and jugglers who declined to perform unless some Brahmin was present in the gathering. They subsisted chiefly on Varttanas or alms begged from the members of that caste.[93] It is believed that they collected it only from the Brahmins of the Agrahara villages.

The beggar community that was attached to the Rajus was the Bhatrazus. The Bhatrazus, originally were the court bards and panegyrists of the ruling Rajus. After decline of the powers of the Rajus, they started to beg from other caste as well, and had less special claim upon them. They carried little books with them and extolled the virtues of the important men of the village in extempore verses.[94] Later on under the British rule they were employed as teachers in the Pial schools.

---

[93] K. Jayashree, The Vipravinodin Community, Itihaas, vol.XVIII, 1992.

[94] Cuddapah District Gazeteer, p.85.

Attached to Komati caste were the two begging castes called Viramushtis and Mailaris.[95] The Viramushtis were the followers of the ViraSaivism. They were mainly employed as wrestlers and bards, and the Mailaris carried around, an image of Kanyakamma and sang in her praise. Several inscriptions after the 16th century, record the donation made by the Viramushtis.[96]

The Kammas supported a special beggar caste, namely the Pichchiguntas. These begged only of Kammas, Velamas and certain Kapus.[97] They were known for being learned in the family history of the Kapus, Kammas and etc.

The prosperous weaving castes had various groups attached to them as dependent castes that received alms from them. Some of them were Sadhana Surulu, Samayamuvaru, Inakamukku, Bhatrazus etc.

The dependent groups attached to the Devangas were Singamavallu, Virmushitivallu etc. They were professional acrobats and mendicants. As these people were Saivites, the Jangams, the priests of the Lingayats, attached themselves to them.[98]

Perikas supported the begging caste of the Varugu Bhattas. These people went around the Perika houses for their dues every year.

---

[95] I. R. Hemmingway, op.cit.
[96] South Indian Inscriptions, vol.XVI, no.193,197,300.
[97] I. R. Hemmingway, op.cit.
[98] Adidamu Surakavi, Ramalingeswara Satakamu, ed. N. Venkat Rao, Shataka Samputi, vol.I, p156.

The Gamallas supported a begging caste called Yenutis or Gavuda Jettis. They went around the Gamallas houses to collect their dues annually.

The Malas had their own beggar caste, namely the Mashtigas, who were gymnasts, the Pambalas, who were the musicians, and the Katikapus, who were jugglers. In some places Chenchus were also included among the Mala beggars.

The begging castes specially attached to the Madigas were the Dakkalis, Mastidis and Tappitas or Bagavatas. The Dakkalis, who were also the dependent caste of the Madigas, earned their livelihood by begging performing rituals, reciting songs and playing music. They also played on a wonderful stringed instrument called 'Kinnera'. It is believed that the Dakkalis were untouchables even to the Madigas. All the above mentioned groups begged only from the Madigas.

MUSLIMS:

The region had witnessed the arrival of Muslims in the wake of Muslim invasion in the first quarter of the 14th century. However, their number increased to manifold when the Muslim rule was established over Andhra Desa. In course of time they became a part and parcel of the region and came to occupy an important place in the social fabric of the place. They belonged to different region of west

Asia Africa. The local population who get converted to the religion was also included in the Muslim society. Almost all of the Muslims earned their livelihood by serving the king. Most of them were employed in the administration and in the army. One very seldom came across an unemployed Muslim in those days as the king always provided some occupation to his co religionists. However, they were divided amongst themselves on racial lines. The Persians felt that they belonged to a superior race and intelligence than the rest. The other races of the Muslim population, present on the soil of Andhra resented this condescending attitude. But the disgruntled forces could not do them any harm as the Persians received patronage and full fledged support from the state of Golconda. However, with the fall of the Qutb Shahi rule over the region, they lost all the privileges. The Mughals and the Asaf Jahs were of the Sunni sect of Islam and did not patronize the Shiah Persians.

The earliest groups of Muslims who were staying in Andhra Desa were called as the 'Deccanis'. They were the Arab Muslims who had reached through the coastal south from ancient times, and also those who had come to the Dessan during the Tughluq period and were naturalized as the citizens of this region. They had mixed up with the local people and joined them in all walks of life. They were the followers of the 'Sunni' sect of Islam. They were the Sunnis with a mystic aptitude and adhered to Sufism. They were conversant with the regional language and had developed a separate Indo-persian dialect called 'Deccani'.[99] During the region of the Qutb Shahs, the Sunni elite was pushed side and was mostly detached from the body politic. The Deccanis or the Sunnis turned to the Sufi monasteries called the 'Khanqahs'. At the Khanqahs, they received their religious education, spiritual guidance, and the chances for their cultural pattern to flourish. They had left the cities as there were no avenues left to them there. Hence, they concentrated in and around the village only. They had been forced to become rural oriented. They had endeared themselves to the village people of the Andhra. They never any good feeling for the new Muslims as they had lost their patronage at the court to them.

Some of the Arabs from Syria, the Pathans and the Mughals, staying at the capital city were known as the Gharibs. The Arabic and the Turkish influence in the Qutb shahi kingdoms of the Deccan in the 16th & 17th centuries cen be seen from the extant materials.[100] the existence of Arabs has been observed inlarge numbers in Hyderabad. Infact, at Hyderabad, the population of Arabs was only next to their population at Delhi. Theyu also had a restaurant

---

[99] Nizamuddin Shirazi, <u>Hadiqatus Salatin</u>,.
[100] P. M. Joshi and M. A. Nayeem, Studies in the Foreign Relation of India, from the earliest times to 1947, in Prof. H. K. Sherwani Felicitation Volume.

named 'Café des Arabs' in one corner o fthe city where one could see them in large numbers.[101]

As most of these Arabian poets were Shiahs by religion, they received patronage at the courts of the Qutb Shahi Kings. They were especially popular at the court of King Abdullah and Abdul Hasan. They had made Hyderabad an important center of Arabic culture in the second half of the seventeenth century. This was due to the influx of poet and scholars drawn from Arab countries, especially, from Syria. The Sayyids, as some of the Arabs were knows as, were a munch respected class and were either employed as teacher or nobles of highest rank.[102] They were good leaders of men. Some were employed even in the army of the Qutb Shahs.

As they followed the same religion of Shiahism as the king of Golconda the Persians received all the best positions and highest pay in the kingdom.[103] There were "several Persians nere the King".[104] They were appointed as Governors of the principalities and also the Commandant of the forts in the Kingdom. The Commandant of the fort of Kondavid was a Muslim.[105] They also did not do any hard toiling work and few of them were farmers. Most of them were employed in high ranking posts and seldom any of

---

[101] J. Dolche, ed Voyage en Inde du Comte Modave, 1773-1776, Paris,1971.

[102] Mohammad Ziauddin, op. cit..

[103] Tavernier's Travels in India, p. 382.

[104] William Foster, The English factories in India, 1637-41, Oxford, 1912, p.222.

[105] Anonymous Relations, p.79.

them occupied any low ranking posts in the administration. They were mostly employed as Supervisors of the King and kept an eye on the officers of the principalities. They were eyes and ears of the King and saw to it that everybody was doing his duty faithfully. They greatly benefited from the exploits of this position. By controlling the lower officials, they did not let complaints against them, reach the higher levels. All the judicial decisions in the provinces, were to be taken in the presence of the concerned parties, by the leading Moslems of the place. Besides, some Hindus were also present there.[106]

They had become big traders and carried on trade in food articles to the places south of Andhra. While describing their way of life, a contemporary foreign writer says that they led a 'seemly' life and gave expensive parties or banquets. They ate all kinds of meat except that of the pig. They were also great drinks of wine.[107] Some of them took a great amount of wine and they often sent their servants or personally went to the factories of the European merchants for the foreign liquor. The expatriate Persians, Arabians, Afghans and Turkish ruling elite in the kingdom of Golconda loved to acquire the imported goods from the kingdom countries.[108] Infact, a sort of race took place between them, whenever new European ships reached the Coromandel coast. They

---

[106] ibid., p.82.
[107] <u>Antony Schorer's Relation</u>, p.59.
[108] S.Arasratnam, p.54.

loved to own fancied items from Europe like in dogs, the dolls the looking glass etc. The merchants had a difficult time in pleasing all the officials of the King.

They acted as money lenders on usury and got 'four per cent per mensem' interest on the advance loans. The interest sometimes was as high as five percent. They lent money even to the Hindu Governors of the administration divisions of the empire. The King, bestowed large sums in religious benevolence to the Persians who were poor, but of noble birth, and had come from Iran in search of better prospects of life. As the court patronized poets from Persia, many a people of very low education and intelligence came over to the Qutb Shahi courts. There are references to poets of very low ranks attending the courts. They stayed at Golconda, enjoyed the life, collected their valuable gifts from the King, and having got the riches left for motherland fully satisfied.[109]

The high ranking nobles of Persian origin were called 'Afaqis'. The Sarkars or provinces and their sub-divisions were farmed out to the nobles of Iranian origin. They were all urban oriented. The role of the Iranians in statecraft and in the international politics was all in all. The King also was not strong enough to control his own Omras. They were very handsomely paid and maintained an army of about five hundred men. Similarly, the lesser soldiers of Persian origin were allowed to maintain two horses and four to

---

[109] H.K.Sherwani, <u>The History of the Qutb Shahi Kings</u>.

five servants. The solders on foot were allowed to entertain two servants. These were the special emoluments given to the Persian only. The Indian soldier was paid less than the Persians' and was allowed to carry only a lance and a spike and no musket.

They were very powerful and often behaved in a very high-handed way. Once when a Hindu banker was asked to pay a huge amount of money when he was illegally detained by an Omra, all the Hindu merchants shut up their shops as a protest. The King was then forced to take action and he returned all the money back to the banker.[110] The King, however, could not punish them and at the most could only levy a fine on them for any misconduct. The Persians following the Shiah faith, were said to have the descended from the Mohammad himself and the King, following the same religion, could not to them any harm, not that he ever wanted to.[111] at the maximum, only a fine could be lived on a Persian man whatever his fault would have been.

EUROPEANS:

They came as merchants to the ports on the coats of Andhra Desa. They belonged to different nations of Europe viz. Portugal, Denmark, Netherlands, France, and England. While the Portuguese had arrived on the land of Andhra

---

[110] M.Thevent, <u>Indian Travels of Thevenot</u>, p.135.
[111] <u>Antony Socherer's Relation</u>, p.56.

only in the seventeenth century, they established themselves on the various ports of the country. Some of the important ports on the coastline of Andhra were Bimlipatnam, vishakapatnam, Kakinada, Jagganthpuram, Coinga, Ingeram, Yanam, Palakaollu, Madapollam, Narsapore, Motupalli, Masulipstnam, point Devi, Nizampatnam or Petapuli, Cginna Ganjam, Cottapatnam, Ramaptnam.[112] The Europeans had established factories at these ports besides the factory at the capital city of the Golconda Kingdom. At Masulipatnam, the different ethnic groups had separate locations viz. Frenchpeta, English Palem, Volanda Palem or the Hollander's place etc.[113] Thomas Rogers of England was stationed at Golconda, chiefly for the purpose of watching the English interests at court.[114] Similarly, all the European merchant companies had their representatives at the capital city. The permission for the factories was taken from the King after giving him some valuable presents. One could not visit the King after without present and gain favours.[115] The King often got angry when the presents did not reach him. Besides, the King the foreigners had to keep the Governors and other important officials happy with their presents.

---

[112] Sinnappah Arasaratnam, <u>Merchants, Companies & Commerce on the Coramandel coast, 1650-1740</u>, p.41.

[113] I. P. Gupta, <u>Mastulipatnam and the North Coromandel Region during the 18th century</u>, in Indu Banga ed. <u>Ports and their Hinterlands in India, 1700-1950</u>.

[114] William Foster, op. cit., p.xxx.

[115] William Foster, <u>The English Factories in India, 1637-41</u>, Oxford Press, 1912, p.143.

These European Companies, had to employ a number of Telugu personnel to help them in their business. They did not follow the local language, custom, and the trading practices of the local people. The 'Dubashi' or the translator was the most important India in their employment. The other people employed were the writers, the Brahmin, cook, tailor, barber, etc. In the hinterlands also a number of Telugu were employed. Weavers, washers, dyers, painters, rice producers i.e. farmers, smiths for making of nails, rope markers and coir makers were given employment. In course of time, the younger white servants were also employed as writers to avoid employing Indians.[116] they were also made to learn the local languages i.e. Telugu and Persian. The young officers were also shifted from place to place in order to "acquire a general knowledge of the Company's business". This must have been done to decrease the dependency on the local people.

The European men led a scandalous life in India. There was no controlling authority over them to control their personal lives. The absence of family responsibilities also was a reason for the debauched life that they lived in India. They kept Indian women as their mistress but did not have any binding responsibility towards them. They could drive them out of their houses at their whims and fancies. They had children from them, yet took very little care of them.

---

[116] Henry Dodwell, Calender of the Madras Despatcheds. 1744-1755, p.222.

Sometimes, the married men also kept concubines. They spent their money on drinks, women and gambled a lot. All the senior servants of the Co. lived a life of extravagancy and were imitated by the junior servant, who often ran into trouble owing to huge debts. The officers were ill paid and they resorted to borrowings from the local people. They could not pay back the amount due to their high standard of living. When the loaning party demanded the due money they embezzled the Companies money. "The maintenance of soe many debauched and wicked persons as have been continued under the name of souldires in the Fort brought a scandal to our nation and religion."[117] The English higher ups were very much worried about their men in India. They passed certain laws from time to time to control their nationals here. The higher ups maintained diaries wherein they noted down the behaviour of each and every man. They passed rules stating that all servants of the company, civil military, must Church every Sunday.[118]

The Europeans behaved cruelly towards their Indian servants. They often beat them up for small mistakes. It was observed that in earlier days, they behaved in the same way as a higher caste Hindu behaved towards the untouchables. "In this city (Masulipatnam) they (foreigners) are allowed to exercise justice themselves, to seize debtors and any others

---

[117] William Foster, <u>English factories in India, 1655-166,</u> p.35.

[118] Henry Dodwell, <u>Calendar of the Madras Despatches</u>. 1744-1755, p.225.

who give them offence, to bring these persons inside the lodge, maltreat them and in short, act as masters."[119] As a result, rules had to be that in punishing a servant, his explanation should also be taken into account and all the disputes should be taken to the Company and settled in an impartial manner.[120] The English at Masulipatnam inflicted corporal that he has been charged with committing a mistake. The authenticity of the offence did not matter.[121] All the men were to stay inside their respective forts or the factories but the order was seldom obeyed.

The permission to many was given very sparingly in the Dutch Co. The rule was that if a man had served his full term with the Company, then permission may be granted but that too very sparingly. This precaution was mainly to see that they did not desert their wives once they found their salaries inadequate to sustain them.[122] The Dutch kept their families in the factories for safety sake. The availability of European girls being very less, the men were forced to marry any one that was at hand. They married 'Castez' or the girls born to Portuguese parents in India. John Field the English chief at Masulipatnam, had married a 'Castez' wife.[123] Later

---

[119] India in the 17th century, Memoirs Martin, Tr. Lotika Varadarajan, p.12.

[120] Calender, 1744-1755, op. cit.

[121] Willam Foster, The English Factories in India, 1630-1633, p0. 171.

[122] Om Prakash, The Dutch Factories in India, 1617-1623, New Delhi, 1984, p. 105.

[123] Strenysham Master's Diary, p. 204.

on the English law-makers disallowed the marriage of the Protestant English with the Catholic Portuguese.

However, some of them also wanted to go back home. "My desire is to retourne for my countrie, I am wearie of India…". This was a letter from one Matthew Duke at Masulipatnam to the Company Headquarters in London on September 7, 1622.[124] In the other hand people like Francois de Raymond, a French commander of the army of Nizam II felt at home in Hyderabad. He lived in great style and luxury at Hyderabad and was interested in Indian culture. Under a fictitions name of Hadji Mustapha he published a French translation of the Siyar-ul-Matakhirin written by Ghulam Hussain Khan Tiba Tibai in 1789 A. D. He died at Hyderabad in 1798 A. D., and was buried here itself.[125]

The Europeans copied the lifestyles of the rich Indians and Persians. They kept a number of servants and rode out in palanquins, horses or chaises for travel that proved to be very costly. Some of them had 'roundells' or umbrellas carried over their heads by their servants. However, this privilege was given in Andhra, only to the persons of a very high rank.

Inspite of the order prohibiting then from venturing out with the umbrellas, the lower staff continued to do so.[126] They also copied the daily routine of the locals to get

---

[124] William Foster, <u>E.F.I, 1622-1623</u>, p. 119.

[125] Lester Hutchinson, <u>European Freebooters in Moghul India</u>, 1964.

[126] <u>Strenysham Master's Diary</u>, vol.I, p.295.

adjusted to the climate of the region. Their day began with the sun-rise. While some to them just washed their heads with cold water, other had bath either with cold or hot water daily. Some took bath only twice or thrice weekly. They also took their afternoon siesta as it become very hot in the afternoon. It was also a custom of the Dutch to wash their mouths after the dinner. In the evening and night they strolled in the gardens for some exercise. At about ten O' clock their day was over.

The Indians held the Europeans in very low terms because of their eating habits and uncleanliness. Venkatadhwari, a contemporary poet considered the British as filthy rats.[127] The poet remarks that they had very low health habits and that they never had bath after their natural calls. Another contemporary writer while deriding the Europeans, said that the French ate raw meat or uncooked meat and drank a lot of Toddy, an intoxicating drink.[128]

RELATION BETWEEN VARIOUS EUROPEAN COMMUNITIES:

There existed a lot of rivalry between the different European Companies doing trade with the Coromandel coast. The Dutch described the English as unworthy of trust. Office orders were passed saying that no relation whatsoever

---

[127] Venkatadhawari, <u>Viswagunadarshanamu</u>, p.264.
[128] Adidamu Suryakavi, <u>Ramalingeshwara Shataka</u>, p. 294.

should be maintained with the English.[129] However, when the relations improved the Dutch, gave banquets in the honour of the English Governor when he paid them a visit at their factory. They never let an opportunity escape their hands in inciting the Indians against the other merchant companies. They were in constant fear of the Muslim officers and never disclosed their profits to them. They did not construct good houses though they had the means to build one. They also did not want to show the arrival of their Indian merchants as it would spark a jealousy in the 'Moores' and they would impose higher duties on them.[130] The relations with the French deteriorated so much that for the sake of better bargains in trading facilities, they fought wars against each other. The French sided with Salabat Jung whereas the English sided with the English. Finally the French were defeated and sole hegemony of the British was established over region.

CHANGES:

In addition to the already mentioned social divisions, some new sub castes were also added to the already prevalent castes, during the period under study. Some were new and developed as a result of the interaction with the foreigners. The new castes were the result of either conversion or due

---

[129] Lester Hutchinson, op. cit, p. 108.
[130] Om Prakash, op. cit., p 279.

to the intermixing of the locals with the foreigners. Ther were also new additions to the social structure of Andhra because of migration from the Hindus from the north. These new castes have not found mention in the contemporary literature. The low caste Hindu converts some to Islam, though become Muslims yet as they continued to follow some of the old Hindu modes of life, they were not treated equally by the Muslims. Similarly, the physical relationship of the Indian women with European men led to a set of altogether new people. They were not accepted by either of their parents' society. They were rather looked down upon by both sides. The arrival of northerners and their settling down within the boundaries of Andhra Desa created a new set of castes in Hinduism. Some of these castes have been discussed below.

(a) **Dudekulas:** A mixed class called Dudekulas occurred during this period. They were said to be converts from Hinduism, and, though they professed the Muhammadan religion, most of them spoke only Telugu.[131] They also followed both Muslims and Hindu customs.[132] They even dressed up like the Hindus and did not put on the trousers or lungi of the Mushammadans. Unlike the Mohammadans,

---

[131] I. R. Hemingway, Madras District Gazetteers, Godavari, vol. I, Madras, 1907, p39.

[132] Cuddapah District Gazetter, p. 69.

the Dudekulas invited all their friends and relatives to a great feast when their dagughter reached puberty. This was a tradition that the Hindus followed. The Muslims on the other hand kept it a secret.[133] Their from of salutation was different, while they bowed to the castes, to their own caste they did their old Telugu from of salutation which was 'Niku Mokkutamu'. They also adopted Hindu names. The names ended with the Hindu suffixes like 'appa' in men and in women the suffix of 'bibi' was replaced by 'amma'. As such the men were named Pullanna, Hussaingadu etc., the females as Roshamma, Madaramma etc.[134] They could not intermarry with other Musalmans and were looked down upon because they were musicians and cotton cleanser. They attended mosques like the Muslims but consulted the Brahmins on auspicious days like marriage.[4][135]Though they accepted the authority of the Qazi's, they also worshipped at the Hindu shrines on important occasions.

(b) **Luso Indians**: In the early period of time when only the Portuguese had come to Andhra, the children born of the of Portuguese father and Indian mother were called by this name or by "Mustezas i.e. half

---

[133] I. R. Hemingway, op. cit.

[134] Thurston, op. cit., vol. I.

[135] Cuddapah, op. cit

breds".[136] Later on the name was applied to all the children born out of such unions. The father could be an Englishman, a Frenchman, a Dane or a Dutch but the mother was to be an Indian. These children were neither acceptable to the father nor to the mother. They were not brought up properly and spent the days and nights with the servants. No education was given to them and when they grew up they were found to be not eligible for any job. They could not work hard as they were not used hard work. Their whole life was spent in drinking and loitering here and there. These were a contemptible lot. Some of them were employed as watchmen and warders in the times of troubles on the outskirts by the European factories.

The European also kept Indian "housekeepers" within their housese as European women were very few in India. The foreigners looked after these women well. They were treated more or less as wives and the servants treated her as the mistress of the house. Sometimes, the European men left much off their property to these Indian women and to their illegitimate children. The total amounted to more that the shares of the legitimate children i. e. children born of their legally wedded white wives. These are visible in the

---

[136] Thomas Bowrey, <u>A Geographical Account of the Countries Round the Bay of Bengal, 1669-1679</u>.

wills left by the European men.[137] This led to the formation of a separate poor Anglo-Indian clan that consisted of a European father and an European mother. The children born to them in different parts of India continued to say here and became a permanent resident of the country. Such a class also existed in the Andhra Desa in the 17th and 18th centuries.

(c) **Converted Christians:** The missionary activity of the foreigners was successful in converting the Hindus to Christianity. They got converted to the different sects of Christianity, like, Catholicism, Protestantism, and other. However, these people also could not give up all the traditional practices of their old religion and continued to follow many of the old practices.

(d) **Katike:** They belonged to the service class and find mention in the Hamsa Vimshati. They were the butchers in Telugu country. They observed both Hindu and Muslim customs. The Katike class was dived into three types viz. the Muslims were called Ganji Kasai and they dealt with beef. The other two sects were the Sultanis and the Surasus. At Kurnool, the Sultanis were Hindus, who were the forcibly circumcised by the Nabob of Kurnoool.[138] The

---

[137] Holden Furber, John Company At work, p. 328.
[138] Kurnool Manual.

Sultanis were the forcibly converted Hindus and the Surasus were the Hindu butchers. The Sultanis did not give up the Hindu customs and traditions as the conversion was forced upon them. It was only from the 19th century onwards, that they slowly started following the Mohammadan customs. They used to dress up as Hindus and only adopted the dress of Muslims later on.

CLASS CONFLICTS:

During the period under study, the left and the right hand castes, or Idangai and Valangai, were absent from the Andhra Desa. However, there was a struggle by the Sudra community for a higher place in the social ladder and they never reconciled to their low position. They were always demanding certain privileges that were being enjoyed by the higher castes. Sometimes they were allowed and at other times they were disallowed. One finds stray references of class conflicts in the coastal region of the country and in the Nellore District. However, in the lower classes there was hostility that continued upto the 19th century. The rise in the social ladder had become a passion in the minds of the people of Andhra.

The French traveler, Tavernier, has written that there was hostile attitude between the military and the agricultural communities and between the labourers and the artisans.

He has mentioned a quarrel among the castes in between 1673 and 1681 A. D. "The artificers including the gold smiths, and the carpenters had been insolent to the higher castes and tyrannical towards their inferiors. The higher castes conspired with husbandmen and labourers to degrade the artificers, and they prevailed on the Muhammadans to help them. Accordingly, the artificers were reduced to the lowest grade of society knows as Halal-chors or unclean eaters. Henceforth, the artificers were not allowed to ride in palanquins at marriage and festivals, but only on horse-back. The poorest Hindu, excepting those of the proscribed caste, had a week's jollity at his marriage, going about in a palanquin, attended by guards, carrying swords and javelins, while others bore ensigns denoting the honour of their caste. But if any artificer or low caste man attempted the like, he was dragged back to his quarters by the hair of his head…."[139]

However in the class of the Untouchables, a lot of ill feeling could be witnessed between the Madigas and the Malas as the former belonged to the left hand caste and the latter to the right hand caste. The fights were basically related to the use of use of certain privileges by either of the two castes. While the Malas resented the use of palanquins at their marriages by the Madigas, the latter continued to

---

[139] James Talboys Wheeler and Michael Machillan, European Travellers in India, pp. 49-50.

carry the bride and the bridegroom through the streets in them and used tinkling ornaments.[140]

Even in the 19th century they were continuously fighting amongst themselves. At Kurnool, in 1886 AD, a Madiga succeeded in obtaining a red cloth from the police Superintendent as a reward. He wore it on the head and rode on a horse in a procession. The Malas resented this and they tried to murder the Superintendent for giving the reward.[141]

The upper caste were also not free from internal quarrels. The Brahmins objected to the entry of the Komatis into the Vaishya fold of the caste system. The struggles continued throughout the seventeenth and the eighteenth century. Even in the nineteenth century, though the Komatis have been included in the Vaishya caste, the Brahmins did not accept them as the third caste of the Hindu society. Disputes regarding their performance of the 'Subah', 'Asubah' i.e. auspicious ceremonies according to the Vedic form was raised by the Brahmins of Masulipatnam in 1817 A. D., and adjudicated upon.[142] They very adamantly wore the sacred thread and uttered Gayatri Mantras inspite of the opposition of the Brahmins.[143]

The Muslim sect also, was not free from class conflicts. Though they were followers of the same religion, often

---

[140] J. A. C. Boswell, A Manual of the Nellore District, Madras, 1873.

[141] Thurston, vol. IV, op. cit.

[142] Moore, Indian Appeal Cases, vol. III, p. 359-82.

[143] Thurston, op. cit. col. III.

differences cropped up, in between the different nationalities. The divergent races tried to gain an upper hand, as the region had become their place of inhabitation too. The Arabs, the Pathans and the Mughals, staying at the capital city of Hyderabad, were known as the 'Gharibs'.[144]

In 1608 AD, an unhappy incident place at Nabat Ghat. The 'Nabat Ghat' incident was a tragedy of errors in which, first the 'Gharibs' were ruthlessly massacred. They were shortly after avenged by a general massacre of the Deccanis. The Deccanis who were especially in the police and the military departments were the worst hit by this madness. They were massacred in large numbers. This incident was followed by a 'Firman' or Order issued by Sultan Muhammad Quli Qutb Shah for expulsion of the Mughal strangers and the 'Hirzakars' or the triflers. This led to the widespread revolt by the Deccanis against the Sultan. However, the revolt was ruthlessly suppressed. The hatred between the 'Afaqis' or the Persian nobility and the Deccanis increased.[145] Later on the under the Asaf Jahs the difference crept up between the Mulkis and the Non Mulkis i.e. the resident Muslims and the non-resident Muslims of Andhra Desa.

---

[144] Mohammed Ziauddin Ahmed, The Relations of Golconda with Iran, 1518-1687, Ph. D, thesis.

[145] ibid.

SOCIAL MOBILITY:

During the period under study mobility was witnessed in the social system of the Andhra Desa. One can find both vertical and horizontal mobility that existed in the social system. It can be described in two ways namely, Social Consciousness and Social Immigration and Migration. While there was a rise in the consciousness of the lower classes regarding their social status and thus a horizontal mobility could be witnessed in the society. The period also witnessed a fall in the exalted position of the foremost caste i.e. the Bhramins. In the vertical mobility, one finds the coming in of a number of people into the region of Andhra. The region witnessed the arrival of a number of foreigners during the period under study. There was also an immigration of Indians from the different parts of India. The main reason of these immigrations was the invitations offered by the Kings of Andhra Desa to them to come and make the place their residence. The region was also very prosperous and attracted the people of different nationalities. The people migrating from Andhra Desa, to different places was another new phenomena witnessed during this period. Some of them migrated to the southern parts, the others had gone overseas in search of livelihood.

The Rise in Social Consciousness Of The Lower Caste And The Degradation Of Upper Castes:

The contemporary political changes like the decline of the Vijayanagara Kingdom from 1565 AD, leading to the rise of the Nayakas, the emergence of the Qutb Shahi Dynasty, the subsequent occupation of the Golconda Kingdom by the Mughals, the establishment of the Asaf Jahi rule over Hyderabad, and finally, the establishment of British rule over Andhra Desa, led to a lot of changes in the social structure of the region. The age old dominance of the upper casts was replaced by the newly literate and economically stronger Sudra community. These changes are vividly reflected in the Shataka literature of the 17th and 18th centuries.

One of the most remarkable change witnessed in the 17th and 18th century Andhra, was the professional mobility in the Sudra community. The traditional caste jobs were replaced by the new vocations. The Sudra were making inroads in the profession hitherto forbidden to them by the Sastras. They were adopting the jobs of the upper castes.[146] The main reason was that the various sub sects of the Sudra caste had taken to education and learning. This gave them the self confidence to take onto new jobs. This

---

[146] Sarojani Regani, <u>The Shataka Literature, Source Material for A Study of the Social History of Andhra Pradesh, 15th-19th century</u>, in Itihaas, vol. XVI, 199, p.42.

process had already started under the Vijayanagar Kings. The Panchanamvaru community claimed equality with the Brahmins and called themselves the Vishwa Brahmins.[147] They had taken to learning and education. They claimed divine origins and tried to climb the social ladder. They claimed that were the descendants of God Vishwakarma and his five sons. They conducted their marriages under their own priests, they wore the sacred thread and challenged the supremacy of the Brahmins. Similarly, the barbers or the Mangala caste claimed equality with the Brahmins. They formed an important part of the temples as musicians and exploited it to their advantage. They called themselves as Nai Brahmins.

Later on, in the seventeenth century the Kapus and the Gollas made an attempt to better their position by taking to reading and writing. Koochimanchi Timmanna, 1690-1760, a contemporary poet of the Pittapur region, says that the Kapus were becoming poets and the Gollas were becoming Pauranikas.[148] These professions had not been ordained to them by the caste system. It was an attempt by these communities to change the existing pattern of society. The fishermen were taking to astrology and the untouchable

---

[147] Dr. R. Soma Reddy, <u>Social Awakening among certain oppressed in Andhra During the Vijayanagar Period</u>, South Indian History Congress, Preceedings of the VII Annual Conference, Quilon, 1988, pp.75-80.

[148] Koochimanchi Timmanna, <u>Kukkuteshwara Shataka</u>, ed. Swami Shiva Sharaswami, Shataka Samputi, VolII, p.9.

Mala caste had become Gurus. The people of the smith caste could be seen as seers, the Sathanis as Vaishnava and the educated weavers had become government servants under the British rule. All these professions had earlier been in the hands of the Brahmins. The job of a priest was also being taken over by the Jains. The poet was not able to comprehend the situation and blamed every change to "Kali Dosham".

The establishment of the East India Co. on the soil of Andhra Desa caused the emergence of the Sudra communities as the economically stronger groups. Though in the traditional caste hierarchy they remained in the fourth place, the economic gain had given them secular power. The most benefited caste was the land owing people. Vemana, the contemporary social reformer, spoke about the importance of the land owning class.[149] He spoke of the accumulation of wealth and said that the acquisition of wealth was a duty of all and to live in poverty was a sin. He said that poverty was fire that burnt not only the person concerned but all those that were near him. The other sub sect of the Sudra caste, which become rich were the Devangas or the weavers.[150] The demand of textiles from Andhra region had increased manifolds after the arrival of the Europeans merchants in the region. This benefited the

---

[149] Dr. Gangadham Appa Rao, <u>Vemana and Sarvajyna</u>, p.67.
[150] Adidamu Surakavi, <u>Ramalingeshwaram Shatakam</u>, ed. Nidadavolu Venkat Rao, <u>Shataka Samputi</u>, vol. I, p.156.

weaver caste a lot and they accumulated a lot of wealth. The new merchants from the Balija sect had become so powerful that they had started using Shetty after their names. The use of the title shows that they had become undoubtedly the leading caste in trade and commerce. The Golla community, too has been described as rich.

Instead of patronizing the Brahmins, the neo rich Sudras spent their wealth on sycophants who belonged to their own caste.[151] The caste of the Dasaris was maintained and sustained by them. They did not want to spend their newly acquired wealth on the snobbish Brahmins. It might be also that the Brahmins would not have agreed to be entertained by them as they have been mentioned to bear a snobbish and condescending attitude towards the neo rich Sudras.[152] The wealth remained in the same caste though it did change hands. The writer of the Shatakas who were mostly Brahmins have all condemned this attitude.[153] The money of the rich were being spent on the dancing girls and the rope-trick performers. The Devangas spent their riches in maintaining the Jangams, the Kapus on the Pambakani community.[154] The Balijas spent their money in maintaining the Dasaris, the Gollas maintained the Pitchukuntis, while the businessman spent his money on the prostitutes. The Shreshti Karnams spent their money for the maintenance

---

[151]   Adidamu Surakavi, op. cit.
[152]   Sarojini Regani, op. cit. p. 45.
[153]   Timmana, op.cit.
[154]   Surakavi, p. 305.

of the Parijala community. The main reason for the lack of patronage has also been given by these writers. The wealth of the neo rich Sudras, was so little that they could not afford to please the Brahmins whose demand were always too high. The principalities of petty chieftains were so small that they could not grant land to the Brahmins. On the other hand, the newly literate Sudra castes were happy to receive even a little amount as a gift. The new "Pandits" were pleased by meagre gifts like a measure of salt, a handful of millet or a glass of butter-milk only.[155] They, being new aspirants and rebels against the age old system, were satisfied with these gifts. As such one can see that the liberated Sudras helped their brethren by patronizing them.

Another remarkable change, witnessed during the period under study, was the degradation of the upper castes, which had till now enjoyed unlimited powers and wealth. The upper castes including the Brahmins, Khatriyas and the Vaishyas felt a change in their status in the society of the Andhra region. While the first two castes faced a downright deterioration in their position in the social ladder, the Vaishyas faced strict competition in trade and commerce from the new communities. Because of the changed political scenario, the Brahmins had lost the patronization of the kings and the powerful people. The Agraharas had been terminated and they remained only in names.[156] The

---

[155] Koochi Manchi Timmanna, op.cit.
[156] Suryakavi, op. cit.

Manyams were reduced in size. The attitude of the people towards the Brahmnis was that of utter contempt. The Muslim kings had their own favorites and donated lands to Muslim officers and the Islamic religious institutions. The Inam lands acquired by the Muslim nobility in the 17th and 18th centuries consisted of the old Agraharams, Manyams and the Srotriyams held earlier by the Brahmins. Later on, these lands were taken away by the British and given to the highest bidder of the land revenue who were called the Zamindars. The position of the Brahmins economically had become very precarious. The contemporary Brahmins writers bemoaned and said that the happy days of the scholars were over and that the good for nothing rulers are squandering their wealth in useless pursuits.[157] They forced take up jobs under the Sudra village headman. The Sudras had become the lords in every village and the Brahmins become the Karnams or the accountants under them.[158] Some were forced to take to the tilling of the land. As such the lofty ideals and the high position of this caste was lost. The petty chieftains also no longer partronized the Brahmins but the story tellers and the literates of the Golla community.

The Brahmins were condemned by the non-Brahmin writers of the Shataka literature for their haughty and

---

[157] Kuchimanchi Timmanna, op.cit.
[158] Venkatadhwari, <u>Visvagunadarsamu</u>, Tr. Venkata Ramakrishna Kavulu, Madras, 1917. P.40, v.2.

hypocritical behavior. The Brahmins have been described as greedy, gregarious and avaricious and who did not mind travelling great distance just to attend a feast held in their honor.[159] Vemana, the social reformer of the contemporary period, also criticized them and said that the Brahmins learnt by heart the scriptures, become proud of their learning and treated the other castes with contempt. He said that the Brahmins called themselves as 'Soomayaajis' or the performers of sacrifices and wore sparkling ear studs, consumed large quantities of goat's meat on the pretext of animal sacrifices, drank 'Soomarasa', an intoxicating drink from a certain plant, and made merry in a most licentious way.[160] Though in the study of the Vedas and the observance of the more important ceremonies of the caste the Telugu Brahmins, were not inferior to their castemen in the southern districts, they were less scrupulous in several minor matters.[161] They smoked and ate opium. They had less influence in religious and social matters over other castes. They did not hold themselves as strictly aloof from the upper non-Brahman castes as in the further southern region. They did not live in separate quarters in the villages. Some of them even allowed the entry of the Sudra into every part of their house except the kitchen.

[159] Ganganapalli Syed Hussain Das, <u>Ganganapalli Husain's Shatakas</u> in Vangoori Subba Rao's <u>Shataka Kavula Charitra</u>, p.451.
[160] Dr. G. Appa Rao, op. cit., p.54.
[161] Godavary Manual, p.52.

The arrival of the Muslims and the Christian missionaries further helped the lower castes to come up in the social ladder. The conversion of the lower caste Hindus to Islam or Christianity immediately enhanced the position of the convert in the general society of Andhra. A reference is there of Ramagadu, a leather worker of the Hindu castes who could not draw water from the village well. He got converted to Islam and became Abul Hassan and since them drew water from the caste well unchallenged.[162]

Social Reform Movements:

The emergence of two important personalities on the scene of social reform in Andhra, further gave a boost to the struggle of the lower castes to reject the age old caste hierarchy. However, one should always remember that during the period under study only an attempt was made to come out of the drudgery of the caste system. It cannot be termed as a revolution. The sayings of Vemana and Veerabrahmam on the scene of the 17th and 18th centuries respectively, can be visualized as an attempt to show the truth to the people and give confidence to them. It can also be said that their works mirrored the mood of the contemporary society. Vemana spoke against the caste system and was deadly against the sectarian strife that took place due to the evils

---

[162] Gordon Mackenzie, <u>A Manual of the Kistna District</u>, Madras, 1883.

of the caste system. He condemned caste and emphatically stated that "it is worth, not birth, that should determine a man's position".[163] He condemned the war of words and the show of supremacy over each other by the Vaishnavites and the Saivites. Neither of these sects tried to stop the immoral activities going on in their sects, but only condemned the other sect for its wrongs. Vemana advised them to stop their bickering or else the Muslims might destroy them. He has criticized the Brahmins for their hypocritical behaviour and wanted to expose them. He showed contempt for the Brahmin ritualistic and ascetic devotees who set their hopes of salvation upon formal ceremonies.[164] He also tried to put an end to the superstitious and the Brahmanical practices, which stood in the way of social progress. He wanted to do away with the caste system and to establish a social order with no distinction of race, caste, religion and class. He says in following stanza:

> *"Kulamu heccu taggu koduvala paniledu,*
> *Saanufadtamayye sakala kulamu,*
> *Heccu taggu maata netterungaga vaccu?"*

The meaning of the stanza is given below.

God has created all human beings equal, of whatever caste they may be. Then how can one tell that one is high

---

[163] W. H. Campbell, <u>The One Great Poet Of The People</u>.
[164] M M. Ali Khan, <u>The Musings of a Mystic</u>, p.5.

and the other is law? Therefore, men should give up all differences of caste and religion and become one caste and one class. All should live in harmony like brothers and sisters. They must forget caste, mingle heart with heart and live with mutual affection and respect.

Swami Potuluri Veerabrahmam popularly known as Brahmam garu belonged to the eighteenth century and he came after the Vemana period.[165] It is believed that he was influenced by the teachings of Vemana. It is also believed that he belonged to the Vishwa Brahmin community. Like Vemana, he was against the caste system. He condemned the hierarchical system of caste and believed that Vedic knowledge could be gained by one and all. The followers of his teaching were from all the classes.[166] The foremost amongst his disciples were Siddaiah, a Dudekula or half Muslim; Kakkayya, a Madiga or untouchable; and Annajayya, a Brahmin. He was against untouchability and idol worship. He strongly criticized superstition.[167] He exhorted his followers to start wearing the sacred thread of the Brahmins and to apply 'bottu' on their foreheads. His disciples were many in number and after his death, they continued to spread his teachings through Tatvalu or philosophical songs. After his death, temples were built

---

[165] V. Ramakrishna, <u>Reform Trends in Andhra: A Historical Survey</u>, p.45.

[166] N Gangadharam, <u>Sri pothuluri Jeevithamu (Kaliyugatilakamu)</u>, pp.91-95.

[167] T, Donappa, <u>Vemana, Veerabrahman</u>, in Andhra Jyoti.

in his name and his followers started worshipping him as a God.

Immigration and Migration:

Migration means to move out of one's country, whereas immigration means to move into a country of one's choice. Migration and immigration have been a world wide phenomena. Throughout the history of India we witness one tribe or the another entering and very few leaving for destinations outside India. Migration and immigration may take place due to unfavourable conditions at home or favourable and lucrative opportunities abroad. Sometimes the local population may oppose this inflow of people into their country from outside. On the other hand, the immigrants may gradually get integrated into the prevailing conditions of their adopted home and become one with the already existing population. This interaction between people of different cultural backgrounds may lead to an unique society which his different tenets drawn from all the cultures.

The sources for the study of emigrating people into Andhra are the Persian manuscripts, the contemporary Telugu literature and the Travelogues written by various Europeans visiting the region. The East India Company Records also provide us with some valuable information. Though the sources are many, yet the desired information is very scanty and one his to be very care in critically analyzing them.

The Qutb Shahis were reigning in Andhra Desa in the 17th century. By 1687 AD Golconda had come under the suzerainty of the Mughal empire. With the establishment of the Asaf Jahi rule in 1724 A. D. the region once again had an independent ruler till the mid 20th century. During the Qutb Shahis, Golconda witnessed an unprecedented inflow of immigrants the received a setback during the Mughal governorship. However, the number of people setting down in Andhra from outside once again got a boost up during the Asaf Jahi rule. The number of migrants leaving the region was unquestionably less than those entering it. Migration was mainly due to unfavourable climatic conditions that resulted in much hardships for the local people, forcing them to abandon the land of their ancestors. While the immigrants brought with them the culture and traditions of different regions into Andhra, the migrating people took the culture and traditions of Andhra Desa to far away places.

Abbe Carre, a French missionary visited Deccan in-between 1672 and 1674 AD. He described Hyderabad as a place "full of strangers and merchants" who belonged to different nationalities and came from different parts of the world.[168] There were merchants from Central Asian countries, from South East Asian countries and the European

---

[168] Abbe Carre, <u>The Travels of the Abbe Carre in India and the Near East, 1672-1674</u>, ed. Charles Fawcett, p. 329.

merchants. Thevenot referred to the Persian and Armenian merchants of Golconda who were very rich and prosperous. The local Hindus were merchants as well as bankers in the capital city of Golconda, i.e., Hyderabad.[169] The Europeans had established their factories in Hyderabad. The English and the Dutch were very successful in their business. Some French and Portuguese were also found to be residing at Golconda. These Europeans were mainly interested in sea borne trade and had established their factories even in ports such as Masulipatnam, Bimlipatnam, Petapoly or Nizamapatanam, Vishakapatanam, Yanam, Coringa etc. which came under the jurisdiction of the Sultan of Golconda. They exported textiles from these parts to their motherlands and to South East Asia. They paid for these textiles in gold, silver and copper. They were immigrants who had come to Golconda mainly for economic gains and were happy to accumulate wealth.

There were other immigrants to Golconda who were accorded grand welcome on their and were always sure of being patronized by the Golconda court. These people came from Central and West Asian countries like Persia, Arabia, Turkistan, Iraq, Afghanistan etc. Some came from Georgia and some from the African countries such as Abyssynia. They were all followers of Islam and belonged to both the sects of Shia and Sunni.

---

[169] Thevenot, <u>The Travels of Monsieur Thevenot into the Levant</u>.

The Qutb Shahis belonged to the Central Asain region and were the followers of the Shia faith. They followed a policy of encouraging immigrants especially from Persia to come and settle down in Golconda. The Persians being Shia too, always received patronage in the Qutb Shahi court. As such intellectuals, poets painters architects, musicians, soldiers, doctors, theologians and other from Persia came in large numbers to Andhra in 17th and 18th centuries. The nobility of Golconda, during the rule of the Qutb Shahs, was of Persian origin with a few exceptions. They formed the nobility and nearly 80% of them were appointed as the supervisors over the other high officials belonging to the Hindu faith. Allama Meer Mohammad Momin Astrabadi and Allama Ibn-e-Khatoon were the two Persian intellectuals who attained the high post of Peshwas in the Golconda Kingdom.[170] The important palaces and mosques of Hyderabad were all built on the styles of Persia by Persian architects. In 1679, the English Governor visited Ellore and described it was as "one of the greatsed towns in thes country ... where are made the best carpets (after the manner of those in Persia) by the race of Persians, which they told us came over about 100 years ago.[171] The Ambassador was stationed always at the court of the King. At the port of Nizampatnam, rich Persian merchants carried

---

[170] Nizamuddin Shirazi, <u>Hadiqatus Salatin</u>.
[171] Strenysham Master, <u>The Diaries of Strenysham Master</u>, vol.II, p.171.

on sea borne trade. They were very proud of their origin. Reference is made to their haughtiness in the travelogues of Europeans. Though many poor Persians but of high birth came down to Andhra Desa from Iran, they never indulged in farming or worked at low positions in administration. They never worked below the post of a supervisor. The state came forward to help the destitute Persians and took care of them. Sherwani says that it become fashionable for people and of Iran to come to Hyderabad. Many undistinguishable poets came down to the court of Hyderabad, stayed for a few years at the court's expense, received high gifts from the kings and went back to Persia.[172]

the Turks were the militarymen and some were also salves. The immigrants fro Abyssinia who were called the 'Habits' had been appointed as nobles under the Brahamani rulers. These continued to hold to their posts under the Qutb Shahis also. The majority of them were the 'Jangju' or the warriors and the were the slaves. The slaves that were brought to Andhra, were generally warriors and later on came to occupy honourable positions. The Afghans or the Pathans formed the warriors' class exclusively. The Arabs or the Sayyids were a much respected class. They were appointed as teachers, leaders and nobles of the highest rank. They belonged to the Shiah faith. Most of them

---

[172] H. K Sherwani, The History of the Qutb Shahi Dynasty, p.333.

were also warriors.[173] The Iraquis were the architects or the 'Mimar', the artists of the 'Naqqash', and the 'Hukama' or the Physicians. The majority of Iraquis were in the army of the Qutb Shahs. The people of Tajkistan or the Tajiks were on par with the Turks.[174]

The land also witnessed the arrival of a Hindu class of merchants, Saurashtras or the Gurjaras to the Golconda to the Golconda Kingdom.[175] They mainly got settled down around areas of the diamond mines of Golconda. The merchants were mainly from Gujarat who "for generations gave forsaken their own country to take up the trade."[176] Even now there are some Gujarati families in Guntakal and other places whose ancestors settled there a few hundred years ago. In Kamalakota itself there is a pond called Gujarati-Gunta and a temple of Venkata Swami built by the Gujaratis.[177] They were quite well to do and had acquired considerable wealth as the contemporary Telugu literature says that the thieves stole the money of the 'Gujaras' or the Gujarati businessmen.[178]

---

[173] Mohammad Ziauddin Ahmed, The Relations of Golconda with Tran, 1518-1687, Ph. D. thesis, p.30.

[174] Yusuf Hussain Khan, Farmans and Sanads of the Deccani Sultans.

[175] Adidamu Surakavi, Ramalingeshwar Shataka, p.305

[176] Henry Howard, <u>The Golconda Diamond Mines</u>, in The Philosophical Transactions of the Royal Society, vol. XII, London, 1677.

[177] S. Sakuntala, <u>Diamand Mining in the Golconda and Bijapur Kingdoms during the 17th century</u>.

[178] <u>H. V.</u>

The presence of Odde Rajulu, Odra Brahmins, Oddyulu and the Kalinga Komati in villages of Vijayanagar and Bobbili indicate the immigrants of people of Oriya origin into the north coastal Andhra villages. They might have immigrated during the rule of the Gajapathi kings when the above mentioned areas were a part of the Ganga and Gajapathi Kingdoms.[179] It has been mentioned that the Gajapati Governor, Raghudeva, of the Rajmahendranagara province established an Agrahara on the banks of the River Godavary for the for the Brahmins he brought from Orissa.

The region also witnessed the migrations of the Hindus from the region of Golconda to the Tamil lands and to the kingdoms of the Nayakas. These were the 'Kalamkari' printers of clothes.[180] their work was the printing of the temple hangings whose themes were mainly based on the Hindu religious mythology. The Qutb Shahi Kings patronized the Persian artists only. They were accustomed to being regaled by sophisticated Persian miniatures and did not find a taste in the Kalamkari painting. Those of the artists who could manage to get employment with the Hindu political successors of Vijaynagara monarchs moved further south. For employment sake these people had to leave the land of their ancestors and settle down in foreign lands.

---

[179] <u>Nellore Jilla Kaifiyattulu</u>, p.220.
[180] Dr. D. N. Verma, <u>The Kalamkaris</u>, in Itihaas, vol. VIII, pp.152-153.

Golconda became a Mughal subah in 1687 AD The Qutb Shahi dynasty suffered a great loss in the battle with the Mughals and Tanashah, the last ruler was imprisoned. All these upheavals, led to a decline in the number of the immigrating population of Hyderabad, especially from Persia. Sunnism was declared as the religion of the Suba. Infact, migrations from Andhra to different places was witnessed during 1687 A. D. to 1724 AD The Hindu Ministers who were appointed by the Qutb Shahi kings. Were put to death. The survivors were forced to flee from Hyderabad. Many of them went over to their ancestral homes where they indulged in banditry and dacoity. A handful of them were employed in the Mughal army. However, they were removed very soon. The Muslim nobles of Golconda were re-appointed in the Mughal army and were given the posts of Mansabdars in the posts of Mansabdarsin the Karnatik and the coastal areas of Andhra Desa. About 24 such Mansabdardin were absorbed into the Mughal army. Muhammad Ibrahim, a Qutb Shahi noble was appointed the Governor of Punjab.[181]

The migration of Telugu Nayakas to Tamil lands and to Mysore was seen in large numbers but they still preserved their ancestral language and made of life and avoid the "peculiar usages of their adoptive country. Yet they are

---

[181] J. F. Richards, Mughal Administration in Golconda, Oxford, p.65.

invariably treated with the most perfect tolerance."[182] The history of such Nayakas become the history of Telugu penetration into the Tamil country. They established the Nayakdom of Madura and Tanjore and aldo left for central provinces. These Nayakas settled down permanently there along with their families. Along with their political leaders, a number of people from all parts of life migrated to the Tamil lands. These included the Brahmins,both Niyogis and Vaidekis, the Kshatriyas, the Vaisyas, the gold smith, barbers and a large number of common folks. The process did not stop at any one time. It continued in the following 17th and 18th centuries too. It opened new vistas for a new cultural movement, where Telugu and Tamil cultures came to be fused into one. They patronized Telugu literary persons like, Shyama Raya kavi, Sripati Ramabhadra etc. The last Nayaka of Madura was Vijaya ranga Chokkanath who was a great writer of prose. His works were Sri Ranga Mahatmyany, Megha Bharatamu, etc.[183]

The Hindu population of Golconda had vacated the capital city as the Mughals had no faith in the Brahmins and the Hindus. The Comtis or Komatis, from the Telugu country, formed a large proportion of the shopkeeping class in Madras.[184] They were brokers, and suppliers, exporters and shippers, traders in food stuffs, retail shop owners

[182] Abbe J.A Dubois, op. cit, p.13.
[183] Khadavali Balendusekharam, The Nayakas of Madura Telugu Conference Publication, p.26.
[184] Thurston & Rangachari, vol.III, p.306.

and money lenders. They are mentioned as 'Beri-Chettis' and were said to be very wealthy. The presence of Balijas, in the south of Andhra, has also been mentioned.[185] The Tamilised Balijas were called as 'Kaveri Chetties'. The Hindu merchants who could not adjust to new administration of the Mughals migrate to the southern parts especially to the Pulicat refion and to the Gingilly coast. The Telugu agricultural community also threw up some merchants like the Reddys and the Naids who were mainly concerned with brokerage and retail trade only. they worked for the European merchants. The European merchants like the English, who could not find favour with the Mughals, too migrated to the south from the coastal ports of Andhra Desa.[186] The structural weakness of the Masulipatnam port was another cause for migration of the European to more secure and natural ports like Vishakapatnam and Porto Novo. The migration of the Pathans and the Persian merchants was also witness from the last decade of the 17th century.[187]

With the establishment of Asaf Jahi rule over Hyderabad in 1724 AD, Andhra Desa once again attracted immigrants. However, there was a difference in the nationality of immigrating families from those who immigrated into Andhra during the Qutb Shahi rule. Immigration took place by land routes rather than by sea route, as the people,

---

[185] Abbe Carre, op.cit/ p.595.
[186] C. Srinivas Reddy, Strucural Changes and the Decline of masulipatnam- A late 17th century Question.
[187] S. Arasaratnam, p. 163.

generally, came from the northern and western parts of India. The majority of them were Hindus by birth. Very few Muslims came over to Andhra Desa in the 18th century. The Asaf Jahs invited traders and merchants from western Indian states of Rajasthan, Gujarat, Maharashtra and administrative officers and writers from northern Indian states of Uttar Pradesh and Bihar, the people who came to Hyderabad were mainly the Khatris, the Kayasths, the Marwadis, the Parsis and the Shroffs. The Maharashtrians and the Tamilians also came to Abdhra in the seventeenth and the eighteenth centuries.[188] These people were absorbed basically in the army and in administrative officers. The Kayasthas were the earliest Hindus to accompany Asaf Jah I to the Deccan. Most of the premier Nobles or 'Umara-I-Azam' during the Asaf Jahi period were the immigrants to Andhra region. Some of them were: the rao Rambha damily who immigrated from North India, Fakhr-ul-Mulk from Persia to Bijapur then to Hyderabad, Salar Jung family who were the Arab Shihs to first come to Bijapur and then to Hyderabad, Shaukat Jung Hiaam-ud-daila family, the Persian Shiahs to the Deccan, Rukn-ud-Daula family Persian Shiahs to Deccan with Asaf Jah I, Shah Yar-ul-Mulk family Persian Shiahs from Bijapur to Hyderabad, and the

---

[188] Dharmendra Prasad, <u>Social & Cultural Geography of Hyderabad City: A Historical Perspective</u>, p.65.

Chandulal family who were the Punjabi Khatris from the north India.[189]

By mid 18th century, only the French and the English continued remain on Indian soil. The Dutch, the Danes, the Portuguese and other had left for places or for their respective mother lands. The English and the French were always fighting amongst themselves for supremacy. They had started interfering in the political and. By the end of the 18th century, the French had been defeated and the British become the rulers of the coastal areas of Andhra Desa. More Englishmen continued to come to Andhra not only as traders' do but also as military officers and administrative officers to Nizam's territory. They also brought their families with them and started to settle down in the regions of Hyderabad. As they realized the potential riches of the country they slowly but certainly started to settle down in the region of Hyderabad. As they realized the potential riches of the country they slowly but certainly started showing their intentions of ruling over the entire country.

When the Northern Circars were handed over to the English the English East India Company by the Nizam II, the Hindu population that depended on the petty Rajas for their survival was greatly affected. One such caste was that of the Bhatrazus which was the dependent caste of the

---

[189] Karen B. Leonard. <u>The Kayasthas of Hyderabad</u> City, Ph. D. Thesis, University of Wisconsin, 1969.

Rajus or the Kshatriyas of the Andhra Desa.[190] They were
the balled singers who sang the songs of royal heroism.
The change of rulers forced the Bhatrazus to migrate from
northern Circars to Mysore. They received patronage from
Hyder Ali, the ruler of Mysore and the other small Rajas
of the region. However, as the Hindu Kingdoms vanished,
they were forced to take to agriculture and very few of them
remained ballad singers. Similarly, an account recorded in
1801, indicates that the new immigrant warrior chiefs in
Triunelveli made special efforts to bring Brahmins from
the northern peninsula into their new frontier settlement.
"..a great number of Brahmins of the different Nadus and
sects came from beyond the Godavari river and from the
eastern provinces on the encouragement of the chief to
civilize and populate their districts."[191] There was a greater
dispersion of the Telugu merchants or the Balajas in Tamil
Nadu. The Brahmins settled in Tirunevelli for favourite
administration posts. The Telugu Pariahs i.e. Malas and
the Madigas, Komatis and Chettys were living at Arani,
the weaving village near Kanchipuram in the Chingleput
district.[192]

---

[190] Thurston and Rangachari, op. cit., vol. I.
[191] David Ludden, <u>Peasant History in South India</u>, p.52.
[192] <u>Madras Public Consultations</u>, 1771.

Migrations of Pilgrims:

From the region of Andhra many Muslims went to the religious places in the modern Saudi Arabia to see the Holy places of Mecca and Medina. As such the arrival of the Arabs to Andhra was not one sided. It appears that a great numbers of Indians were going abroad to visit the pilgrimage centers also to learn and knowledge, and some settled down in those places only to teach. Sheikh Ali Myttaqui and Shaikh Tajuddin Sambhali, a celebrated Indian saint, and author of many books and a scholar learned in different branches of learning including agriculture and culinary art and about whom biographies were written, settled down at the place of their visit in Arabia.[193] There are references to the capture of the vessels carrying the pilgrims, by the Portuguese and other Europeans. The royal ladies also went for pilgrimages to the distant places. In 1638, Khanam Agha and Shahr Banu, relations of the King Sultan Abdullah Qutb Shah wen on pilgrimage to Arabia.[194]

Slave Trade

One noticeable feature of those times was the migration of slaves from Andhra Desa to the different parts of the world. However, the people did not migrate to foreign countries on

---

[193] Joshi & Nayeem, op. cit.
[194] Muhammad Ziauddin, op. cit.

their own but were forced by the natural calamatis. The Arab merchants, in earlier times, had bought slaves from the coastal area and sold them in the West Asian countries. This trade was later on, picked up by the Europeans as well. Incessant wars, lack of rains, famines and utter poverty forced the parents to sell their children to these foreigners who took them to the East Asian countries and made them to work on plantation. Famines due to wars or droughts in Andhra Desa occurred in the years – 1629, 1630, 1659, 1685, 1713, 1747, 1787, 1804, 1813, etc.[195] Methwold says that children were exchanged for few grains of rice and were taken to the port city of Masulipatnam where they were sold again to the merchants at a much higher price.[196]During the famines whole villages were depopulated due to death or desertion. The peasants sank into debts and had to sell themselves.

The Dutch profited the most from the slave trade. They found it more lucrative than the trade in the textiles and goods. In the letters written to the Dutch factories on Coromandal coast, there was always a demand for more men from Jacarta and Banda in the East Indies. They also put hindrances in the way of other traders engaged in the slave trade. The demand was for young and middle aged men was very great, and sometimes as many as thousand

---

[195] M. Pattabhirama Reddy, A. P. Historical Review.
[196] Methwold Relations, p. 39.

slaves were asked to be procured.[197] Sometimes females slaves were also sent to these far away places. Migration of slaves to different west Asian and to South East Asian countries was of a regular nature. The region continued to be affected by droughts and famines at regular interval of times. References in the <u>Hadiqatus-Salatin</u> speak of drought for a continuous period of 5 years.[198] The Dutch records too speak of heavy mortality in Golconda in 1635 A. D. The people sold as slaves generally belonged to the Sale caste of weaving community, the workers on the agricultural fields, the petty land owning community and the labourers etc. There were directions for sending as many slaves as possible from Masulipatnam. The European Companies took the services of the Hindus and the Muslims also in the procurement of slaves. One noticeable feature of the slave trade was that the availability of slaves declined when the Andhra country was not facing any drought.[199]

When the English East India Co. acquired the rights to the collection of revenues in the coastal Andhra region, it tried to first regulate the traffic in the salves trade. It tried to bring about a systematic deportation of salves from the regions of the coastal Andhra. But it did not have desired effect. The traders continued to indulge in illegal trade practices. Later on, it passed stricture against the trade

---

[197] Om Prakash, <u>The Dutch Factories in India, 1617-1623</u>, p. 170.
[198] Mirza Nizamuddin Ahmed Saidi, <u>Hadiqatus Salatin, 1614-1644</u>, ed. Syed Ali Asghar Bilgrami, pp. 82-86.
[199] Om Prakash, p. 209.

itself. In 1789 AD, the collection of children and adults, for exportation as slaves, to the different parts of India and abroad was prohibited by a proclamation. This was act was repealed in the year 1790 AD, by the Madras Government. Finally with the arrival of the nineteenth century and with a demand for welfare rights the English government was forced to bring out legislations prohibiting the slaves trade completely in the different parts of India. As such in the year 1843 AD, the Act, which made the traffic in slaves a criminal offence was made.[200] With this, finally, the trade in slaves in Andhra Desa and in the other parts of the country, came to an end.

---

[200] Sarada Raju, <u>Serfdom in South India during the Rule of East India Co</u>, in <u>Itihaas</u>, 1973, pp. 133-143.

Chapter III

RELIGIOUS LIFE

In the seventeenth and eighteenth century Andhra Desa, religion formed the most important part a man's life. Religion gave an identity to a man's life. The religion followed by a man bound him to follow certain rules and regulations. He could not break them. Sometimes, the religion followed by a man put obstacles in his way, yet he could not do away with it. He was helpless even if it took away his right of being a human being. He could change his religion but could not deny it. If gave him a social status. It served as the food the soul and taught a man how to lead his life. It teaches him to be compassionate toward his fellow beings.

The main work of a religion is to keep the followers of a particular order together and to try to help each other in difficulty. As such, is gave confidence to people as they felt that they belonged to a group and in times of need, the group would come forward to help them. There are also instances of the people of a religion standing together to enlist their grievances to the higher authority that was generally accepted.[201] The two main religion of Andhra in 17th and 18th centuries, were Hinduism and Islam. The ancient religions of Buddhism and Jainism continued to exist in the region, but on a very small scale. The entry of the Europeans in the seventeenth century, brought Christianity into Andhra Desa. In course to time the work of missionary father made Christianity an important religion of the region, in a very short period of time. The period under study saw wide ranging changes in the religious life of the people. The old religious orders received a setback with the arrival of new religions. The new political regime was the main reason for the decline of Hinduism. On the order hand the new political forces of the region, help in the advancement of their particular religions. When the Muslim were the rulers of Andhra Desa, Islam was the most important religion the region. Similarly, when the region was under the European rule, Christianity was benefited. However, the predominant

---

[201] Masulipatnam District Records, the Muslims of Masulipatnam appeared before the Governor to ask him to stop the playing of music before a mosque by the Hindus.

religious order the times was Hinduism as still majority of the common people of the region continued to profess it. Hinduism with its different sects, sub-sects and cults of worship, was the most popular religion, however, the Muslim rulers declared Islam as the state religion.

JAINISM AND BUDDHISM:

The ancient religions of Jainism and Buddhism had become almost extinct in Andhra Desa. Jainism was already in a declining stage under the Jijaynagar Kings in the sixteenth century. In the 14th century itself their influences had become limited to a very few places like Warangal and Penugonda. By the 17th century the religion continued to exit in t he Telugu country but only stray references connected with this religion can be found. We find reference of Jainism in the contemporary Shataka poems. As their religion was on the decline, the Jain's priests had started imitating the Brahmins or the Hindu holy men. The Jain Gurus had become a mocking stock for the people as they copied the Brahmins and did not behave in an honorable way. They have been described as ignorant in their religious texts. Instead of preaching their own Jain texts, their priests were giving philosophical discourses on the Hindu religious books. A Jain scholar named Venkata bhat use to give discourse on the Puranas. [202] This shows that the religion

---

[202] Koochi Manchi Timmanna, p.9

had lost the following of the masses and hence their Gurus had to eke out a living by speaking about the doctrines of another religion i.e. Hinduism.

The Jain priests went out to seek converts to their sect preaching principle of Daya or mercy. They used to have "a piece of muslin thrown over their mouth to prevent the entrance and destruction of animal life". [203] They would solemnly walk through the streets with a black staff in one hand, and a fan in the other, to fan the spot on which he proposes to sit down so that no living being is killed. [204] They were always dressed up in a white robe and walled without covering their heads. Some of the religious centers existing during the period were Kolanupak of Nalgonda district and Penugonda of Anantapur district. They were from the Vijayanagr period, but continued to exit even in the 17th and 18th centuries too. The devotees must have come to visit the shrines in large mumbers.

The number of Buddhists, in the Andhra Desa of the seventeenth and eighteenth centuries was very few. There are references of the religious order in the Vijaynagar inscriptions of the 16th century but none in the period under study. The contemporary Shataka literature, which speak about t he Jains, is silent as far as Buddhism in concerned. Hewever, records prove that some of the Buddhists lived near the borders of the Maharashtra State. They called themselves

---

[203] Wilmott and Bilgrami, p.350
[204] ibid.

as Vaishnava- Vira or Buddho-Vaisnavas.[205] While most of them were merchants by profession, others had taken to agriculture and were farmers.

HINDUISM:

During the 17th and 18th centuries, Hinduism was the most predominant religion in the Telugu country. It consisted of different cults of worship. The term Hindu as such was not prevalent and the people living in the area under study were generally known by the sect that they belonged to. The important sects prevalent in the period under study were the Vedic religion, Saivism and Vaishnavism. Beside these major cults, there were also some minor cults present in the Andhra Desa, whose deities were worshipped mainly by the lower castes. Some the minor cults were the Village Goodness cult, the Cult of Sati worship, and the cult of worshipping the trees and the plants etc. the mojor sects were further divided into a number of smaller sects. The followers of each cult worshipped the deity of their own cult. However, the cults along with their different sects acknowledge but one Supreme God. It was clear to all that the different deities were only the different forms of the same God. Vemana, the contemporary social reformer, said the there is only one God who has been visualized by his

---

[205] Wilmott and Bilgrami, p.350

devotees in different forms. Therefore they should worship one and only God. He said:

> *"Pasula vane veru paaloka varnmau,*
> *Puspajaati veru puja okati,*
> *Darsnamulu veru daivambadokkti"*

The meaning of the stanza goes like this. The colour of the animals is different but the milk is of the same colour. The flowers are of different varieties but the worship is one. In the same way, the religions are many but the God is one.

However, the important of Hinduism was on the decline. It lost the state patronage with the downfall of the Hindu Kings. It became full of obsolete ideas and disunity and the political authority to control its degeneration was absent. The various sects and cults of the Hindu religion did not have any unity amongst themselves. The religion had become outdated. When the Telugu region came to be occupied by the Muslims, Hinduism became an inferior religion. The declaration of Islam as the state religion in the 17th and 18th centuries further led to the deteriorating of the ancient religion. The priests who were the propagator of the religion were reduced to poverty as a result of the lack of the patronizing authority. They were forced to shift to other mundane professions. While most had to take to agricultural, some succeeded to get official positions in the government. Several of them earned their living by begging at important pilgrimage centers.[206] The grant of the Agraharas was absent. However, during the period of Madanna and Akkanna who occupied important governmental positions under Abul Hasan, the last king of the Qutb Shahi dynasty, Hinduism was revived to a certain extent. They not only patronized the temples but also granted Agraharas to the Brahmins. They helped in the restoration of the holy place of Tirupati. They also got several choultries constructed for the benefit of the pilgrims who wanted to visit the pilgrimage centers and had come from far away places. On the important pilgrimage routes, food was supplied to Brahmins on the orders of Madanna.[207] The establishment of the Mughal suzerainty and letter on the rule of the Asaf Jahs over theregion resulted on the further decline of the temples. The French hegemony over the coastal region of the Telugu country created panic amongst the Hindus as the French behaved in a fanatic way. There are instances of their iconoclastic actions against the Hindu religious institutions. When t he Northern Circars and the Ceded Districts passed over to the English, both the Hindu and Islamic religions suffered a setback in these regions. The position of both religions became almost equal. However, the mosques and other Islamic institution continued to flourish in the Rayalseema and the Telangana areas which were under the Muslim rule.

---

[206] Francois Martin, p.751.
[207] ibid.

HINDU CULTS:

The Vedic religion was the remnant of the old ritualistic religion. This cult was limited to the Brahmins of the region. It mainly consisted to the sacrifices performed by them for pleasing the Gods. However, if they wished they could teach others some of the Mantras of the Vedic religion. The presence of Vedic religion in the seventeenth and eighteenth centuries in Andhra Desa can be visualized while going through the contemporary literature. The temples following the Vedic cult had Agnivatiakas for the performance of daily Pujas. The Brahminsaslo maintained an altar or a Homakundam in their homes for the daily worship. The daily rituals of worship were performed with the chanting of the Mantras.[208] However, there was a considerable decline in this sect during the period under study. The lack of patronage of the Brahmins, by t he Muslim Kings of Golconda and the stoppage of donations of Agraharas to them resulted in a setbak for this cult. The Brahmins resorted to dubious means to earn their living. Some of them performed the Yajnas for teaching the Mohini Vidya to their disciples. The knowledge of this Vidya enabled a man to attract the lady of his choice towards him.[209] The gullible man would mention the lady of his choice and t he teacher would draw the face of the lady on the floor and tried to summon her. The ruin

---

[208] H.V.

[209] ibid

of the temples also resulted in the decline of Vedic religion. The easy an simple principles of worship of the new religions like Islam and Christianity also caused a setback for the old ritualistic religion.

Saivism was as sub set of Hinduism and its followers were the worshippers of Lord Shiva. During the period under study, it was also on the decline as only the smaller chieftains who were the vassals of the Vijaynagar kingdom were patronizing it. The Hande chiefs of Anantpur and the Nayakas of Velur, modern North Arcot district, were staunch Saivites. They patronized the Saiva teacher and the Saivite religious institutions. Similarly, China Bomma Nayaka of Velur patronized the Saiva teacher, Appaya Dikshita (1553-1625 A.D.) They continued to be the adherents of Saivism inspite of t he changed political scenario. Inspite of their suzerainty under the Vijayanagr rule and with the Kings becoming Vaishnavas they did not change their patronization of Saivism. Some of the sub sects of Saivism were Pasupata Saivism, Kalamukhas, Kapalilka; Veera Saivism also called Lingayats. Veera Saivism was further divided into two schools, namely, the Basava School and the Aradhya School. However, in the regions under the Qutb Shahi Kings, the sect was not enjoying an equal status. Later on in the regions under the Vijayanagar regime its importance declined as the royal Kings had become the patronesses of the Vaishanava sect.

Vishnavism was one of the major religious sects of Hinduism. The main deity of this cult was Lord Vishnu. The people prayed to the main deity and his various Avataras. The important temples belonging to this sect were located at Tirupati, Ahobalam, Sri Kurmam, Mangalagiri, Simhachalam etc. It continued to be a major sect in the period under study. The different sub sects of Vaishnavism were Vaikhanasa and Sri Vaishnavism. Even the triblas like the Chenchus were involve in the religious activities of this sect. The main deity of the Chenchus was God Narsimha. The different schools involved with Vaishnavism were the Madhwa School, the Vallabha School, Vithals, Chitanyas etc. Even the Sathanis had started declaring themselves as Vaishnavas and had started behaving like them.[210]

There existed a great rivalry between the two major sects of the period. There was no unity amongst the following of the different cults and all were devoted to the development of their own cults and their deities. The followers of Saivism held their sect to be greater than Vaishnavism. There was continuous bickering going on between them. Each sect criticized the other for the laxity of morals, but was oblivious of the wrongs in it. There were no reforms made in any of the sects, and both the sects were suffering from unaccountable corruption. Vemana (1565-1625), cautioning them had said that if they did not end their sectarian strife then they

---

[210] Koochi Manchi Timmanna, <u>Kukkutshwara Shataka</u>.

would suffer very badly at the hands of the Muslims.[211] One glaring fact of the contemporary period was that all the three major sects of the Brahmanical religion were losing their importance in the society. The number of their followers was reducing. They remained popular only amongst the upper castes of Hindu social system. The lower castes including the Sudras and the untouchables mostly worshipped the local deities that were not connected with the major cults of the Hindu religion.

The most popular cult of the Telugu country was the cult worshipping the village deity. Very village had a Grama Devata or a village God of its own. It consist chiefly of female worship. All the villages and the towns of Andhra Desa have temples dedicated to a Goddess. The people mainly prayed to the deity to save them from natural calamities like famine, pestilence, cattle diseases, and epidemics of cholera, small pox or fever. The different castes, too had their own special deities, for eg. Komati, Kamsala Gamalla, Idiga, Mala and Madigas had their own village Gods. However the village Goddess was only one and it was prayed by the entire sub sects of the Sudra caste. The titular deity of a village that was always a Goddess was called by different names in different villages. While in one village she was Gangamma, in other she was Ellamma, or Maremma, or Sunkulamma, or Mulipokamma etc. These Goddesses were purely local and fund no mention in the ancient texts of the Hindu

---

[211] C.P. Brown, ed. <u>The Verses of Vemana</u>, Book I, Verse no.7.

religion. There was no regular philosophy, the institutions were crude and the simple form of worship satisfied the religious need of the people. The priests for the performance of the rituals came from the Sudras or from the pariah caste of the Malas or the Madigas. The management and worship were in the hands of the non-Brahmins. Some of the castes associated with the worship were the Tammalas,[212] Balijas,[213] and Jangamas,[214] Sacrifices of animals were performed to appease the Goddesses. It was a periodical festival. Every year Jathras would be taken out throughout the village and all took part in it. This cult was very popular with the common masses. The women often took oaths in front of the deities to make their wishes fulfilled.

"The Grama Devata is exclusively worshipped by other castes and not by the Brahmins."[215] The Brahmins neither took part in the festivities nor performed the Puja associate with them. Through the upper castes were not associated with it, they could not overlook it either. They had to live in the village and as such they paid obeisance to the Grama Devata. However, we find no mention of any attempts to shop practice by the upper castes of the village. Maybe the too took their blessing during the Jathra celebration, along with the other villages.

---

[212] Mc. Mss., no.124,pp.33-34
[213] ibid., no.107, p.55
[214] ibid, no153, p.28
[215] <u>Madas Census Peport,</u> 1871, p.137

Another small cult, which was present in the region, was connected with the worship of the Sati goddess. The villagers prayed to the women who had performed Sati Sahagamana along with the dead body of their husband. They were referred as Perantala. "… And hardly a village is without its shrine to some Parantalamma, or who committed Sati".[216] The village to which these women belonged to constructed temples in their honour. Every year, on the day of her great sacrifice, the villagers would congegrate at the temple in her memory. The prayed to her and narrated her deeds and took part in the celebrations of the feasts in her honour.

HINDU RELIGIOUS INSTITUTIONS:

The religious institutions of all the Hindu cults present on the soil of Andra Desa were the temple. The temple signified the abode of the Gods and commanded great respect from one and all. Every village and every town in the Andhra Desa had atleast one temple. In the period under study, the temple existed but on the low scale. They must have been in shatters as the patronesses of the temples had lost their old glory and power. The fund for the repairs of the temples must have been to procure. However, all existing temples had Puja performed in them. The devotees went to the temples and satisfied their spiritual pursuits. The temples contained the idols of the deities and the people offered their

---

[216] Vishakapatnam Gazet

obeisance to them. While describing one temple, an English officer has written in the 17th century that, "within they are very dark, as having no other light but the doors, and they stand always open. And prove in some places the best receptacles for travelers; one small room only reserved, which the Bramene that keeps it will small intreaty unlock, and shew a synod of brazen saints gilded, the tutelary saint of the place being seated in most eminencie, …".[217] The devotees offered different kinds of items to the God, like oil, sugar and other edible things. The idols of the Gods were made according to their mythological incarnations. Sometimes they represented the figure of half God and half beast, for example the idol of Lord Narasimha was half man and half lion. This could have forced the foreigners to describe them as monsters. "The country of Masulipatan (as all the rest of the Coast) is so full of Idolaters, and the Pagodas so full of the lascivious Figures Monsters, the one con not enter them without horror".[218] At Vijaywada, were many temples that were I existence and were people were still offering prayers and the gifts to the Gods. Tavernier, describers one temple at Jijaywada and says that it was having no walls but only pillars. Another temple was situated on a hill. In the middle of this temple was the idol of a God who was sitting cross legged? This could have been a Saivite temple and the idol must have represented Lord Shiva. Another

---

[217] Methwold's Relations, p.20.

[218] Thevenot, p.147.

temple that attracted a large number of pilgrims was the temple of Lord Narasimha at Mangalagiri.[219] The temples maintained Brahmins and their families. These priests and their families consumed all the offering made to the Gods by the devotees. Some of the rich devotees also donate silver items to the God. Many pilgrims from far and near also visited the temples, locatged in different parts of Andhra Desa, during the annual celebrations.[220] An epigraph of 1603 A.D. says that the Hande chief, Hande Demappa Nayaka, constructed shrines and halls in the Mallikarjun temple of Sri Sailam.[221]

PILGRIMAGES:

The system of visiting the pilgrim centers was also prevailing. But their numbers had their numbers had also gone down. The Hindus assembled at holy places situated on the banks of rivers to take holy dips in the water to wash away their sins. They pilgrims traveled great distances and on auspicious days, came to the sites of pilgrimage that was termed as "Tierton" i.e. Tirthas. Some of the most celebrated holy places were Tirupati, and the temples on the banks of River Ganga.[222] Whenever, the Hindus went on a pilgrimage they went in big groups. The rich and the poor

---

[219] Francois Martin, p.750.
[220] Tavernier, p. 203.
[221] B.AR/1943, no.50.
[222] Annonymous Relations, p.71.

went on pilgrimages and there was no distinction of classes. Pilgrims' procession from as fas as Thatta in Sindh visited the Holy place of Tirupati during the rule of the Qutb Shahi Kings. The pilgrims also took the replica of the God they intended to visit, in a palanquin.

The pilgrimages provide to be a costly affair. The governor of Madras, P3eddala Lingppa, visited the temple at Tirupati and to cover up the huge expenses that he had incurred there, he attacked the English and the Dutch.[223] The pilgrims seldom carried any victuals with them, as the villagers on the way offered them food.[224] An officer of the East India Co., Enugula Veeraswamy, went on a pilgrimage from Madras to Kasi. Kasi was situated on the banks of the river Ganges, in north India. The only method of transport was the bullockcart and palanquin. He took almost one year for the completion of the journey. Hence, it was a strenuous work to go on a pilgrimage to distant places.[225]There was also the fear of the fanatic Muslims who always tortured the Hindu pilgrims. However, the Hindus never hesitated to visit the various holy places situated in the distant lands. They climbed mountains, crossed rivers and bore untold miseries but never stopped going on a pilgrimage.

---

[223] <u>Memoris of Francois Martin</u> p. 733
[224] Tavernier, pp.227-229
[225] Enugula Veeraswamy, p.ix.

DECLINE OF TEMPLES:

The temples had flourished greatly during the rule of the Hindu Kings of the Vijayanagara Kingdom. With the establishment of Muslim rule over Andhra country, the number of temples considerably went down. They patronized Islam and its religious institutions. Though the Kings were not religious bigots yet they preferred their own religion to prosper. The number of mosques increased in the Telugu region, while the number of temples declined considerably. However, we find regional variations in the fortunes of the temples during the17[th] and the 18th centuries. In the Telangana area, which saw Muslim rule throughout the period under study, the temples were much affected. The existing temples were destroyed on the order of the first Qutb Shahi King, Sultan Quli. In the Nalgonda distict, the temples at the Devarkonda fort was burnt to ashes.[226] He was described as destroying thousand temples and building mosques in their places.[227] The celebrations in the exiting temples also suffered a setback. The people were afraid of the consequences of patronizing Hinduism, though we find no edict or rule prohibiting Puja in the temples. In the coastal areas of the modern Andhra region, the temples continued to exit in large numbers.[228] With the establishment of Mughal

---

[226] Anonymous, <u>Tarikh-i-Golconda</u>, Ms., g.70.
[227] ibid.
[228] Thevenot, p.147.

rule the secular fabric was torn apart and the strict rule of the Shahriat was established. The Hindus fled the region in large numbers, to further south, in order to escape the wrath of the Mughal army. However, with the establishment of the Asaf Jahi rule over the area, once again limited secularism was established. In 1800 A.D. the coastal areas called as the Northern Circars and the Ceded districts were brought under the English East India Company. In the earlier years, the British showed neutrality towards all regious. However, later on they succumbed to the pressure of the Christian missionaries and worked for the propagation of Christianity. As such, the fortune of the temples in the coastal areas of Andhra continued to waver with the change in the political situation. In the Rayalseema area of the region, the rule of the Hindu Kings continued for a longer period of time than the other two regions. The region continued to be under the Vijaynagar Kings for a considerable period of time and later on the Nayakas held their sway over it. The Christian missionaries tried to spread their religion first in this region but were not very successful.

There were very few temples built during this period. The temples that were built were from private donations only. The Government did not patronize the construction of temples. On the other hand, few of the Muslim leaders and the army generals felt that it was their religious duty to destroy the temples of the non-believers. Some of the mosques were built on those places, where had earlier stood a Hindu temple.[229] A Persian inscription on a mosque at Udaygiri goes like this "…. In the year 1871 (sic.) of the Hijra i.e. A.D.1661, Hindu temple was pulled down and on its ruins this mosque was set up."[230] It is significant to note that some mosques were built on the very ground of the demolished temples. When such structures are observed carefully, one can very easily visualize that the foundation structure of the mosques are of Hindu style. The Jimma Masjid in the Kurnool fort was built by one Muslim called Abd-ul-Wahab Sahib, on the very foundation of a Hindu temple.[231] A manuscript found in the Srikakulam district, states that, during the time of Muhammad Quly Padshah, his general, Amin ul Mulk, came on a military expedition and conquered the whole region upto Navata and Chavuki.[232] This general of the Qutb Shahi army, caused the destruction of the famous Hindu temple of Srikurmam and also destroyed other important buildings. He is said to have constructed Dargas and mosques at Srikakulam.[233]

The temples were destroyed and the building materials form the destroyed temples were utilized even for the construction of secular buildings, besides being used to construct new mosques. When Neknam Khan captured San Thome or Mylapore near Madras, he thought of fortifying it

---

[229] Anonymous Relations, p.71.
[230] Nellore Manual, p.425.
[231] C. F. Brackenbury, p. 192.
[232] T.V. Mahalingam, ed. Mc.no.95 p.20.
[233] ibid.

and also to build a mud gate.[234] The Kaifiyat of the Kurnool Ilaka, states that the bricks and stones of the demolished temples were either used for building mosques or for the construction of the forts by the Muslim officials.[235] The existing temples, located in the Muslim areas, always faced a threat from them. The Muslims did not care for the sentiments of the Hindus. They would enter the Agnivatikas of the temples and smoke tobacco there. They utilized the fire from these Agnivatikas for lighting their cheroots. They also carried away the utensils of the temples and used them as kitchenware in their houses. The temples of Pottnuru, Vemsasinghi, Janri, Chodavaram and many others were destroyed by the followers of Islam.[236]

During the temporary rule of the French over the coastal areas of Andhra Desa, the Hindu temples witnessed further destruction. Venkatadhwari, a contemporary poet has written that the East India Company was not favorable to the Brahmins.[237] The English the French and the Muslims had created social and religious terror in Andhra Desa.

The French were not inclined towards the Hindu religion.[238] At times, they behaved in fanatic ways. They always tried to shop all Hindu worship in the regions that came under their control. They dismantled the

---

[234] <u>Memoirs of Francious Martin</u>; vol.I
[235] Mc. Ms. Kurnool Kaifiyat.
[236] Gogulapti Kurmanadha Kavi, p. 288.
[237] Venkatashwari, <u>Viswagunadarshanamu</u>, p. 294.
[238] <u>Guntur Kaifiyats,</u> ed. Dr. V. V. Krishna Sastry. P. X.

Kasiviswanadha temple at the Voleru village in the Guntur district, and constructed a Christian monastery at its place. The stone inscription of the temple was also shifted to the monastery by the French East India Company,[239]

In olden days there was no taxes on the temples and on the Aradhya Brahmins. However, the Muslim Zamindars levied taxes on both at some important religious centers.[240] At the temple of Srisailam, half a rupee was collected as religious tax from the Brahmins. During the festival days, on the behalf of the government, further collections were made by different officials like, Amins, peons and others.[241] Taxes were collected from the pilgrims on the routes it self by these officials. The Sirkar officials collected fees on behalf of the priests of the temples, paid them a small amount and appropriated the rest. The fee paid to the priests for performing the Abishekhan to the Lord, was collected by the officials and only the fourth share was allotted to the priests.

The decline of temples is also indicated by the reduction in the strength of their trust boards. At Tirupati, the total number of Sthanattar of Venkateshwara temple was 12 in the sixteenth century. It became only 6 in the year 1638 A. D. It further reduced down to only 4 in the year 1684 A.D. During the Qutb Shahi rule there were no endowments

---

[239] ibid.
[240] Mc. Mss. <u>Sri Sailam Kafiyat,</u> p.17.
[241] ibid.

made to the temples after 1638 A.D.[242] Another interesting observation made during the period was that the Hande chiefs of Velur, joined hands with Ibrahim Quli and ransacked the Ahobilam temple in the year 1584 A.D.[243] As a result the worship of the God was completely stopped there. The construction of the Gudipudu temple and the Veleru temple could not be completed because of the official Amin Malka.[244]

The Manyams enjoyed by the Hindu temples were also confiscated.[245] The Tadaparthi Kaifiyat, adds, that the Ramavesvara temple was blown up by the Muslims.[246] The valuable articles from the temples were also carried away by the plunderers. The jewels of the Gods set with gems, gold and silver vessels granted by the Hindu Rajas, to the processional images of both upper and lower Ahobilam temples, were carred away by the Muslims.[247] The articles that escaped notice of the plunders, were later on carried away by the King of Golconda, Ibrahim Qutb Shah.[248] The Aragal of King Pratap's palace, consisting of four granite supporters, was removed to Mecca Masjid at Hyderabad. The

---

[242] S. K. T. Veeraraghavacharya, History of Tirupati, 1978, pp.11 & 40.

[243] S.I.I. Vol.XVI, no. 296.

[244] Mc. Mss 20, (SA), pp.8-37

[245] Ibid., p.238.

[246] Ibid., pp.86-89

[247] Mc. Mss., Kaifiyat of Ahobalam, Cangalamari taluq, Kandanavolu Ilka.

[248] Ibid.

Bhadragiri Satakam was written in about 1750 AD, and it narrates the atrocities of Muslim 'Saradars' on the Brahmins in the holy town of Bhadragiri.[249] The atrocities committed by the Muslims in the religious town of Tirupati, have also been recorded in the Telugu literature of the contemporary period.[250]

Another Hindu institution was the Agrahara. The Agraharas were villages that had only Brahmins as inhabitants. The Agraharas were the grants of the Kings or the nobles given to the religious men for the services rendered towards the Hindu religion. With the decline of the Hindu Kings, the gift of Agraharas to the Brahmins stopped. Infact, these lands were snatched from them and handed over to the Muslims during the reign of the Muslim Kings. In the wake of the Qutbshahi expansion a number of Agraharas were confiscated. The Kaifiyat of Pedapudi in the modern Guntur district states that the Qutbshahi Government or the Turakanyam, established after the fall of Vijaynagar rule, confiscated all Inam and Srotriya lands and also the Pedapudi Agrahara.[251] Under the East India Company, the Zamindars had become the rich men of the principalities. However, they also were indifferent to the Brahmins and did not maintain Brahmin scholars by granting them Agraharas.[252] The main reason could be that

---

[249] Bhalla Perakavi, pp.290-291.

[250] Vaddikasula Venkanna Kavi, p.291.

[251] Mc.Ms.no.101, p.105.

[252] Surakavi, ed. Venkat Rao, p.144-145.

they did not want to hurt their political bosses who were Muslims.

The Mathas were the living quarters of the saints who had taken up the cause of religion and had given up living the ordinary life. The leader of the Matha, was generally a Brahmachari or a bachelor. They stayed in the Mathas that were far from the general towns and village and were situated near a temple that was a pilgrimage center. One such Matha was at the temple of Ahobalam. The head of such Mathas were called as Jiyyars. These Mathas were on the decline as the Muslims continued to loot them. The Jiyyar of the Tirupati Matha was killed when Abdullah Qutb Shah led on expedition to the place. It caused horror in the minds of the Nambi, the Jiyyar's Deputy and the Parpatyadar of the temple.[253]

FAIRS & FESTIVALS:

In the Hindu religion, the festivals are celebrated more for social unity as all the people come together during the celebrations. The caste prejudices were more or less forgotten and every one tried to make the most out of these festivities. The Hindus of the Telugu country celebrated a number of festivals throughout the year. The birthday of their leading heroes and saints were celebrated, the common festivals and

---

[253] A. R. Ramachandra Reddy, <u>Historical Riddles of Venkatachala Vihara Shatakamu,</u> in Itihaas vil. XVI

the local village festivals were also very much enjoyed. Some of the famous festivals were Makar Sankranthi,[254] Dassera celebrated in the Ashwin month,[255] and the Sivarathri.[256]

The festival of Sankranthi was celebrated for three days and was a very important festival for all. The first day was celebrated as Bhog, the second as Sankranthi, and the third and the final day was the Kanumu or the Pasula Panduga.[257]When the festival arrived, the harvest season would be coming to an end and the godowns would be full of paddy, corn and other gains. Hence during the festival different kinds of food was cooked by the people. It was a celebration of the plenty. The women prepared a special dish called Pongali and offered it to the Gods. The Pongali was prepared with the new rice, and jaggery. This sweet dish was very important and it was prepared in every home. The dish was prepared in new Kundas or earthen pots.[258] The milk was left to boil over the new pot and fall to the ground as it was believed to be a good omen and promised happiness and fulfillment in the coming year. The festival was every popular, especially amongst the farmers and the labourers in the fields. It was a celebration of their work in the agricultural fields for the entire year. On the third day of the Makar Sankranthi, the animals were decorated.

---

[254] S. S. & H. V.

[255] S. Pratap Reddy,

[256] Mazhar Hussain.

[257] S. S. & H. V.

[258] H.V. ch. V. p.14.

The bullocks were decorated and taken to the fields for ploughing. Hence the third day was called as the Pasula Panduga in Telangana and Kanumu in the Rayalseema area.

During the celebrations of the temple festivals, Santa or fairs were arranged. The shops were beautifully decorated and were full of delicious sweets and the salty eatables. The shopkeepers arranged these items in stairs so as to attract the buyers. Large number of people came at the fairs to sell their products and to make profits. The potters brought pots to sell at the fairs and made brisk business. As the Pongali was prepared in new pots, the demand for the earthen pots would be very high during the festival of Sankranti. Large queues could be seen at the shops for the various items.[259] The people spent a lot of money on new clothes and on new ornaments. The women made and bought necklaces of pearls, beads etc. and decorated themselves during the festivities.

The Jathras, or fairs were conducted in t he village or towns, during the celebration important temple festivals. Though they were termed as Jathras, in reality they were the temple car festivals. They were taken out after or during the celebration of every festival. Every villager took part in the Jathras. Some of the famous Jathras of the Hyderabad city were the Lachmi Narasimha Swami Jathra, the Vir Bahadur Swami Jathra, the Venkat Narsimha Swami Jathra and etc. During the Shivarathri festival a big Jathra was

---

[259] S.S.

taken out by the people. The images of the deities were taken out in Rathas or wooden cars that were drawn by the villagers. Some persons pulled the ropes of the chariot while the others performed the Porludandau i.e. they lay in front of the chariots and turned their body round on the ground, fulfilling the oath taken in the presence of the deity. The people standing nearby removed the small pebbles from the ground so that the people doing the penance would not be hurt. The Gods were taken through every street and corner of the villages or towns. It was a festivity for all the castes, and the taboo of caste system was forgotten for the time being. At the village of Kolkulapalli, a Jathra of Lord Narasimha was celebrated every year.[260] The village of Kolkulapalli, was situated about 60 Kilometers from the city of Hyderabad. At the Narasimha Jathra, lighted poles were carried by the people in their hand during the night. The musical instrument called Talam was played and Artis were with lighted cottons in a plate of oil, and carried most probably by the womenfolk in the Jathra. Such festivals were celebrated every year. Tasaddika, or a fixed sum of money was paid by the government to the temple, to draw the card during festivals. The East India Company government also continued this system in the Ceded Districts.[261]

---

[260] H.V.
[261] A. Jagganadhan.

Another important festival of the Telugu people was the Vithunati Panduga.[262] It was a festival of the agricultural lands. It was concerned with the sowing of the Cholam seeds. The Purohita or the Brahmin priest was asked to select an auspicious day and time for sowing of the seeds in the field. The festival was celebrated with a lot of gaiety and enthusiasm by the men and the women of the villages. The sowing of seeds in the field was done by all the communities irrespective of their castes. It was the festivals that made the people one and during the Vithunati Panduga, the people addressed each other in close terms. The Pedda Reddy has been quoted as addressing the Brahmin as Bawa or cousin. The women called each other as Vadina or sister-in-law and as Atta or mother-in-law. Nobody seemed to bother about the usual courtesies and joked with each other as if they belonged to the same family.

Among the local festivals of the time, Batakamma was quit an important festival. This festival is celebrated mainly in Telangana area and this must have been the practice during the period under study. Batakamma is festival celebrated by the women even to this day. Actually, Batakamma was the local name of Devi Anasuya or Parvathi or Sita. It started in the month of August or September after the celebration of the Ganesh Chaturthi and ended in October or November before Dassera.[263] The women wore grand make up, put

---

[262] S.S
[263] Dr. Rashid Musavi

on costly dresses, and decorated their hairs with flowers. They proceeded toward a stream or a river, in a procession, dancing and singing all the way. The song they sing goes like this, Batakkamma, Batakkamma, Oyalu. The festival was beautifully described in a play called Chand Bibi by Vizir Hussain.[264] The women of the coastal Andhra and the Rayalaseema region celebrated the Bommalakoluvu during which the dolls of different kinds were arranged and displayed in a beautiful way.

In most of the villages of the Telugunadu, the Jathra were conducted for the Grama-Devata or the village deity. The contemporary Telugu work <u>Suka Sapatati,</u> mentions the Jathra of the deities Gangamma, Pochamma, Yellamma etc. conductd by the people of the various villages of the Andhra country.[265] Men and women both took part in these Jathras. They sang, danced and prayed in front of the temples dedicated to the deities. Animal sacrifices formed a part of the village temple rites. During the celebrations, a number of goats and sheep were sacrificed at the altar of the deity and their blood was scattered on the floor and on the roads. The shepherds brought their stock of sheep and goat to the fairs. The sacrifice of the animals made at temples increased the demand for them manifolds. The cocks were also sacrificed amidst the chanting of the Mantras by the priests. The women made Pongali and offered it to the Gods

---

[264] ibid.

[265] <u>S.S</u>

as food. They also threw the milk of the Pongali on the floor of the temple. A lot of incense was burnt during the performance of the Puja.

An important item in these Jathras was the dance of the Shiva Shaktis.[266] These men and women dancers were said to have been possessed by the Goddess or Shivams and performed a very speedy and violent dance in the processions. The words uttered by these Shiva Shaktis were said to be truth, and everybody listened to them with attention and devotion; as it was believed that the Goddess herself, was speaking through the mouth of these persons. Several suspecting women brought their husbands to these jathras to make them to take an oath in front of the deity to remain faithful to them. Many of the believers followed the path of Moodh Bhakti or blind faith. Some of the devotees cut off the parts of their body and offered it to the deity. It was called as Mokku or a bribe that was given to the God in return for the wishes fulfilled. The toes of the leg or the fingers of the hands or sometimes the foot or the hand itself was cut off and offered as a gift to the deity. A Jathra has been mentioned by the Portuguese religious man Abbe Carre, at a place called Macheron or Macherla.[267] He says that there was a large temple of the Hindus. The festivities continued through out the night and later on in

---

[266] ibid.
[267] The Travels of Abbe Carre., p.353.

the morning, they carried the idol in a palanquin all around the village streets.

The Hindus celebrated their festivals with great pomp and show but in Hindu ruled areas only. In Muslim Kingdoms they always maintained a low key. An unknown Dutch employee of the Dutch factory at Nizampatam, writes, "The Brahmins hold in honour some of their temples, called by them pagodas, but not in such great numbers, or with so many ceremonies, as in the Gentu country where the Muslims have no authority."[268] However, in the village there was less restriction and the Hindus were celebrating them with great joy. The reasons could be the absence of Muslim regulating authority.

ISLAM:

Islam, had considerable following in Andhra Desa during the period under study. It was declared as the religion of state in both the centuries under study as the rulers were the followers of Islam. The higher strata of the Andhra society in the 17th and the 18th century were the followers of the Islamic faith. As such it received all the patronage from the state and the ruling elite of the region. The establishment of the Qutb Shahi kingdom in the sixteenth century had already made Andhra Desa an Islamic centre. In the following century, the region became

---

[268] <u>Anonymous Relations</u>, p. 71.

an important center of Muslim religion and culture. About the cultural glory during the reign of the Qutb Shahi Kings, H.K. Sherwani says that, "The reign of Muhammad Quli Qutb Shah was marked ... by the blossoming of all that was latent in Tilang-Andhra in the field of literature, art, architecture, song and dance, and the culminative effect of all these tendencies was the planning and construction of the new capital....Hyderabad....a standing and lasting monument of his own fine taste and to the glory of the epoch dominated by the rulers of the Qutbshahi dynasty".[269] This was carried on further by his successors of the dynasty. However, the cultural aspect received a setback during the Mughal occupancy of the region. The religious work was never stopped. During the Asaf Jahi period, the cultural and the religious talents were once again revived. These two centuries, on the whole, marked an important phase in the spread of Islam and its religious institutions in the Telugu country. The city attracted a number of foreign Muslim immigrants who came here in search of fortune. This swelled the ranks of the already existing Muslim population, and this in turn strengthened Islam in this area.

The believers of Islam were divided into two main sects-the Shiahs and the Sunnis. The followers of Ali, who was the cousin and son in law of the Prophet, and the lineal descendents of Ali were termed as Shiahs. The persons who did not accept these principles were the Sunnis. However,

---

[269] H.K. Sherwani, pp.171-173.

both of them accepted the basic tenets of Islam, which was preached by Prophet Mohammad.[270] Islam had entered the Telugu-speaking region even before the Muslim forces occupied the region. The Qutb Shahis were the followers of the Shiah sect and hence Shiism became the state religion under their rule. They ordered that in public worship the names of the 12 Imams should be read.[271] The Kings tried to strengthen their sect by inviting foreign Shiahs to their kingdom. As such people from west Asian regions started infiltrating the Telugu region. The Persians belonged to this sect. They filled all the important government posts under the Qutb Shahis. The King bestowed large sums of money on the Persians who were from noble ancestry but were men of small means.[272] When Andhra Desa came under the Mughal occupation and later on when the Asaf Jahs became the independent ruler of the region, Shiims lost its place of importance. The Mughals and the Asaf Jahs belonged to the sect of Sunnism and hence declared it as their State religion. The Shiah sect received a setback and Sunnis were in the limelight. They were given all the important post in the administration. The immigration of foreign Muslims came down drastically during this period. On the other hand, Muslims from north of India stated coming down to the south.

---

[270] William Theodore De Bary, Sources of Indian Tradition, p.376.
[271] Henry Briggs, vol. III, p. 354.
[272] Schoerer Relatins, p. 56.

The division between the followers of the two sects of Islam was so great that each tried to outdo the other. When the Shiahs were in power, the Sunnis became rural oriented and preferred to lay back. Similarly, when the Mughals established their rule, several Shiahs migrated to the other places and left Andhra Desa. The Shiahs and Sunnis differed in their methods of offering prayers. However, both of them offered prayers in religious places called Masjids or mosques. The population percentage of the Shiahs was in minority as compared to the population of the Sunnis in this region. The reason could be that the Shiahs were mostly foreigners. The Persians formed the majority of the Shiahs in Andhra. The Sunnis were the earliest arrivals in the Telugu country. They consisted of Pathans, Afghans, Arabians, and others. The local converts also were mostly Sunnis. There was no good feeling lost between the two sects. The Persians were every haughty and did not mix freely with the local inhabitants of the region. The Sunnis accepted Andhra Desa as their motherland and mixed freely with the local Telugu population. The principle of brotherhood of Sunnism had attracted a lot or converts from the locals.

MUSLIM RELIGIOUS INSTITUTION

The Muslims constructed Masjids in villages and towns that had Muslim population. Antony Schoerer, writing about the Golkonda kingdom, observed, "In the towns, and also in the villages, are many of their churches, called Masjits, for travellers and residents, for Amy Moslems live all through the country".[273] The first Qutb Shahi ruler, Sultan Quli, built one thousand mosques.[274] The Muslim elite built mosques in new place with a religious zeal. It was considered a religious act to build mosques in new places. Hence, whenever they occupied a new territory or created a new village or town, the Muslims took it as their duty to construct mosques there. When they constructed any public building also they never forgot to construct a mosque in it. A mosque was built along side the Darul Shifa, which was meant to be a medical hospital and college. Similarly, at the Charminar, which also served as a college, a mosque was built at the top. Even at the tombs of the Qutb Shahi Kings, mosques were constructed.

At Tadaparthi, when they came to power, the Nawabs of Arcot and the Nawabs of Kurnool constructed several masjids in the areas under them.[275] Similarly, the Muslims built villages and passed orders that the revenue from the new village would go to benefit such a mosque. In the same manner a village named Neknamabad, was built by Nekanam Khan, the Governor of Gandikota, and was made over to the mosque at Gandikota. The revenue of the village was utilized for the maintenance of the servants

---

[273] Schorer Relations, p.57.
[274] Anonymous, Tarikh-I Qutb Shahi, (Ms.) p.70.
[275] Mc. Ms. Tadaparthi Kaifiyat.

of the mosque.[276] The Muslim ladies were also not far behind their menfolk in the religious works. Queen Hayat Bakshi Begum, the mother of Sultan Abdullah, built a new town called Hayatabad, near the capital city Hyderabad, and therein built a mosque.[277] Another Qutb Shahi lady, Khaireeyat -un-nissa Begum, who was the daughter of Muhammad Qutb Shah, founded a place called Khairatabad and also built a mosque at the place. She dedicated it to her teacher, Mullah Abdul Malik.[278] Similarly, a mosque was built by Kultusum Begum, the wife of Prince Quli Mirza at Kultusumpura, a place, which was also her creation.[279] During the Asaf Jahi rulers also, the women always did religious works. The courtesan of Nizam II, Mahalakha Chanda Bibi, built a mosque called Saniye Baital Haram, near Purana Pul in 1203 H.

The establishment of Muslim rule in Andhra Desa marked an important stage in the position of the mosques in the region. The mosques were generally very large in area and they catered to the needs of a large number of people. The Muslims visited mosques to offer prayers. On ordinary days they offered four prayers at different hours in the mosque. On Friday of the week, they offered five prayers and the religious place use to be crowded of the people on that day.

---

[276] Rafat –e –Rizwana, op. cit.

[277] Rafat –e –Rizwana, op. cit.

[278] Rafat –e –Rizwana, op. cit.

[279] ibid.

The mosques continued to be in the same influential position throughout the two centuries of Muslim rule over the Telugu country. They became very prosperous and influential religious institutions. The changes in the ruling dynasties over the region, did not in any way hinder the growth of the mosques. Infact, the number of mosques in Andhra Desa increased with the change in the ruling dynasties.

The mosque had its own organizations and functionaries for the management of its affairs. The trustees of the mosque were appointed by the founders themselves. When Hayat Bakshi Begum built the mosque at Hayatnagar, the Imam and the Moazzim of the mosque, were appointed by her. They were generally appointed on hereditary basis, with the right of succession to that office given either to the spiritual disciples or to the sons of the occupants of that office.

They supported a number of poor religious men who had made Islam their way of life. A type of holy men, belonging to the poor families, stayed in the mosques and learnt the Quran, the holy book, by heart. These people were married. They, along with their families, were maintained by the offerings of the people, at the mosques. Another important group of religious men were the Faquirs or the Dervishes i.e. the mendicants.[280] They were found in large numbers in the kingdom of Golconda. They lived in unhygienic conditions and never did any work. They were not married. They used

---

[280] Tavernier, p. 383.

to give sermons in the mosques, in the evenings, sitting on a carpet. Their disciples collected food for them from the villagers and fed them.

Another religious institution of the Muslims, was the Khanqahs. These were the residential places of Sufi saints. The saints along with his followers lived here. The family of the saints also resided at the khanqahs. During the Qutb Shahi dynasty, the influx of Sufis from the western Asian countries was witnessed. Sufis continued to flourish under the Mughal rule and under the Asaf Jahi dynasty. Infact, during the Asaf Jahs, the number of the Sufis was the maximum in Andhra Desa.

The Khanqahs had a number of attendants staying within the premises. For example there were the barbers, washermen, and other attendants. The descendants of these people served the descendants of the saints for generations. The barbers also played the music at the Dargah of the saints during the celebration of the Urs festival. These attendants were all maintained on the revenues collected from the lands donated by the rich and powerful followers of the saints. The Kings and his nobles, the provincial Governors, the high officials and others gifted land to the Sufi establishments. Sometimes, the attendants were themselves granted Inam lands for the performance of free sevice in the Khanqahs. These places also served as propagators of the local language, culture and traditions of the people as the Hindus and the Muslims stayed there under one roof.

The pontiff was the head of the Khanqahs. He was known as Shaikh or the Pir. He presided over the religious congregations in it and gave instructions to his disciples. He administered the Khanqah and enjoyed absolute authority over all present in the premises.[281] The spiritual disciples of the saint were known as Murid.

All the religious institution of the Muslims, like the Masjids and the Sufi Khanqahs, provided food and lodging for the poor, the needy and the travelers. There was also the provision of free haircut, bath etc. The needy also received alms and clothes like lungis at these places. From time to time, public feeding was also undertaken.[282]

Another important Muslim religious institution existing in Andhra Desa, during the 17th and the 18th centuries, was the Dargah. A Dargah is a Muslim shrine or tomb of some reputed holy person and which is the object of pilgrimage and adoration. All the renowned Sufi saints of the period came to have tomb-shrines built by their disciples. These shrines, in the course of time, became important centers of worship and pilgrimage for not only their spiritual disciples but also to the laymen.

The inducements for the people to visit these Dargahs were the desires for having children, recovery from sickens,

---

[281] K.A. Nizami, <u>Some Aspects of Religion and Politics in India during the Thirteenth century</u>, p.206.

[282] R. Soma Reddy, <u>History of Religious Institutions in Andhra Desa from A.D. 1300-1600</u>. Ph. D. thesis, Osmania University, 1980)

preservation from any grievous calamity and danger or any other event exciting grateful feelings. The Muslims belonging to both the upper classes and the common masses, used to vow, especially in times of crises, to offer some thing to a particular shrine, if the desires were fulfilled. These shrines, like all other religious institutions were patronized by the Muslims rulers and their subjects alike. The present practice of celebrating the Urs festivals of some of these shrines and making a pilgrimage to them, among the Muslims and non-Muslims, is a continuation of the same tradition.

Each Dargah had a Mutawalli who was generally a descendant of the saint to whom the Dargah belonged. Some times, the saints themselves, appointed the Mutawalli of his tomb, before their death. These Mutawalli were always the descendants of the saint. If the deceased saint had no children, one of his near relatives or the chief disciples was appointed as the Mutawalli. This post was held on a hereditary basis. The Mutawalli was the owner of the properties of the Dargah, which included the building, lands, etc. He also decided all-important matters concerning the affairs of the institutions. He was assisted by the Sajjada and the other menial servants.

The Ashurkhana was another Islamic institution that comes under the scope of the present study. It belongs exclusively to the Shiah sect. The recorded history shows that the Ashurkhanas were first started to be built during the reign of the Qutb Shahi Kings-- Ibrahim Qutbshah and Muhammad Quli Qutbshah.

The Ashurkhana is defined as "the building which houses the Alams or the conventional copies of the standard carried by Iman Hussain".[283] At present they number about half a dozen, and are situated mainly in and around the city of modern Hyderabad. All the Ahsurkhanas had Alams, but the one at Maula Ali is said to contain the impression of the hand of Hazrat Ali, on a stone. Some of the Ashurkhana are The Maula Ali Ashurkhana, Ashurkhana-e-Nal-e-Mubarak, Bagh-e-Hazrat, Hussaini Alam of Golconda, Badshahi Ashurkhana, and the new Hussaini Alam Ashurkhana.

These institution became very popular in the 17th century A.D., when a number of them were set up in the city of Hyderabad and in the other towns and villages where Muslims lived. These buildings though religious in character, played an important role in the cultural and economic life not only of the Shia Muslims but the entire population. Zore writes that the complete population whether Muslims or non-Muslims, used to pay homage in the Ashurkhanas and all the differences between the rulers and the ruled and the cultural, creed and caste were wiped off.[284]

The chief functionary of the Ashurkhana was the Mutawalli who was appointed by the government and the post was hereditary. He appointed his assistance called

---

[283] H.K. Sherwani, p.313.
[284] Mohiuddin Qadiri Zore, Hayat-e-Mir Mumin, p.46.

Mujaver, who was the caretaker of the institution. On the days of the Muharram festival a few menial servants like sweepers, watermen, light-men etc., were appointed on daily wages.

MUSLIM FAIRS & FESTIVALS

Some of the famous Muslim festivals were Shab-i-Barat, Birthday of Prophet Mohammed, Nauroz, Id-ul-Fitr, Id-ul-Zuha etc. During the Qutb Shahs, Moharram, was observed as a mourning festival. The Qutb Shahs belonged to the Shiah sect of Islam so mourned for the death of the martyrs at the battlefield of Karbala. Some of the fairs that were conducted during the Asaf Jahi rulers at the capital city Hyderabad were Maula Ali Mela, Baf Sharfuddin Urs, Yusuf Saheb Sharif Saheb Urs.[285] The other famous festivals were the Khat Darshan Jasne Haidri and Moharram. There was a fixed calendar of ceremonies, maked by banquets, the distribution of gifts to nobles, and public displays. Four major darbars were also held on Nizam's birthday, Nauroz or Persian New Year's day, and on Id-ul Fitr and Id-ud Zuha. During these festivities the Nizam received honours at the Id Durbars, while on Nizam's birthday and on Nauroz, all others received awards.

---

[285] Mazhar Husain, List of Urses, Melas, Jatras etc, in H.E.H. the Nizam's Dominions, 1349F.

The mourning of Muharram lasted for 40 days.[286] "The Moors of Golconda celebrated it with more Fopperies than they do in Persia."[287] The rulers of Andhra were more serious and meticulous in the celebrations than the Muslims of their ancestral region. It was on old custom in the Qutb Shahi dynasty to observe the festival. They observed every rule of the Moharram. Every believer was to put on black dress for all the days and the slippers were not to be worn. The Kings followed these rules and the nobility and the common man followed the royalty.[288] Black dresses were distributed to the poor as they could not afford to buy it. All pleasures were given up by the King and the nobility during the days of mourning. Similarly, all the people were to desist from all kinds of enjoyment. The musical instruments were covered and stored up and no music or dance was performed in the Kingdom. Royal orders were issued not to kill any kind of animal for eating purpose. The butchers' shops were ordered to be closed. No trader was to sell nay intoxicants like opium, toddy and tobacco during the mourning period. The smoking of Hookahs was not allowed. Even the barbers had to close their shop as the cutting of hair was not allowed. All these restriction applied both to the Muslims and the Hindus.[289] The lighting arrangements

---

[286] Nizam-ud-din Ahmad Saidi, Ms. Hadiqaturs Salatin, pp.41-49

[287] M. Thevenot, p.149.

[288] Dr. Zor, Mukaddame Qulliyat Sultan Muhammad Quli Qutb Shah, p. 143.

[289] Ms. Hadiqutus Salatin, pp. 41-49.

were systematized during the days of Muharram. There was great zeal an enthusiansm in the public and attractive Taazia made with golden threads were taken out. "They erect Chappeals in all the Streets with Tents, which they fill with Lamps, and adorn with Foot-Carpets; the Streets are full of people, and all of them almost have their Faces covered with Sifted ashes."[290] The Ashur Khanas were decorated very tastefully. The pathetic songs called Mersiah ware rendered by the singers in mourning, in the Mehfils or religious gatherings. While describing the celebrations, the French traveler, Thevenot, has written that the people took out huge processions on the streets. Some of them dragged huge chains, which used to be wound around their waist and was very painful to carry. Almost all of them carried swords. The rich carried the real swords, the poor had only wooden ones with them. The other processionists carried different representations of the Muhammad and Hussain, the Martyr.[291]

The ceremony was always marked with bloodshed. This festival was mainly related with the sect of the Shiahs. They ware the followers of Hussian, who was killed at the battle of Karbala by the forces of Calif Yezid. The Sunnis who were followers of the victorious forces, would laugh at them. This was enough to ignite the passion of the mourners who quarreled and fought with them. People were killed in

---

[290] Thevenot, p. 149.
[291] ibid.

dozens. However, no one ever regretted this fight as is was believed that the gates of Paradise were open throughout the fen days of Moharram. Anyone killed in the fights would be welcomed in heaven.[292] This would occur every year when the feast of Moharram was celebrated.

The birthday of Paigamber Mohammad, the Icon of Islam, was celebrated with great gaiety by the Muhammadans during the rule of the Qutb Shahi Kings. It was again a festival of the Shiahs. It was celebrated on the 12 Rabi Awwl. In this festival all pleasures were to be enjoyed. The whole city of Hyderabad was decorated and Aiyanabandi was done.[293] The King took took part in the celebrations and gave away lots of things in charity. Langars were established and the poor got free food there. In the celebrated hall, the King kept the portraits of the Iranian King and his nobles on the right side of his seat. The portraits of the Mughal King and his nobility were kept to the left side of his seat. This was done to show the obedience of the Golconda King towards both of them. The portraits were a symbol of their presence in the celebration hall.[294] A portrait of a white horse symbolizing the Prophet going to paradise, was also present there. In the morning, the performers of acrobatic feats were called from far and near to entertain the King and the public. The Baazigars, the Nat-Natnis and the Reshambaz

---

[292] Thevenot, p.149
[293] Mirza Nizamuddin Ahmed Saidi, Ms. <u>Hadiqatus Salatin</u>, p.50.
[294] Hadiqatus Salatin, p.52.

performed their feats. The jesters called as Lobatbaaz also entertained the audience. During the night, the King and the nobility were entertained by the dancing girls who were referred to as Luliyan. They used to be dressed up in beautiful clothes and applied perfumes all over their body very extravagantly. They generally danced in circles accompanied by ear soothing music from India and Iran. Later on food was served and without any distinction, the rich and poor ate from the same vessel.[295] Betal nut was also given to all. The celebration continued for almost a month. Processions were taken out with the King leading it, the nobles, the public, the dancers and the musician followed from behind. During the celebration of the Prophet's birthday, the King distributed red dress in the public.

The other famous festival was the Nauroz. It was the Parsis. New Year and was introduced in the Deccan by the Qutb Shahs. It was celebrated by all. The Qutb Shah Kings held grand Darbar and it was attended by the Rajas and the Amirs who came to pay their homage to the King.[296] A ritual called Panjeri was performed. The royal Begums and the ladies also took part.[297] Delicious food was cooked and distributed among the poor and the hungry, free of cost. The celebrations were also glamorized by the dances of the nautch girls. There were gaiety and grandeur every where.

---

[295] ibid.

[296] Sadiq Naqvi, Muslim Religious Institutions and their role umder the Qutb Shah, pp.238-239.

[297] Kamtar, Dastaane Nabab Nizam Ali Khan, 1221 H.

The festival was equally popular during the reign of the Asaf Jahi Kings. The records mention that, the second ruler of the Asaf Jahi dynasty, Nizam Ali Khan Bahadur, celebrated the festival on 20 March 1768, which was a Sunday.[298]

The most important festival celebrated by the Muslims was the festival of Id-ul-Fitr. It was a festival celebrated both by the Shiah and the Sunni sections of Islam. Before the celebrations, the Muslims fasted for almost a month on the occasion of Ramadan.[299] All the followers of Islam whether young or old, piously fasted for the entire month. They donated very liberally to the poor during the fasting month. The month of Ramadan ended with the celebration of the Id. All the people went around greeting their friends and relatives on the festive occasion. The rich and the poor wore new dresses and had special food cooked for the celebrations.

The order important festival was the Iddu'z Zuha or Bakrid i.e. the festival of the goat. The slaughter of animals was compulsory as it was a festival of sacrifice. The goats and sheep were sacrificed in large number and everybody indulged in gaiety and festivals. The meat of the animas ware devoured by the Muslims. The religious law says that one third of the meat was to be distribution among the poor, another one third should be given to the poor relatives

---

[298] The Chronology of Modern Hyderabad, 1720-1890. CRO Hyderabad Government, 1954.
[299] Thomas Bowrey, p.96.

and one third was to be eaten by the family of the person performing the sacrifice.[300]

The fairs that were conducted in the Islamic religion were the annual Urs celebration. Urs are the anniversaries of the Sufi saints that were celebrated with much fanfare in the Andhra Desa. One interesting thing about the celebrations was that, they were celebrated by Muslims and Hindu followers of the Sufi saints. The Urs celebration of Maula Ali held a very important place in the list of festivals of both the Qutb Shahs and the Asaf Jahs. The ceremonies were performed every year. The first mosque was built there by Sultan Ibrahim Qutb Shah on the request of one of his subordinate named Yakut. The Kings also paid their obeisance there. During the rule of the Qutb Shab, a daughter of a nobleman, Syed Muzaffer became the caretaker or the Mujawer of the shine. Her name was Syeda Bano. The lady known for her piety led a secluded life in meditation and prayers over the hill. When she gave up salt in her food the people started calling her as Phiki Bi or the saltless lady.[301] During the Asaf Jahi period, the shrine was patronized even by the nobles of the court, both Muslims and Hindus. The nobles built their suburban villas to stay near the shrine during the Urs period. They also contributed to the development of the shrine. The house

---

[300] Sadiq Naqvi, op. cit., p.234.
[301] Dharmendra Prasad, Social and Cultural Geography of Hyderabad city: A Historical Perspective, pp.133-135.

for beating drums was built by the Hindu nobles while the Ashur Khana was built by the Muslim nobles.[302] Besides the Maula Ali Urs, the Urs of Hazarth Mir Monin, Barahana Shah Saheb Urs, the Yousuf Saheb and Sharif Saheb urs, Baba Shafuddin Saheb Urs were the other famous religious festivals of the Muslims of Hyderabad.[303]

The Urs were celebrated not only in Hyderabad but all around the Andhra Desa. The Dargah of the Kadi Ziauddin Multani and the Dargah of Syed Sah Jaml Bagdad Warangali, situated in the Urs village in the Warangal District, had their annual Urses celebrated with great enthusiasm and religiosity. The Dargah of Baba Fakhruddin of Penugonda in the Anatpur District, is referred to in a Persian record of 1673-1674 AD.[304] It was known popularly as the Babyya Dargah and was important for both the Hindus and the Muslims. Both the sections of the society came to celebrate this Urs and seek the blessings of the saint. Similarly, the Dargah of Galib Saheb at Rajkonda, Nalgonda District and Shah Ali Pasha Dargah of Alampur in the Mahbubhagar District were great religious centers. At all the Dargahs mentioned above, the Urs is celebrated with great religious sentiments even till date by both the Hindu and the Muslim communities.

---

[302] ibid.
[303] ibid.
[304] A.R. 1967, no2.

PILGRIMAGES:

The Muslims also went on pilgrimages to the holy places. The most important pilgrimage centers of Islam were the holy cities of Mecca and Medina, where the shrine of Prophet Mohammad is situated. These two centers were situated in the country of Arabia and the pilgrims were taken to the far away holy centers on ships that belonged to the King of Golconda.[305] These ships, carrying the pilgrims, were often attacked by the Portuguese pirates but this did not deter the enthusiasm and zeal of the pilgrims. The pilgrimage was made yearly. Every year, the King of Golconda, sent "a proportion of rice as an almes to be distributed amongst the pilgrims."[306] This was considered as a very holy act by the Muslims. The ladies too visited the Holy cities. The ladies belonging to the royalty also paid a visit to these holy centers. Some of the pilgrims settled down in these holy places and did not come back to Andhra Desa.

CHRISTIANITY:

The religion of Christianity was brought to the Andhra country, by the trading merchants from Europe. The merchants, traders and the seamen were indifferent towards their religious functions. However, in the later periods not

---

[305] Memoirs of Francois Martin, p. 718.
[306] Methwold's Relations, P.37.

only did they succeed in regulating their own religious lives but also influenced that of the local population. They took the maximum advantage of the freedom of religion doctrine, which was followed by the Qutb Shahi Kings. In a short period of time, they were able to spread their religion amongst the people of the region. However, it was left to their religious men called missionaries to bring about this change. A considerable number of the local population got converted to Christianity. An interesting fact about these conversions was that the people got converted without the use force. They willingly adopted the new religion. The reason for this was the elasticity of Christianity that the missionary fathers followed. They allowed the people to continue some of the old Hindu practices. The converts were allowed to follow certain custom and rituals of their old religion. This gave a very comfortable feeling to the people. They felt that they had not left their old religion but had adopted some more good points in it. The converts included some from the upper castes also. In the earlier period of time, the Christian missionaries adopted the lifestyle of the Brahmin priests and behaved as one. They dressed like a Sanyasin and took only vegetarian food. All this was done to attract the people to their religion. However, the positive approach was replaced by a negative one in the later years. The later missionaries started to abuse Hinduism and this created a bad feeling in the minds of the local people. To this the Indians protested and tried to stop the works of conversions. The earliest missionary belonged to the Jesuit sect. After the end of the seventeenth century, the region witnessed the arrival of the Protestant missionaries. The Christians of the period under study, in Andhra Desa, belonged to both the Catholic and Protestant sects. The population following Christianity as their religion included the various European nationalities and also the native converts.

a. <u>ARMENIANS :</u>

"The Armenians are settled here on account of Trade; they are Christians of separate Communion".[307] The Armenians were the earliest arrivals in the kingdom of Golconda. They were devotional Christians who settled in places where they could freely exercise and follow their religion, without any interference from outside. They settled in the Golconda Kingdom during the rule of the Qutab Shahi dynasty. The discovery of the Armenian cemetery in Hyderabad in the 1970s gave the evidence of the Armenian settlement in the city. The existence of the cemetery of the children, which has an elaborate memorial structure done on it, gives us the evidence of the existence of an Armenian nobleman who lived here along with his family.[308] They were mainly traders and some of them indulged in the slave

---

[307] John Fryer, P.96.
[308] Mohammad Abdul Waheed Khan, Armenian Cemetry Discovered in t he Old city, Hyderabad, The Andhra Historical Research Society, vol. XXXIII.

trade.[309] They followed the Orthodox Church and were neither Catholics nor Protestants.

b. <u>ENGLISH</u> :

"The English, of the Orthodox Episcopacy".[310] They were all Protestants. In the earlier years, the Britishers were not much inclined towards their religious functions. They would even go to the church in a drunken condition. The reason could be that there was no clergyman in the factories who could preach to them the goodness of Christianity. Those who needed to go to church for the Baptism of their children, for marriage or for burial of the dead and for other purposes, went to the Portuguese churches. As the Portuguese followed the Catholic religion and the English were Protestants, this was not liked by the their superior officers. Later on the authorities in London took some tough stand as far as the religion of their men in India was concerned. Some of the steps are mentioned as following. The Board of directors of the East India Company used to dispatch Bibles and Catechises to the various factories on the Coromandel coastline. These were dispersed amongst the youth and soldiers.[311] It was ordered that all the English men and their families should not be married, buried or baptized

---

[309] S. Arasaratnam, op.cit.
[310] John Fryer,p.96
[311] The Diaries of Streynsham Master, 1675-1680, p.263.

by the Roman Catholic priests. They were asked to follow the Protestant religion. Any one who did not follow this order was to be sent back home.[312] The marriages of all English men were to be performed in the Protestasnt church and their children were to be educated in the Protestant religion only. In 1671 A.D., Thomas Whitehead was appointed as the Chaplain of the Masulipatnam factory and he looked after the religious things. At Narsapur, the families of two English missionary men lived completely among the natives teaching and talking to them and distributing books. They learnt the local language and also ate the food of the local people. They did without bread or meat and had rice, fish, fowls and vegetables. They, by doing this, tried to influence the natives to turn towards Christianity.[313]

c. **PORTUGUESE :**

"The Portugals, of the Romish Church".[314] The Portuguese belonged to the Catholic sect of Christianity. They followed the dictates of the Roman Church. They continued to follow their religion after coming to Andhra Desa. During the rule of the Qutb Shahs, the Portuguese had established their Church at Golconda. It was reported that in 1670 A.D. the Portuguese had a chapel

---

[312] ibid.
[313] Hilton Brown, The Sahibl- The life and ways of the British in India as Recorded byTehmselves.
[314] John Fryer,p.96.

at Masulipatnam, in the Kistna district and that some "blacks" worshipped there.[315] There in the churches, lived the Portuguese priests. As a matter of fact, the priests were allowed to have a church in their dwelling places itself. The King of Golconda, had allowed the concessions to the Portuguese only. These priests helped the needy Europeans irrespective of their religion. One of such church was located at "Millapour" of Malkapur.[316] The Europeans living in the Andhra Desa employed converted Christian Indians as their servants.[317] There were two Catholic churches in the capital city of Golconda, one at "Millapour" and the other at "Royal aldea".[318] At the latter place one could find a number of Christians residing. It had become the residential area of most of the Christians of Golconda. The majority of these were Portuguese.

d.DUTCH:

"The Dutch, most Calvinists".[319] The Dutch were the Protestants who followed the teachings of John Calvin. In the early years of the trading companies only the Dutch had a minister or a clergyman in their factories.[320] None

[315] Gordon Mackenzie, <u>A Manual of the Kistna District,</u>
[316] <u>The Travels of The Abbe Carre in India & the Near East, 1672-1674</u>, p.326.
[317] ibid.
[318] Abbe Carre, p.350
[319] John Fryer, p .96.
[320] Gordon Mackenzie.

of the other trading companies cared much for the religion of their motherland. There were no chaplains in the other factories. In 1615 A.D., the Dutch East India Company had issued orders to it resident Chaplain in Palakol to the effect that it was part of his responsibility to care for the spiritual needs not only of the Dutch in the area but also of the Telugu people. But at the same time it is well known that the famous Palakol Pagoda or Gopuram was financed and constructed by the Dutch themselves.[321]

e. FRENCH:

They were the followers of the Catholic sect of Christianity. They behaved in a intolerant way with regard to other religions. The French were very particular about the spread of their own religion in the Southern parts of India. Under the French, a systematic method was followed, while spreading Christianity. In 1718 A.D., a church was established at Madiguba in the Anantpur district by the French. In 1787 A.D., a French lady built the Church of St. Catharine at Masulipatnam.

CONVERSIONS:

When Andhra Desa came under the rule of the Musims, Hinduism ceased to be the state religion. Its place was taken

---

[321] Job Sudershan, <u>Great Cloud of Witnesses</u>.

over by Islam. We find the Qutb Shab rulers of Golconda and the Asaf Jahi rules of Hyderabad following a policy of non-interference in the religion of its subjects. They allowed the Hindus to follow their own religion. However, as the followers of Islam they never stopped the proselytizing attutute of their other Muslim brethren. Their loyalty was always with their own religion.

There is no evidence of forced conversions of the local population of Andha Desa during the Muslim Kings. However, there were some conversions performed on the people defeated in the battlefields. The Muslim priests knows as Kahtiff i.e. Khatib were a powerful religious body.[322] They were present in the King's court and in different villages and towns of the Kingdom. They were a powerful constituent in the decision making body of the kingdom of Golconda, and their support was essential for the king to be on the throne. As such, the King took every shep to keep them in good humour. They received annual grants from the government for their maintenance. Some of these Kahtiffs also belonged to the Sufi order. The main work of these Muslim priests was to propagate the tenets of Islam amongst the no-believers, to influence them with the teachings of their faith and help in getting converts from the ranks of the non-believers. They felt it their duty to spread the message of brother hood and equality of Islam amongst the people of Andhra and to get as many converts as possible to their faith.

---

[322] Schorer's Relations, p.57.

The Muslims who were not associated with Islam in a religious way, also took it upon themselves to convert the Hindus to their own religion. The Muslims merchants got children from the Northern Circars Districts for conversions to Islam, and after conversion these people were taken away for use as slaves and as Lascars on the ships.[323] In Nellore district, the Muslims purchased servants in their childhood itself. The parents sold these children in bad times such as during famine, droughts etc. Similarly, the Muslim generals when succeeded in conquering a new territory took upon themselves to get the defeated people converted to Islam. Such conversions were always of a forced nature. In such cases, the forcibly converted Hindus retained most of their original traditions and customs. As example can be had of the Dudekulas people. They followed a mixture of Hindu and Muslim culture.[324] They could not come back into the Hindu fold even if they so desired. After a period the time they slowly adjusted to their new religion.

However, some to the lower caste Hindus, got voluntarily converted to Islam, in order to come up in the social order. In Islam there is no distinction of caste. It teaches us the concept of brotherhood and equality. As such all restrictions hitherto imposed on a person gets removed when he becomes a Muslim. They become equal to others in their society. In

---

[323] Sarada Raju, <u>Serfdom in South India during the rule of East India Co,</u> in Itihaas.

[324] Edgar Thurston and K. Rangachari, <u>Castes and Tribes of Southern India.</u>

such cses, the converts became more Muhammadan than the original Muslim. Ramagadu, a leather worker who could not draw water from village well, got his self converted to Islam and became Abul Hasan. After conversion, he drew water from the same caste well unchallenged.[325]

The various trading companies from Europe did not have much religions zeal. The early Europeans too were not much interested in their religion. As a matter of fact, they never hesitated to escape the religious duties. It was left to the missionary activists to spread Christianity in the Telugunadu. Among the Europeans, the Portuguese were the first to bring Christianity to the soil of Andhra. In 1597 A. D., they built the first Catholic church at Chandragiri which was under the Vijaynagara rulers. Venkata II was the Vijayanagr King, at the time. He was much influenced by the new religions and always held discussions with the different missionaries that were present in his court. He even allowed them to convert his subjects to Christianity. The Portuguese fathers tried their level best to convert Venkata II to Christianity but were unsuccessful. The fathers visited different parts of the Vijayanagar kingdom, spreading the doctrines of Christianity amongst the people. They opened their religious centers at various places in his kingdom.

These missionaries conducted themselves in a very becoming way and influenced the public with their high standards of living. The Catholic fathers followed the

---

[325] Gordon Mackenzie.

pattern set by Father Robert de Nobile, who called himself the European Brahmin, wore saffron robes and obstained from the non-vegetarian food. He publicly announced that by becoming a Christian, no one renounces his caste and nobility. The fathers who followed him in the later years, learnt the local language and spoke to the people in their mother tongue. They wrote books in Telugu that contained the teachings of Lord Jesus Christ. Several poems on Christmas were also written. Some of the books of Christanity were written by the local converts. However, the number of converts from the public was not much.

The early Christian missionaries, both Catholics and Protestants believed that Christians would be more successful in India if the upper and the clean castes were converted to Christianity first. They also felt that by approaching the lower castes of the society they would be antagonizing the upper strata of the Indian society. Some of the Catholic missionaries even disliked the conversion of the untouchable castes and spoke openly against it. In this connection the comments of Father Clement Bammand, who was very popular among the Telugu Christian around the year 1820 AD is very important. He said that "it is very difficult to convert the Pariahs; it is a waste of time to preach to them". He recommended that the conversions should be directed toward to people of the Sudra caste. While recruiting the local clergy in the church also the same method was followed.[326] However the Protestant missionaries realized their foolishness early. While the Catholics have continued the same policy even in the twentieth century.

The French tried to bring about a systematic expansion of their missionary activity for the conversions of the people of Andhra. The French Jesuits ware the first missionary fathers to give the tenets of Christianity to Andhra Desa.[327] However, it was only in the eighteenth century that they brought their mission to this part of South India. The French Jesuits came to the Andhra region in the 1730s. They were very successful in spreading the Catholic faith and in getting converts from the Hindu religion. The Missionaries used the colloquial or the popular Telugu and hence established immediate rapport with the flock. The fathers book Indian names so that the people might understand them and also that they would not be looked upon as foreigners, but as local priests. In 1735 A.D., the Tumma family of the Reddy's clan was the first to be converted to Christianity, amongst the people of Andhra.[328] This family had migrated from Bellary to Guntur. The Gopu family of Reddys was the second family to be converted by the Jesuit fathers. A Brahmin family called Nedimanindla, was converted to Christanity by the French Jesuit monk, Gyana Bodha Swamy.[329]

---

[326] Solomon Thanugundla, <u>Historical Development of the Evangelisation work among the Telugus of India</u>.

[327] Samuel Purchas, <u>Purchas His Pilgrims</u>, p. 308.

[328] Gordon Machenzie.

[329] Samuel Purchas, p. 295.

With the increasing number of converts who mostly belonged to the down trodden class, it became necessary to translate the Bible into Telugu. The French fathers learnt the local tongue. The knowledge of Telugu helped them to translate some sacred subjects like the Biblical history and several poems on Christianity in the local language. They wrote it down on paper or on the palmyra leaves. In a very short time, a number of translations of the Bible, in Telugu, appeared. Later on, the Hindu converts, too, started writing works in praise of the newly found God. The members of the Gopu family composed beautiful literary works on Jesus and on Christianity. The members of the Nedimanindla Brahmin family, later on became Dubasis or translators, while some of them were appointed as the Dewans.[330] One such work was Vedanta Rahasyam in which the inferiority of the Hindu Gods was shown.[331] The Christian God, Jesus, was referred to as Parameshwara or Sarveswara and was shown as being superior to the Hindu Gods. The book described the incarnation of Sarveswara as Isu or Jesus and was composed by a local convert, Ananda, a resident of Mangalagiri. He belonged to the higher Hindu caste. He dedicated the book to Dasa Mantri, a Brahmin convert to Christianity. Another such took was by Pingali Ellanarya

---

[330] ibid.

[331] Prema Nandakumarm, <u>Religious Movements in South India</u> in South India Studies, dr. T.V. Mahalingam Commemoration Volume.

and it was called as Tobhya Charitra. In this book, the life of St. Thomas was described.[332]

The French Jesuits collected their followers and lived in areas that were under the French troops. As such converts from Mysore, Mahratta and the Muhammadan areas flocked to Guntur, which was held by the French army from 1752 to 1779 A.D. The French army was located there and hence peace prevailed. There was also immigrations of the Hindu converts from the Tamil lands to Guntur. There were also some migrations of Christians, from the Telugu lands to further south either due to famines or due to the cruel Zamindars. A Telugu colony of the Telugu Christians could be found at Chingleput.[333]

The neo converts retained certain Hindu customs even after their conversion to Christianity. They never ate beef, continued to wear the sacred thread, and did not allow the women to touch the Bible during their monthly periods. The children continued to be married very young i.e. below fourteen years of age. The Brahmin girls, especially, continued to be married before puberty. The division of the caste system was maintained. The higher caste converts never married in the family of the lower caste converts. The Christian converts from the sub-sects of the Sudra caste were well integrated with the Hindus of the same sub-sect. they continued to marry in the Hindu households. The major

---

[332] Ibid.

[333] Gordon Mackenzie.

difference one finds is that while the Thali in the Hindu marriage were kept with the Purohit, here the Thali or the marriage locket was kept with the church. All the other customs were same as in the Hindu marriages. The Brahmin priest, the Intichakali or the washerman, Mangali i.e. the Barber, the Kummari i.e. the Potter, and the Carpenter attended the marriage and played their traditional ritualistic roles.[334]

The converted Hindus who were earlier staunch followers of the Hindu religion, could not easily break away from the old religion. They continued to support the Hindu temples that they had built earlier. They donated money for their maintenance and also for the construction of new ones. They also celebrated the Hindu festivals and took part in the Jathra with much gaiety and fanfare. All the above-mentioned customs, termed as the Malabar Rites by the Europeans, were abolished by the Pope in Rome. However, the Hindu converts continued to follow them. Dr. Heyne in the year 1814, wrote "In giving to the Hindoos the Christian religion, allow them to retain their castes and they would be bound to embrace it without reluctance, and in considerable number". Hence it was felt that to attract the people of Andhra Desa towards Christianity, they should be allowed to follow certain tenets of Hinduism. Most of the Hindus satisfied their curiosity by listening to the foreign preacher,

---

[334] G. Prakash Reddy, Caste and Christianity: A Study of the Sudra Caste Converts in Rural Andhra Pradesh, pp.113-128.

but never came near them. Sometimes the missionary fathers felt this attitude of the Telugu very tiring and frustrating.

The missionaries of the Protestants sect of Christianity came to the region only after 1800 A.D. i.e. in the nineteenth century.[335] They adopted a different way of spreading their religion. Unlike the Catholics they started abusing the Hindu way of life. They started showing to the people the drawbacks of their religion and showed the goodness of Protestantism. The priests preached it to the people and also wrote literature against Hinduism. Songs having anti Hindu religion contents were written. However, this had a negative influence on the people and there were resistance offered to the conversions.[336] The negative approach of the Protestant priests, was not liked by the people at Madras, and hence they tried to shop the conversions. There is only the mention of a Gauda Brahmin i.e. a Bengali Brahmin being converted to Protestantism.

However, the Christina missionaries, either Protestants or Catholics, were busy with their work through churches, chapels, educational institutions, orphanages, and asylums and later on by hospitals and medical services in the region. They no doubt, did commendable work for the benefit of the people, in the different parts of Andhra Desa.

In the nineteenth century, the missionary activities in India received a setback. As the conditions were not

---

[335] Samuel Purchas and Gordon Mackenzie.
[336] Samuel Purchas.

favourable in Europe, the missionaries could not be sent to India. The absence of priests created a vacuum in the religious activities of the converted people. There was no one to help them with their prayers and no one to exhort them to their religious duties. The result of all this was the re-conversions of the newly converts back to Hinduism.[337] The method of re-converting the Christians to Hinduism was known as the Suddi method in the local language.[338] There were no new conversions made in the 19th century. The Christian societies had started establishing educational institutions. Missionaries startd their educational activities from the year 1804 itself. Is was only in the second half of the nineteenth century, that the missionary activities of converting the locals were once again revived.

CHANGES

The existence of diverse religions in the region brought about a number of chages in the religious conditions of Andhra Desa. Some of them were positive while the others were of a negative nature. They are illustrated below.

One of the significant changes witnessed was that there was a shift in the popularity of the ancient Brahmancial religion. The reasons were many for the unpopularity of the ancient Hindu religion. The destruction of temples, the

---

[337] Gordon Mackenzie.
[338] S. Pratap Reddy, Andhrula Sanghika Charitra, p.335.

loss of patronage to the Brahmins, the fear in performing the various religious functions in the Muslim ruled areas, and various other factors led the people away from the old religion. The end of the Hindu political rule over the region resulted in the loss of the patronizing authority of the Hindu temples and their priests. The Brahmins, were losing their foothold in the society. They were forced to undertake other professions, as their old job as priests was fast losing ground. With the establishment of the rule of the Muslims in the region, the hold of the Brahmins on the temples too was lost. Previously, the lower castes and the follower of other religion were not allowed inside the temple. When the political authority passed into their hands, the Muslims started entering the temples.[339] The lower castes followed suit in no time. They entered all the other areas of the temple except the sanctum sanctorum. We find the Brahmin authors to the Shataka poems, lamenting that the Lord Venkateswara watches the sins committed by the Mlechas i.e. the Muslims, in a silent manner without taking any action.[340] This shows the dejection and helplessness of the priestly class in protecting their religious institutions.

The development of social consciousness among the lower castes led to the degradation of the position of the Brahmins and some of the other upper castes. The work

---

[339] Mc. Mss., <u>Sri Sailam Temple Kaifiyat</u>, p.18.
[340] Vaddikasula Venkanna Kavi, <u>Shatru Samhara Venkatachala Shatakamu</u>.

of the contemporary social reformers also opened the eyes of the people. Vemana, one of the contemporary social reformers, preached in different ways that devotion to God coupled with knowledge, was far superior to blind worship. He also proclaimed unambiguously that the worship of the one God i.e. Ekesvaroopasana was the best and the noblest means to salvation. Vermana asked the people to develop their critical faculties and acquire worldly knowledge. He exposed the hypocrisy, deceit and trickery of the priests, and of the Brahmins of his days.

While doing so he portrayed his thoughts in the following couplet:

"Pattu batta gatti pattenaamamu betti,
Vatti bhraanti cendi Vaisnavudai,
Lotte traagi yatadu lokula jeracuraa?"

He condemned the cruelty and injustice that existed in the society of his time on account of religious practices. Vemana was, therefore, a man of the highest order, who strove unceasingly all his life to build a perfect society.[341]

The village deities had gained more importance among the local population. "But in every case the real religion of the people throughout the Ceded Districts finds its expression not so much in devotion to orthodox Hindu Gods as in the

---

[341] Dr. Gangadham Appa Rao, <u>Vemana and Sarvajna,</u> pp.24-25.

worship of titular deities of the village."[342] This was true for also the regions that were not under the British. The Gramadevatas, Ammas, or village deities are numerous and all are of the female sex.[343] The people identified themselves more with the village Gods. The age-old faiths like Shaivism and Vaishnavism had given place to heterodox creeds and the people had started worshipping the local deities.[344] The Brahmins had lost the prestige and popularity; and the "Agraharas" were dying fast.[345] When the people of the Gods were themselves in trouble then the Gods could not enjoy the same popularity as before. The rituals associated with the village deities, did not need a Brahmin priest for performance of the puja. The priests of these local deities, generally belonged to the Sudra caste. Sometimes, even the pariah castes such as the Malas and the Madigas performed the ceremony. It saved a lot of money. They could perform all the religious practices in less amount of money, as the priests belonged to the lower castes and being poor, were satisfied with little money. Unlike the Brahmins, it was not necessary for the local priests to show off their knowledge or riches to the devotees. There was no hypocrisy of any type. It increased the self-respect of the villagers, as the Gods belonged to them and not to the Brahmins. There were no

---

[342] Brackenbury in A. Jagannadhan, <u>Some Aspects of Sicio-Economic Conditions in the Ceded Districts: 1800-1810.</u>

[343] Vishakapatnam Gazette.

[344] Koochi Manchi Timmanna Kavi,op.cit.

[345] Adidadmu Surakavi, p.144-145.

hard and fast rules and no dogmatic rituals that had to be followed in worshipping the local deities. The festival time was to enjoy and make merry. The entire village took part in it and it was considered a universal ceremony.

The sectarian strife between the Shaivites and the Vaishnavites had helped the Islamic religion.[346] The so-called upholders of Hinduism i.e. the Brahmins were continuously fighting amongst themselves with regard to their particular sects and Gods. The people were fed up of the principal of compartmentalism of caste and internal crisis of the Hindu religion. Some of them were attracted towards the new religion called, Islam. The teachings of Islam opened up their minds and they started demanding the status of equality in the social field. The birth of social reform movement happened during this period. The teachings of the Sufi saints, coupled with the teachings of the Hindu reformers like Vemana and Veerabrahmam influenced the local public. These changes were more evident in the lower castes. The new principle of equality preached by the Muslims, had a greater influence on the people suffering from the rigid principles of Hinduism. They felt better with the new religious doctrines. Vemana, while flaying the ignorance of the lower castes, says that men are easily led by falsehood than by truth. He was as theist, but did not believe in idol worship. All this led to conversions of Hindus to the different religions that came to Andhra

---

[346] Adidamu Surakavi, op. cit.

Desa. The single dominance of the Hindu religion was badly shaken. The new religions were fast making inroads into the religious framework of the region.

On the positive side, the 17ᵗʰ and 18ᵗʰ centuries saw the intermingling of the various religious and cultural ideas that came to Andhra and made a permanent base here. As Hindus and Muslims lived as neighbhours, they were naturally affected by the living style of each other. The proximity of the people helped in creating a healthy opining of each other. The result was that they stared celebrating the religious festivals of each other. The Hindus of Andhra celebrated the first ten days of Muharram with same austerity as the Muslims. The tribes such as the Lambadas, also celebrated the festival. Telugu folk songs about the Moharram are sung to this day in the villages. The Hindus took part in the festival and observed all the austerity associated with it. The babies born during the Moharram were named as Faqir Appa, Hussain Rao, etc. Telugu folk songs on the festival were composed by contemporary poets such as Ramanna & Balaiah, and the poetesses' viz. Immam Akka, Vanoor Bee etc.[347] Songs wuch as the Jangnama, Panjatan-i-Pak and certain Marthiyas are sung upto these days by the local population.[348] One such poem goes as follows:

---

[347] P. Rama Raju, Muharram folk songs in Telugu, p.57.
[348] T. Donappa jana Pada Kala Sampada, pp.127-30.

Peddala Panduga Rawe

Peerla panduga rawe

The meaning of the couplet is that "come, the festival of the great man; come, the festival of the Peer." [349] The tribals, especially the Lambadis, sang songs in the praise of the martyrdom of the people at Carbala.[350] On the other hand, the Muslim royalty, nobility and the common man did not hesitate in taking part in Hindu festivals. During the rule of the Asaf Jahs, the Prime Minister of Hyderabad, Mir Alam Bahadur, had gone to Poona. He attended the Ganesh festival on 31st Austust, 1794 AD at Poona.[351]

RELIGIOUS TOLERANCE:

Some of the Muslim rulers of Andhra were liberal in their religious policy. There was freedom of religion in the state. William Methwold writes in the first quarter of the seventeenth century that "Religion is here free and no mans conscience oppressed with ceremony or observance".[352] The people of different religions were living peacefully in the kingdom. There was no tax or harassment of any kind. The religion of the state was Islam but it was not forced upon the

---

[349] Sadiq Naqvi, Qutb Shahi Ashurkhana of the Hyderabad City, p.72.
[350] ibid.
[351] Newsletters, 1767-1799.
[352] Methwold's Relations, p.12.

subjects. Every man was free to profess his religion and this was true to all faiths. Though we find that conversion were taking place in the Andhra region, they were not done in large scale. However, they did not behave in a fanatic way, they did not force the non-believers to accept their faith. People were free to profess their own religions. However, during the wars, certain followers of Islam did take liberty with the locals who were treated as good for nothing. But, it was not a state policy and the rulers were more or less magnanimous to the other religions. The King's were very much concerned about the religious sentiments of the people and they always had an interest in the festivals of their subjects and themselves took part in most of them. The Qutb Shahi Kings enjoyed the Hindu festival as much as their Islamic ones. We find references of the Royals of the Qutb Shahi dynasty, taking part in the celebrations of Hindu festivals such as Basant, Deepawali etc. Sultan Muhammad Quli Qutb Shah celebrated "Basant" in a very grand way. He would enjoy the arrival of spring along with his women.[353] He loved the yellow dresses that the ladies wore during the celebrations. The shops and the streets were beautifully decorated. People used to sprinkle coloured water on each other. Similarly, the Muslims borrowed the system of burning fireworks in the celebrations of the Shab-I-Barat. A lot of fireworks were burnt on the night of this festival. The houses were decorated with light and the entire night

---

[353] Muhammad Quli Qutb Shah, <u>Kulliyat.</u>

was spent in merry making and gaiety. Most probably, the Muslum have borrowed the concept of light and fireworks from the Hindu festival of Diwali.[354] Some of the Sultans of the dynasty donated handsomely to the Hindu temples. A farman of the Sultan Abul Hassan Tana Shah, dated 12th Rabi I, 1095 A.H./18th Feb.1684 A.D., bearing a royal seal, addressing the officials of the Chandi paragana and Ramraj Shankaria, Governor of Carnatic, records the grant of 50 Kochals in the three villages, for the maintenance of the temple of Sri Bhasamara Malleshwar Swami. It is also mentioned that a village called Malleshwaraswami Puram should be laid out in the neighbourhood of the temple and its revenues should be utilized for the upkeep of the said temple.[355] Abul Hasan, the last king of the Qutb Shahi Dynasty, also made large grants of money to the Hindu Temples. It has been recorded that an amount of nearly Rs.64, 925 was given, most probably as an yearly allowance to the temples.[356]

The Asaf Jahs, too celebrated the Hindu festivals along with their Hindu nobles and subjects. The Nizam conspicuously participated in four Hindu festivals, namely, Basant, Dasserah, Divali and Holi.[357] The Hindus were

---

[354] H.K. Sherwani, <u>History of the Qutb Shahi Dynasty</u>,

[355] <u>Farmans and Sanadas of the Deccan Sultans, 1408-1687 AD</u>

[356] Girdhari Lal Ahqr, Ms. <u>Tarikh-e-Zafrah.</u>

[357] Karen Leonard, <u>The Kayasthas of Hyderabad City: Internal History and Their Role in Politics and Society from 1850 to 1900</u>, Ph. D. thesis, University of Wisconsin.

awarded honours during these festivals. Some Hindu holidays were declared as major public events. The Hindu family of the noble, Raja Rae Rayan, traditionally sponsored a public procession on Dasserah. The Nizam officially sanctioned leave for Hindu noblemen who wished to go on pilgrimages or attend temple festivals. The domestic ceremonies, even specifically religious ones, occasioned invitation and visit between noblemen of different religious backgrounds.[358] However, the domestic environment of the Hindu officials, in the Asaf Jahi reign, did not reflect the court culture. The domestic culture of the Hindus, had its own set of rules. While they followed the Islamic etiquette in the court, at their homes they were traditional Hindus. They celebrated all the Hindu festivals at their homes along with their family members.

The festivals and commemorations popular in Qutb Shahi days continued to flourish and were common to all levels of the populations. Once patronized by the Qutb Shahi Sultans, these occasions were tied to permanent shrines and landmarks in all parts of the city; and they continued to be patronized by the Asafia rulers.[359] The most important was Moharram, the commemoration of the martyrdom of Iman Husain at Carbala in 680 A.D. Alams or relics allegedly associated with the events at Qarbala had been installed in shrines by members of the Qutb Shah royal

---

[358] ibid.
[359] Karen B. Leonard, op.cit.

family and by highly placed nobles. The Alams were taken out in procession during the ten days of Muharram and were paraded about the city to provoke displays of mourning and to receive offerings from the populace. Other important events in Hyderabad were Urs and the Melas at the tombs of Muslim saints and the annual festival jatras at Hindu temples. Though the Asaf Jahis were from the Sunni sect of Islam they never hesitated in offering their respect to the martyrs of the war at Carbala.

The Sufi saints were respected by the common people and the royalty. The Sufi saints were the advocators of secular religion. Though they were followers of the Islamic religion, they never hesitated to learn and adopt goodness of other religions. They were not religious bigots. They imparted their philosophy of brotherhood and unity of religions to their followers. They also endeavoured to learn the language of the local people in order to converse with them on the mysteries of the Sufi philosophy. During the rule of the Qutb Shahs, Akbar Shah, the son of Syed Shah Raju II, the pontiff of a Sufi Khanqah at Hyderabad, wrote Sringara-Manjari. This work was written in Telugu as well as in Sanskrit. This shows that the study of the local languages like Telugu and Sanskrit were cultivated in the Khanqahs in Andhra Desa.[360]

The Sufi saints were believed to have possessed spiritual powers, and as such the local people were drawn towards

---

[360] H. K. Sherwani, p. 605.

them without any discrimination of Hindus and Muslims. The devotees approached the Saints for blessings. The general public was much influenced by the Saints and as a show of respect to them they granted donations of lands on a collective basis. An inscription of 1608 AD. records the grant of 100 bighas of land by the residents of the village Siddhavatam Sima to a Muhammadan saint named Peer Zadda Saheb.[361] Even after their demise, the people continued to visit their Dargas or the burial place.[362] The devotees continued to recall the teaching of the Saints and in their memory flocked to the place where they lay buried. The people came in large numbers and the gathering took the shape of a fair with a religious background. It started to be called as Urs. It was celebrated every year on the death anniversary of the Sufi Saint. These celebrations were secular in nature and both the Hindus and the Muslims came to celebrate it. For the Urs celebrations, the Hindu Basavis or the dancing girls used to perform at the dance programmes. They were granted jagirs and hold them still.

The Sufis not only had influence on the general public, bur their philosophy appealed even to the Kings and the Nawabs of Andhra Desa. Before his marriage, the Qutb Shahi King Abul Hasan Tanashah was a member of the Khanqah of the Sufi saint Shah Raju II, which was situated in

---

[361] Topographical list of the Cuddapah district, no.932, p.601-602.
[362] ibid

the capital city.[363] Local Nawabs like the Mayana Nawabs of Kadiri, patronized the saint Hazrat Syed Shah Zaheeruddin Hussaini. They granted Inams and Jagirs for the saints and their followers' maintenance. They also created Gumbads or domes on their Dargas as a show of their respect. The Nawabs of Kadiri constructed seven mosques in the honour of these saints. The mosque at Kadiri, depicts Hindu style of architecture from inside while it has Islamic style of architecture in front. It is believed that the masons who were employed to construct the mosque were the followers of the Hindu religion and hence the mosque has interiors in the Hindu style. The exterior portion of the mosque was made by the Muslim designers and as such the outlook of the mosque is Islamic in style.[364] The Penukonda inscription refers to the grant of villages to the Darga of saint Babanatha by the Hindu ruler of the Vijayanagara dynasty, Venkata II.[365] It was believed that the Sufi saint Babanatha had taken refuge in a Hindu temple. He refused to vacate it inspite of the use of force. Finally the temple had to be converted into a mosque for the saint who continued to stay there along with his followers.[366]

The Asaf Jahis, being Sunni, had great belief in the Sufi saints. The Sufis played a very important role in bringing

---

[363] Topographical list of the Cuddapah district, no.932, p.601-602.
[364] Syed Basha Biyabini, p. 99-104.
[365] Anantpur District Records.
[366] K. Satyanarayana, A study of the History and Culture of the Andhras, p.338.

the people of all religions together. They were respected and honoured by both, the Hindus and the Muslims. The Shrines and Urses of the saints were also celebrated by all and sundry. Some of the famous Urses of Sufi saints of the Asaf Jahi period were the Moula Alil Mela, Baj Sarfuddin Urs, Yusuf Saheb Sharif Saheb Urs etc. The Hindus visited the shrines and tombs of the Muslim saints. At Moula Ali's tomb, the Hindu noblemen of the Asaf Jahis, viz. Raja Chandulal, Raja Rao Rumbha and the others constructed monuments. They continued to do the same at various shrines of the Sufi saints. They also re-started the celebration of Mohrram that had been stopped during the Mughal Governorship of the Andhra region. Rai Nanak Ram, Kayastha official of the Asaf Jahis, was a great devotee of the Sufi saint Moula Ali. He used to stay in the Shrine, at the Kohe Maula Ali for the all the four days of the Urs celebration.

Beside the celebrations of the festivals of the Hindus, the Muslim Kings did not hesitate in appointing them to the high posts in their administration. Under the Qutb Shahs, the Telugus rose as high as to occupy the post of the prime Minister of the kingdom. The provincial administration of the kingdom was essentially in the hands of the Hindu officers.[367] The Brahmins had become indispensable to the administration. The Hindus were also employed in the army of the King. During the region of Muhammad Quli, Rai Rao was the commander of the important fort of Kondavidu. The

---

[367] H. K. Sherwani.

period of Abul Hasan Tana Shah is especially remarkable for the appointments of Hindu nobles. The Mir Jumla or the Prime Minister was a Brahmin named Madanna. He started his carrier as a Shroff and by dint of his merit rose to the position of the Mir Jumla. The Hindu officers too received patronage by the Sultans in grant of the Inam lands and other awards. Several firmans of the Qutb Shahi Kings donating awards to Hindus have been discovered. A firman of Abdullah Qutb Shah dated 29 Jamadi, 1038A. H./13th February, 1629 A. D. orders the grant of orders the grant of Deshpandiagiri together with the grant of land in Inam, rusum, etc. in perpetuity to Appa Kondu son of Timmanna from the district of Kondmel Sarkar of Muhmmad Nagar Suba, Hyderabad. The farman bears the royal seal.[368]

The Asaf Jahi Kings too encouraged the immigration of Hindus from other parts of North India. The people who came to Hyderabad were the Khatris, Marwadis, Kayasths, and others. During their early rule, the highest posts concerning revenue and civil administration were entrusted to Hindus requiring perfect loyalty and confidence.[369] These official were held in the highest esteem and enjoyed the same privileges as their Muslim brethren and were include among the highest nobles of the state.[370] The later powerful rulers' i.e. the English too could not do without the help

---

[368] State Archives, <u>Farmans and Sanads of the Deccan Sultans, 1408-1687 AD</u>

[369] Dharmendra Prasad. P. 64.

[370] ibid.

of the Hindu officials. During the trading activities also the European could not do without the employment of the Hindus as Dubashis or translators, as middlemen and also as servants.

When the powers of governance passed from the Muslims to the English, they too brought in certain changes in the religious conditions of the region. In the beginning of their reign, the English were neutral to the religion of the land. They presented shawl to the Hindu Gods, fired salutes to the prophet Mohammad, and etc. The collectors of the different units to the administration attended the religious functions. But after the year 1833 A. D., the Christian missionaries protested and agitated against this attitude. As such, after 1833 AD, the English neutrality towards the native religions, was no longer discernible in the English East India Co.[371]

SUPERSTITION

The prevalence of Superstition was a common feature amongst all the communities of the region. The Hindus, the Muslims and the English all suffered from this and indulged in different ways and methods to negate to negate the effects of the evil eye.

---

[371] Y. Vittal Rao, Religious Conditions in Andhra, in the Journal of the Andhra Historical Research Society, vol. XXXVII.

Different forms of Superstitions existed in the Telugu country. To counteract these several types of practices too had come into practice. Bhoot Vidya was resorted to by the people to free themselves from the evil effects of Chandragraha and the other Grahas.[372] The work of the Yogini was to cure illnesses by giving them some ash and also to foretell the future fortunes of the people. The Brahmins too benefited from this attitude of the people.[373] They taught them the Mohini Vidya, which was said to give manpower to attract women of his choice.[374] We come across the term Dari Kattu in the contemporary literature very often. The people resorted to it if they wanted some bad omen for some their enemies.

Talismans were commonly worn in order to drive away the evil. [375] A usual as kind is flat piece of mental with a figure of Hanuman on it. Another made of leather with the skin of a lizard got from a Madiga stitched into it, is hung round the shoulders of week and sickly children. Women and houses were supposed often to be possessed of devils, and which only a professional sorcerer can exorcise. Yerukala women were in great request as exorcist.[376] In cases of illness supposed to be due to the ill will of a fod or spirit, three handfuls of rice are carried round the invalid, and are then

---

[372] H. V.

[373] ibid.

[374] ibid.

[375] Godavari Manuaal, pp, 46-47.

[376] ibid.

placed in a winnowing fan, which is held by both patient and the sorceress. The latter then scans the formers; face, professes to be able to read there the name of the offended spirit, and advises as to the propitiation to be made. The belief in witchcraft is exceptionally strong, and almost every ill is thought to be due to the person's being bewitched.

Childbirth was surrounded by a number of Superstitions.[377] A pregnant woman should not see an eclipse, or her child will be born deformed. The labour pain was relieved by turning the face of the bull god in a Saivite temple away from the emblem of Siva. It was also lessened by touching of a ring made of a mixture of gold, silver, copper, lead and iron made by a dasting blacksmith on the day of an eclipse by the woman in pain. Some drems are supposed to foretell events. Thus it is a good thing to dream of being bitten by a cobra, especially if the bite drew blood.

People who had lost two children and were expecting to have a third, generally begged small pieces of gold from their neighbours with which they made a gold ornament to put in the nose of the new born baby. The child was called, if a boy, Pullayya or Pentayya, and if a girl, either Pullamma or Pentamma, meaning respectively 'used up leaf-plates' or 'refuse'.[378]

During the eighteenth century itself the war against superstitious practices had started. The contemporary social

---

[377] ibid.
[378] Godavari Manuaal, pp, 46-47.

reformers preached the people against them. Vemana, the social reformer exhorted the people to rid themselves of all superstition and the meaningless practices connected with religion. He taught them that devotion coupled with knowledge was far superior to blind worship.

The Muslim Kings would not proceed anywhere without asking the Brahmin Jyotishian and the Persian astrologers to look for an auspicious date. The Kings did not occupy their thrones without consulting their astrologers. During droughts he would ask his subjects to pray in the open fields and lakhs of rupees were given in alms to the beggars to seek divine blessings in the form of rains.[379]

The foreigners too suffered from superstitious practices. Sir Streynsham Master sent in all seriousness to his daughter, lady Coventry, along with the most elaborate directions for use, "in an Indian silk bag and paper, an Eaglestone good to prevent miscarriages of women with child, to be worne about the Necke".[380] In an another incident, an Englishman was reported to have reported to have restorted to black magic in order to recover his missing property.[381]

---

[379] Mirza Nizamuddin Ahmed Saidi, pp.82-86.
[380] Dennis Kincaid, <u>British Social Life in India, 1608-1937</u>, p.22.
[381] William Foster, <u>English Factories in India, 1655-1660</u>, p.263.

Chapter IV

POSITION OF WOMEN

The position of women underwent great structural changes during the 17th and 18th Centuries in Andhra Desa. With the foreigners from West Asia and from European Countries making Andhra Desa their permanent place of abode, the region saw a growth in the variety of its womenfolk. Till the Vijayanagar Empire was having its sway over the region, Andhra Desa consisted of only the Hindu population and as such only Hindu women to be found in the region.

However, with the coming in of the Muslims and the Christians, the woman belonging to different religions and countries coloured the canvas of Andhra Desa population.

These women came to Andhra Desa along with their spouses and other male relatives who had come to the Deccan to try their luck in different professions. They continued to follow the religion and traditions of their motherland and used to dress themselves in their own clothes. This resulted in the growth of a hybrid culture. With the advent of the foreigners, rare factual position of the women of the Andhra Desa came to light which later-on became one of the interesting topic of study for the foreign scholars. The foreigners tried to bring some positive changes in the life of the contemporary women of this region. The region witnessed some initial far-reaching changes in the position of women during the seventeenth and eighteenth centuries. However, large scale changes could be witnessed only in the 19th century, when the trends of social reforms got initiated.

In this chapter, the status enjoyed by the Hindu, Muslim and the European women is discussed. The system of keeping women in Parda, which was brought by the Muslims, was a new concept for Andhra Desa. The marriage customs and rituals, the system divorce, widowhood, Sati Sahagamana, and the importance enjoyed by the public women in the society are some of the other concepts that are covered in this chapter.

The position of women in the 17th and 18th centuries, continued to be the same as written in the Manu Smriti. The dictum laid down by Manu that a women does not deserve freedom and should not be independent of man was still being followed by the people. The women themselves were great followers of this dictum. As such their condition continued to be bad. They continued to feel that they were the lesser mortals and that they must have some male members to support and to take care of them. Their attitude was self defeating and as such their progress was never to be self-made. The men were engrossed in their own mundane affairs to be bothered by any revolutionary ideas. Another significant aspect of the position of women in Andhra was that the contemporary social reformers also did nothing to better their cause. Vemana, who spoke about all the prevailing evils in society had not even spoken against the child marriages. In fact, he glorified those women who lived according to the ancient customs and traditions of the society. It was left to the foreigners like Muslims and the Europeans to improve the condition of Hindu women of Andhra.

The Hindu women continued to play the role of a good daughter, a good wife and a good mother. They were a part of the family and had no individual identification. The society viewed them only in their traditional role of a wife and mother. They lacked separate identity. They were identified with the family. People lived in large joint families where the father-in-law and mother-in-law were the highest in hierarchy. Next came the eldest son and his wife, followed by the others in that order of hierarchy. The eldest son's wife being the eldest daughter in law managed the household and looked after the needs of one and all. In Vemana's writing, it can be seen that the goodness of a women was weighed with regard to the way she treated her husband. A women was a good women if did not talk back to him and who treated his family members as her own.[382]

The women were not taught any occupational techniques. Thought we find instances of women taking part in the weaving industry and in the agriculture fields and in other professional activities. Many of the women from the lower castes were also employed in the diamond mining industry of Golconda. However, they seldom took interest in any professional activity on an individual basis. They were only helpers of their men who actually did the main jobs. The women of lower caste comparatively enjoyed a better position and freedom than the upper caste women. In the lower castes, both husband and wife had to work for livelihood and as such the women were respected by their husbands. The economic status of the women being recognized, it gave them a sort of equal say in the matters concerning the family. They also enjoyed the rights of re-marriage after divorce and widowhood. They could move outside, they could sell wares in the market, they could seek a livelihood by telling the fortunes of others, some sold flowers, etc.[383] Some were also employed as servants in richer households.

---

[382] C.P. Brown, <u>Verses of Vemana</u>, p.288.

[383] <u>H.V</u> & <u>S.S</u>

The position of higher caste women was deplorable. Most of the time they stayed indoors. They were not supposed to work outside. In times of difficulty also they had to stay inside unlike the lower castes who immediately took to some occupation or the other in bad times. They had no property rights. The marriage system was polygamous and men were free to visit prostitutes at their free will. There was no stigma attached to a man visiting a prostitute, or keeping a concubine. In fact, it was symbol of economic propesperity as only rich men could maintain a mistress. In higher caste there was no system of re-marriage of widows, or the system of divorce. They never learnt any art. They were barred from learning anything else except the household chores like cooking, sewing, cleaning and decorating the house with Muggu, looking after the children and the elderly. They were taught to pay obeisance to all the elders in the family and learn not to reply back to their elders. The husband was the wife's God and she could never disobey him. The mother-in-law was never satisfied with the work of her daughter-in-law and went on grumbling and criticizing her. In <u>Suka Sapatati</u> we find, a daughter-in-law resorting to black magic in order to stop her mother-in-law from talking too much.

The contemporary Muslim literature also described the qualities that is present in a women and the qualities that should be imbibed by her. They described as a masterpiece of God's creation but her nature was very complicated and could not be understood by a common man. As he could not understand her he called her Devil, unwise and cunning.[384]

However, there are certain types of women who are always loyal to their husbands and treated them like Gods. If she succeeded in making her husband happy then her importance in the family and the society increased. They never hesitated in praising the loyalty of wives towards their husbands and said that only loyal woman were good women.

PURDAH

The women were more safe in Andhra during the Vijaynagara empire. A young woman was completely safe on the street even if she was decked in ornaments from head to foot. There was a peace and tranquility in the Hindu empire. Women were in the service of the Emperor as cooks, sword fighters, wrestlers, trumpeteers and palanquin bearers, etc.[385] Some of them also acted as soothsayers and astrologers. There are references of women acting as accountants who wrote accounts inside the palace gates.[386]

There were women trumpeters and pipe players. However, the profession that attracted women the most was that of music and dance. The rulers of Vijaynagara were very much interested in music and dance.

---

[384] Mullah Wajhi, Sabras, ed. Jved Vishist.
[385] Sewell, pp. 248-249.
[386] ibid., p. 382

A large number of women dancers and musicians were in the service of the kings and nobles. The temples too had their own dancers who were called as the Devadasis. They were also ably awarded by the temples and the Kings for the services towards the God. Besides the Deva Dasis, the royal courtesans there were the ordinary prostitutes in the kingdom.[387]

The establishment of the Qutb Shahi dynasty over Andhra Desa in the 16th Century brought about certain changes in the life of the women. The freedom of movement that they had enjoyed during the Vijaya Nagara Empire came to be curtailed. The Muslim rulers of Golconda did not allow their women to roam about in the open. They were followers of the religion of Islam which says that a woman should always be behind a curtain or Purdah. The patronage given to women dancers, musicians and literateur was no longer available. The rule applied to the women of the Muslim religion only but the prevailing conditions were not condusive to the women of other religions also. The lack of encouragement and the loss of importance in the public life further deteriorated their condition. While the Hindu woman was suffering from the evils of widowhood and Sati, the Muslim woman was behind Purdah throughout her life. The upper strata of the Muslims, especially the nobles and the high officials always kept their women in tight security and in utter seclusion. As soon as the girls attained the age

---

[387] Elliot, <u>History of India</u>, pp. 111-112.

of 12 or 13 years, they were put in seclusion. When the children, both girls and boys attained the age of seven, they could see either of the parents only. The house of a Muslim had two separate quarters, one for the men and the other for the women. It was impossible for one to cross over to the other without permission. A boy started living in the gent's quarters from the age of seven and saw his mother only on some important work or on a festival. The brother and sister could not meet and play together. The father could not see nor talk to the daughter daily. Fryer says that "at seven years the son being taken from the mother, the sister from the brother, and not a father, though fourscore and ten suffered the interview of his daughter...... "[388] Whenever, the Muslim ladies went out they were carried in Palanquins by the bearers, and these were always closed. The public had never seen the Queens nor the wives of important persons come out in the open. The rich and poor never allowed their women to roam about freely in the open.

There is a beautiful account of the Parda system in the travelogue of the French traveler, Travernier. The wife of King Abdullah Qutb Shah and his mother wanted to be treated by a Dutch surgeon. The King had described his talents and the old Queen mother and Queen wanted to be operated on by the Dutch Surgeon called De Lann. Before the European Doctor was brought in their presence, his hands were washed and when they were dry, they were

---

[388] John Fryer, p. 89.

rubbed with "sweet oils" so that all the infections and other evils would be destroyed. He was then brought before the Queen mother and the young Queen who were sitting behind a curtain. They took out their hands from a hole made in the curtain and did not show him their faces. The eunuch guards of the female quarters stood there till the European was treating them. They watched every move he made. Finally, the Queens granted several gold coins to De Lann for the treatment. This was also handed over to him by the guards.[389]

"The Moors are by Nature plagued with Jealousy, cloistering their Wives up, and sequestering them the sight of any besides the Capon that watches them."[390] One could find several women in the house of a rich Muslim. The Harem, as the ladies quarters were called, were full of different types and ages of women. The high class ladies were all cloistered up in their homes without ever leaving it. As a single person had several wives and concubines in his Harem, a lot ill will and jealously could be seen in between them.[391]

The Persian men and the other high ranking officials felt that their ladies were personal properties and if anybody even looked at them it would lead to bad name for the family. They employed several persons to look after their

---

[389] Tavernier, pp. 232-233.
[390] John Fryer, p. 88
[391] Mullah Wajhi, Sabras, ed. Javesd Vishist.

female section of the house. However, no males were employed in the ladies residential quarters. Neither the King nor his leading men had any faith on any other man when their ladies were concerned. As such they employed the eunuchs who were very faithful and zealously guarded over the female members of their employers. Whenever a King wanted to call any of the ladies of his harem, it was done through Kutnis. An old woman was employed as the messenger to visit the Royal Zenana chambers and convey the message of the King. These old women were called as the Kutnis.[392] The Guards of the ladies' quarters were also females, as no male member was employed in the Harem. The officers employed in the Zenana quarters were women and most of them belonged to the royalty or the nobility. A sister of the last Qutb Shahi King, Abul Hasan, Swas the "keeper" of the Zenana quarters.[393]

In a Urdu Mathnawi of the period, Saif-ul-Mulk, the author Ghawwasi says that during the marriage celebrations also the women did not come out in the open. He has described that the hands behind the Purdah were active and were throwing flowers of a hundred kinds on the bridge and the groom, while describing the Muslim marriage system. During the marriage ceremonies also the men and women stayed in separate quarters. All the rituals were performed

---

[392] Ghawwasi, Mina Satwant.
[393] Francois Martin, p.761.

from behind the curtains. The Muslim ladies, wether young or old were confined to their homes only.

If an emergency arose then the ladies covered themselves totally from head to foot and only then came out. This applied to both the upper and lower class of Muslim women.[394] Later on they started putting on a black outfit called Burqah, and only then went out. It covered their bodies from head to foot. A thin veil was in the front, for their eyes to see. The woman had to be always accompanied by a male companion while going out. If the rich ladies went out they were always carried in an "enclosed palanquin" by the bearers.[395] The palanquins would be covered from each side and no one could look inside it. Anybody doing so would only be inviting his death.

A Muslim woman had no liberty whatsoever in their life. The houses of the Muslims were constructed in such a manner that it was quite impossible to see what was going on the street. The rooms were small and excessively hot. Sometimes, little boys and girls were employed to work as servants to the wives. There was practically no work for the ladies. Hence, they spent their time in serving their husbands and in nursing their children.[396]

The contemporary paintings also affirm to their ideas. The women are shown smoking Hookahs, drinking, playing

---

[394] John Fryer, p. 89
[395] Francois Martin, p. 759.
[396] Thomas Bowrey, pp. 63-64.

or listening to music.[397] The life shown in painting is very easy going and luxurious. The women were provided with all the luxuries of life but did not enjoy the basic liberty of even looking outside world. They were enclosed in the four walls of their homes and were in no way linked with the outside world. They had a carefree and monotonous life. Each day did not differ from the one that had already passed without any change.

The lower class of the Muslim women did not observe such strict regulations of seclusion in their daily life. "The seclusion of women in Muslim families was an institution in upper class Muslims and court oriented families".[398] The system of Parda could not be enforced strictly for them. The main reason could have been the economic backwardness. The lower class could not afford to built separate quarters for their women in the house. As such, they stayed in the same rooms as their men. This would certainly have facilitated them to exchange ideas and understand what was going on outside the four walls of their houses. They even helped their men in the professional works. There are references of the Muslim women of the nineteenth century indulging in the weaving of cotton turbans and cotton carpets. When they could do this in this in the 19th century, then they would be working even in the earlier centuries. Some were also

---

[397] Jagdish Mittal, <u>Deccan Painting as a source of history</u> in V.K.Bawa, <u>Aspects of Deccan History</u>, Institute of Asian studies, Hyderabad.

[398] Karen B. Leonard.

employed as servants to the rich ladies and went on errands for them outside.

The Hindu women enjoyed more liberty than her Muslim sisters. The common people gave their wives more liberty. During the time of marriage the bridegroom was obliged to promise the parents of the bridge that he would allow his wife to move about freely in the town and to visit her neighbours.[399] There was no restriction on the movement of women amongst the lower caste of Hindus. They were employed in various occupations and helped the man in income generation. "The Gentues observe not that strictness, both Sexes enjoying the open Air."[400] A Hindu woman was free to go out into the open alone or accompanied by another woman or man. She did not cover herself while going out. In fact, she did not even cover her head when she went out.

The middle and the lower class women were allowed to mix freely and take part in the different activities like attend the market, assist the men in the agriculture fields bring water and firewood, attend to the cattle, and performance all the ordinary in door and out door of life.[401]

However, some of the upper caste Hindu women had started staying indoors after the advent of the Muslims in Andhra Desa. The Rajus who claimed to be of Khsatriyas origin, strictly kept their women under Gosha

---

[399] S. N. Sen, ed. Indian Travels of Thevenot and Carreri, p. 136.
[400] John Fryer, p. 89..
[401] Nellore Manual, p. 213

or in seclusion.[402] The reasons could not be found out as no reference to the cause for this practice is given in the contemporary literature.

The Bhadragiri Satakam gives us information about the atrocities committed by the Muslim Generals, Sardars and Officers on the people of Bhadrachalam.[403] The atrocities of Muslims on the people of Tirupati has been described in the other Telugu works of the same period.[404]

Maybe because of the atrocities of the Muslims, the Hindu women had started staying indoors. The writers even criticized Lord Venkateswara for watching silently the atrocities committed by the Muslims on their women and on them.

The European women did not believe in the concept of Purdah. They did not stay in seclusion on any pretext. They enjoyed everything that a man could enjoy doing.

They did not have any restriction of movement and there are records that testify that women travelled alone in different ships that sailed from the ports of Europe, to come to India. However, they had to maintain the customs and traditions of the land that they had come to. When the Qutb Shahi King Abdullah Qutb Shah visited Masulipatnam, they had to go out of the room whenever the king or his nobles paid a visit to their quarters.

---

[402] Thurston and Rangachari.

[403] Bhalla Perakavi, Bhadragiri Satakam, p. 290-291.

[404] Vaddikasula Venkanna Kavi, Shatru Samahara Venkatachala Vihara Satakam, p. 291

When King Abdullah Qutb Shah visited their quarters in Masulipatnam, the women were asked to leave the rooms of their factories. However, in their society there was no concept of the system of Purdah.

MARRIAGE

The custom of marriage was the most important phase in the life of a woman. An unmarried woman was a bane on society. Marriage, gave a woman status and position in the society. Once married she had to remain in the house of her husband till the end of her life. The relationship with her parent's house remained only nominal after marriage. She visited them only on festivals or on some important occasions, when she was invited. The permission of her husband, in leaving the house was of utmost importance. The husband was not only the lord of the house but also the lord of his wife. His authority was final. The wife was only an advisor in the household affairs. However, her advice could be taken or left a it was the sole prerogative of the husband. She could give her piece of mind only when asked for otherwise most of the time she only abided by the decisions taken.

In Hinduism, polygamy was permitted but was seldom practiced. A man married twice only when he did not get any children from his first wife. Sometimes he married three to four women for the sake of children. Adultery was not common but it was not completely absent from the society. The men took it for granted and were not punished for going astray.[405] On the other hand, the punishment for adultery in women was severe. The goodness and morality of the public kept such evils away from the society. The quality of chastity was considered to be the highest accomplishment that a woman could have. Vemana reflected the views of the contemporary society when he said that a girl of great beauty with various accomplishments was compared to a devil if she was not faithful to her husband.[406] An ordinary girl who was sweet tempered, modest, and had a sweet tongue will be loved and respected by her husband who will only see her inner beauty and be blind to her outward ugliness. The Hindus married according to the choice of their elders. The marriage was arranged by the parents and the boy or the girl never questioned the decision taken by them. The couple to be married never even saw each other before the marriage.

The children will be never questioned the decision as it would amount to distrusting their own parents. It was considered not good to question them on this subject, as till now they had taken all the major decisions. The concerned boy and the girl were only to give their consent. The castes married into themselves only. "Every occupation married in the same occupation."[407] While writing this, Bowrey

---

[405] Methwold's Relationship, p. 14
[406] Vemana Shatakamu
[407] Thomas Bowrey, pp. 29-31.

meant to emphasize that each caste married into its own. A marriage between different castes was not only forbidden, but was even unthinkable. It would lead to Varnasankara which meant the breaking of the traditional caste system and their mixing together. This was considered as the greatest sin that anyone could commit.

"Children are married very young, at from 4 to 9 years of age."[408] Child marriages was the custom of those days. It was mostly a phenomena of the upper and the richer castes. The parents married their children very young. The richer the family, the younger was the age of the bridge and the groom.[409] Every parent tried to get his daughter married off at a very early age. The marriage of young daughters was considered a holy act which guaranteed the parents a sure abode in heaven. As such the girls were married off before they matured. Similarly, the boys were also married at an early age. If the parents were unable to fetch an alliance at the recommended age then it was almost impossible for a girl to get married. If a daughter crossed the age of 12 then, it would be very difficult for the father to find a suitable boy for her.[410] The custom had following amongst such castes that adhered to the Brahmanical way of living. Most of the upper castes followed this custom. In tribal and lower castes

---

[408] <u>Anonymous Relations</u>, p. 70
[409] Thomas Bowrey, pp. 29-31
[410] John A. C. Boswell, p.227.

this system was not in vogue and the girls were married only after puberty.

When a father was unable to find a suitable match for her then he would be forced to find a gullible man to marry his daughter. As such sometimes, the young girls were married to aged man. They looked like their fathers, and most of times these girls would go astray.[411] Their moral habits were badly affected by this prevailing social custom which was to be blamed.

Another evil that was a result of this practice was the early motherhood of these young girls. A contemporary European traveler, Thomas Bowrey, while writing about early motherhood of these young girls says that they conceived as early as 11-12 years and by 25 or 30 years of age they grew old. Early motherhood led to the early exhaustion of the reproductive organs in females and as such a woman of 25 years looked like an old woman of 50 years and above. They could not bear children after 25 to 30 years of age because of the same reason. A contemporary Telugu work sites examples which throw light on the ills of child marriages. The difficulties faced by the huge responsibilities often resulted in great hardship for the young husband and wife.[412] In Hamsa Vimshati the ills of child marriages and its resultant difficulties were retold by the poet.[413]

---

[411] Chowdappa's Sataka, p. 41..

[412] Anonymous Relations, p. 70

[413] H.V. story no. 5.

After marriage, the child bride was not taken to the husband's place. She stayed in her father's house till she grew up. She continued to stay with her father till she matured and attained the age of leaving for the husband's house. When she was grown up, she was taken to her husband's house with great pomp and show. The boy and his relatives came to take her to her new home. Once she was taken there, she stayed in her husband's house, throughout her life. During 17th and the 18th centuries, the family was always a joint family. The newly arrived bride stayed with her father in law, mother in law, the brother in law, the sister in law, and co sister in the house.

The family members lived as a one unit and they shared all their profits together. It was taken as a pious duty to serve the old parents.[414] The daughter in law served the old people and did the house hold work.

She also treated the servants of the house in a very cordial way. From very early age they were taught to cook, arrange the house and do all the household chores without any complaint. They were also generally illiterate. They did a lot of work in the house. The girls were taught to milk the cow and to utilize the products got from it. "They marry very young, not knowing their Wives though till at riper years they come to consummate their Hymeneal Rites".[415]

---

[414] Methwold's Relations, p.25
[415] John Fryer, p.95

Most of the non Brahmin castes of the Telugu speaking people were split into endogamous subdivisions. These subdivisions had to marry amongst themselves and no marriage was allowed outside the endogamous subdivision.[416] On the other hand, the exogamous sections of these subdivisions had to marry outside these groups only. These exogamous groups were known as Inti-Perulu or House –Names. All the sub sects of the Sudra caste followed the marriage custom of Menarikam. This was the custom of marrying the girls to their maternal Uncle. They tried to find alliances in closer family circles only. However, this custom was not followed by the Brahmins and the castes adhering to their way of life.

BRIDE PRICE AND DOWRY

In the Sudra caste and in the lower castes the custom of giving bride was prevalent.[417] it was known as the Kanyasulkam. The father and the son went to the girl's house and asked the father of the girl for her hand in marriage. The bride price something's included ear rings, bracelets, and other jewels, clothes for the bride and her mother and also some present for the father. The boy's family also bore up with the expense of wedding.[418] The parents of the girl

---

[416] I. R. Hemmingway, p.49
[417] Thomas Bowrey, pp. 29-31.
[418] Methwold's Relations, p.24

in such marriages did not give anything to the bridegroom or to his family.

The custom of dowry existed only in the Brahmins and other upper castes of the Andhra Desa. In the upper castes, the father of the bride went to the boy's father with the marriage proposal. The bride's side paid dowry to the groom's side when the alliance was settled. In the upper castes the bride carried the Stridhana or Sare meaning dowry, along with her during the departure to her husband's house.[419] It was also known as Varakatnam.

The Brahmin's followed the Muhurtam or Nakasastra, Rasi and Gana. They were very particular about the auspicious hour and day for the celebration of the marriage. The horoscope of the right girl also was significant. If the horoscopes of the girl and the boy did not match then the wedding would not be performed. Everything had to be compatible and only a marriage could take place.[420]

MARRIAGE CEREMONIES

The marriage system of the Hindus in the Telugu country was celebrated with great pomp and show. It caused a lot of expenditure. People spent a lot on celebrating marriages of their children. It was a time when family name and honor was at stake, and every person tried to show off

---

[419] Nellore Manual, p.227
[420] S.S

that he belonged to a decent and respectful family. In order to keep up the family reputation, the parents spent a lot of money and often landed in huge debts. They vied each other in celebrating marriages and each wanted to out class the other. There were two stages in a marriage, namely, Vivaham and Punassandhanam. The ceremony called Vivaham was performed when the children were young. All the ceremonies concerning marriage were solemnized and they were betrothed to one another when they were no more than small children. When the boy and the girl were grown up, the Punassandhanam was performed. It was the ceremony which made the girl to leave her parent's house and enter the house of her husband. The marriage began with the engagement ceremony. During the engagement a ring was offered to the girl.

All the guests were earlier invited through Shubhalekha or Vignapana Patrikalu i.e the invitation cards. On that day, everybody feasted on a special dish called Pallakollu which was made of milk.[421]

On the day of the wedding, the bride and the bridegroom were bathed after applying turmeric on the entire body. They were assisted by elderly married woman called Muttaiduvalu. The woman sang various marriage songs called Ettili, Dhavalamu etc. for the good fortune of the bride and bridegroom. When the bridegroom entered the house of the bride along with his relatives and friends,

---

[421] Nellore Manual, p.227.

they were welcomed by an elderly lady who washed the bridegroom's feet. Later on he was bathed in oil and group of married women sang Mangalaharati for his good fortunes. The bride too, got ready with an oil bath and turmeric paste was rubbed all over her body to give her a fair complexion. When she was ready she sat in a new basket filled with grain. She was carried to the wedding- stage in the basket by two of her close relatives. The next stage was eating of the Madhuparkam, a preparation of a mixture of curd, ghee, water, honey, and sugar by the groom.

When the bride and groom were on the wedding stage, a curtain was drawn in between the two so as not to allow them to see each other. Next, the father placed a coconut and fruits into the bride's hands and took her hand into his own. The mother-in-law poured water on his and his daughter's hands. Finally the father handed over the daughter's hands to the bridegroom who accepted her after chanting some mantras. The bride and the groom sprinkled some cumin seeds and sugar on each other. The curtain separating them was removed. After this the bridegroom tied the Thali ot Mangala Sootram round the brides neck which was followed by Talambralu or the throwing of pearls on each other's heads. As pearls were unaffordable by all, clean rice was used as pearls and the ceremony was celebrated.

The next stage was the Saptapatha or the seven steps that are taken by the bride. Each step had a distinct importance, the first for obtaining food, the second for obtaining strength, the third for solemn acts of religion, the fourth obtaining happiness, the fifth for the sake of the cattle, the sixth for the increase of wealth and the seventh for the priests for performing sacrifices. With this the marriage ceremony was solemnized. On the same evening, the bridegroom came out under the open sky to watch the Arundati Star or the polar star. On seeing it, the bridegroom said Heaven is stable, the earth is stable, these mountains are stable, may this woman be stable in her husband's family. The bride then saluted the bridegroom. After the marriage a sumptuous feast was arranged this was known as the Buvvambanti, which was attended by the relatives and the friends.

Amongst the Razus or the Kshartiyas, written contracts of marriage were exchanged. The wedding was performed at the bride's house. The bridegroom had to wear a sword throughout the marriage ceremonies and he was to go round the village before the ceremonies began.[422]

The different Sudra sections followed more or less the same rituals for their marriages. However, in the Naidu caste the bridegroom took the dowry to the brides place i.e. bride-price was paid to the father of the girl. In the caste, the bridegroom merely put the Thali on the bride's neck, while his sister tied it from behind. Similarly, in the Kapus a ritual called Pradhanam was followed by which the bridegroom's father asked the bride in marriage for his son. In this caste marriage were generally celebrated in the bride's place. On

---

[422] Godavary Gazetteer, p. 53

the last day the married couple pretended to plough and sow seeds in the fields.[423] A practice called Ariveni was observed at the wedding of all the Sudra castes. In this, the bride and the groom offered their Puja to the earthen pots which represented the Gods. The number of pots varied from 9 to 21 and they were of different shapes and sizes.

Another important custom that was to found in all the castes was called Alaka Wherein, on some pretext or the other, the bridegroom and his party took offence of the bride's party on the night of the 4th day. They withdraw in affected anger and came out only after the bride's relations offered them some presents and a re-conciliation was brought about.

The lower castes amongst the Sudras, more or less followed the same rituals in their weddings. However, certain important differences are the following. Among the Golas or the shepered caste, the bride and the groom went to a Brahmin who cast their horoscopes and fixed the day of the marriage. In the Chakali or the washer man's caste, the Thali was first blessed by the head of the caste. It was he who then asked the groom to tie it round the bride's neck. The marriage practices of the Kamsalies or the smiths and the carpenter's castes resembled most closely, the practices of the Brahmins. In the Perika caste, the bride and the groom were made to fast on the day of the marriage. Instead of the

---

[423] ibid., p. 55

Thali, a necklace made of 101 cotton treads with seven knots was tied to the bride's neck by the groom.[424]

In the fifth caste or in the untouchables like the Malas and the Madigas, marriage was performed mainly at the bridegroom's house. The bride goes to the house of the bridegroom immediately offer the marriage. No Brahmin priest officiated at the marriage of either the Mala or the Madiga. In these castes, girls were married at any age and it was the grooms' father who asked for her hand for his son.[425] Among well-to-do Malas, the bridegroom went with pomp and music to the brides house, but the more common practice was for the bride to come to the brides place. After praying to the pots in the Ariveni custom, the bride with her bridesmaid and the groom with his best man sat on a dais facing east. After few rituals performed by a barber, the couple were bathed in oil. As in other marriage the bride put on silver toe rings and Thali round her neck by the groom.

They also worshipped the Arundati star. On the fifth day, a goat was sacrificed signifying the end of the marriage ceremony. The Madiga too followed the same customs in their marriage ceremonies. However, the marriage of the Madigas was very noisy, as a lot country liquor was consumed by all the invitees.

---

[424] ibid. p. 57.
[425] <u>Nellore Manual</u>, p. 241.

TRIBAL'S MARRIAGE.

In contrast to the upper castes of the Telugus, the marriage ceremony of the tribal's was very simple. There were no ritualistic burdens. There was also no dowry and there was not much expenditure. Furthermore, it lasted for just one day. One significant aspect of the tribal marriage was that there was no child marriage. The girl and the boy were both grown up. It was not arranged by the parents. Marriage was performed to the wishes of the bride and the groom. The young people were free to select their life partners. The ceremony was not considered as a time to show off the family wealth, nor was it considered to keep up the family pride during the performance of the rituals. It was a very simple function attended by the entire village. Amongst the tribal's of the Andhra Desa the marriage ceremonies were more simple and fast. In the Chenchu tribe, marriages were performed in three different ways.[426] In the first type the boy and the girl with mutual consent retired to the forest for one night. In the morning, on returning to the Gudem or the village they were married. The parents invited the relatives and friends and presented the bride and the groom with new clothes etc. After hosting a feast for all those present, the marriage was solemnized. In the second instance, after clearing a circular piece of land, a bow with

---

[426] Edgar Thurston and K. Rangachary, "Castes and Tribes of Southern India", vol. II, Madras.

an arrow is fixed to the ground. When the shadow of the bow and arrows touches its bottom they the boy and a girl were married. They went round the bow and arrow and then took the blessings of the elders present. The third way of marrying was the Aryan way of consulting a Brahmin by the elders of the family. On the auspicious day the bride and the groom sit on a pial, made for the special purpose.

They throw rice on each other's head in the Talambralu ritual, after the Thali is tied around the bride's neck by the groom. In the Yanadi tribe, marriage was performed after mutual consent of the boy and the girl. The girls were married after puberty and the marriage tie was very loose. The practice of adultery was very common. The Yanadis were polygamous and it has been noticed that a man could have as many as seven wives. The marriage was solemnized by tying the Thali around the brides neck by the groom. The women loved to wear bangles, but being poor only few ladies could afford to wear bangles which were in great demand. In the tribe of the Koyas, a youth who has been refused in marriage by a maiden carried her off by force. The marriage was held in bridegroom's house. It was solemnized by tying a Thali and a saffron colored thread. The widow and the divorced woman were allowed to remarry. In the tribe of the Konda Reddis marriage by capture was recognized.[427] However, when a parent did not like a match, he absented himself from the meeting with the suitor's party and sent

---

[427] Godavary Gazetteer, p.67.

a bundle of cold rice after them when they have departed. Amongst the tribal's of Yerukalas, Sukalies or Lambadas and Dommaras etc., tying of Thali solemnized a marriage. While the Yerukalas were polygamous, the Dommaras were monogamous but kept a number of concubines. The girls were always married after puberty and their wishes of selecting a life partner was most of the time respected by the parents and the elders of the tribe.

MUSLIM MARRIAGE.

The Muslims formed an important part of the region in the seventeenth century and eighteenth century. The marriage ceremonies differed a lot from the Hindu style of celebrations. However, there was also a lot of similarly in both the sections of the population. In the Muslim families also, the marriage were fixed by the parents. The boy and girl accepted the decisions of their elders.

The details of Muslim marriages are to be found in the book called Shahi Shadi written by Raja Gridhari Prasad in Persian. Raja Girdhari Prasad was an important official of the Asaf Jahi King Mahboob Ali Asaf Jah VI. He witnessed the marriage of the sister of Asaf Jah VI i.e Najils-un-Nissa Begum which was solemnized in the year 1892 A.D. The book gives us a detailed account of the marriage practices during the Asaf Jahi rule. Though the Asaf Jahi rules were followers of the Sunni sect of Islam, their cultural practices more or less resembled that of the entire Muslim community. The Kulliyat of Mohammad Quli Qutab Shah also gives us a vivid picture of the Muslim marriage. Besides, the Mathnavis like <u>Behram and Gulandan</u> by Wajhi throws light light on the rituals followed by people in Muslims wedding. All these works dealt with the weddings performed in the royal households. However, the literature of the period is silent as the wedding of the common people are concerned.

One of the remarkable things that one comes across while analyzing the contemporary records is that, the royal weddings were never performed alone. The royalty and nobility always made it a point to marry off one or two or more daughters and sons of the poor people. During the marriage of Najils-un-Nissa Begum, the King got the marriages of several poor girls performed too. This was a great benevolent act on the part of Nizam Mhboob Ali. The precedent was set by royals and followed by the nobles. The celebration of marriage continued for more than a month in the higher ups. In this time further alliances were fixed. People came to know about prospective brides and grooms in the marriages. The parents could watch the behavior of their future daughter-in-law in a congregation and could fix up alliances after having been fully satisfied by the girl's and her family's behavior and mannerisms. Muslim marriages were all conducted from the house of the bridge only. The people also sent out Madowatniyan or female emissaries to seek good proposals for their sons. The Madowatniyan reported to them the riches and the claims of such and such maidens.[428] These emissaries were paid by the boy's father for their work.

In the Muslim marriages, the groom's father paid the bridge Mehr or an amount of money for marrying his son. The amount of Mehr was decided on the qualities and physical beauty of the girl and her family background. Sometimes several proposals reached a girl's house and it was the Mehr amount that generally settled the proposal in the name of so and so.

The first step was called the Rasme Rukha which was the proposal of marriage sent by the bride's father to the groom's father. The letter had the groom's name written on it and was placed in a tray with some amount of money that was sent as a token. Later on, a letter with the consent for marriage was sent to the bride's house by the groom's father. This was followed by Mangni, or the engagement ceremony where on a fixed date a ring was presented to the groom by the girl's father. This was a time for celebration and people enjoyed drinking different kinds of Sherbets or soft drinks. On the Namak Chasi day the groom's side threw a lavish party for their friends and relatives. On this day, the alliance was made public and all people were informed about the marriage. Betel nuts were exchanged and distributed among the friends and the relatives.

---

[428] Nellore Manual, p. 258

The next important ceremony was called Rat Jagga which was the night before the marriage wherein the women did not sleep during the night and enjoyed good food along with relatives and friends. Next came the Rasme Haldi wherein turmeric paste was sent from the boy's house to the girl's house. It was applied to the girl's hand and feet as turmeric is said to enhance of beauty.

The bride was later on bedecked with jewelry made of flowers. In Dhamal as the name suggest religious people like the Fakirs etc. and relatives were called and given dinner. The Fakirs danced, sang and walked on fire the whole night for celebrating the alliance.

The actual celebration of marriage started with Rasme Saanchak, where the groom's side sent trays full of dry fruits, Mewa, Mithai, jewells, clothes and cosmetics for the bride. Gifts of clothes, cosmetics, sweets, good and rich food, betal nuts and betel leaves were sent for the bride. The gifts for the groom from the bride's side were sent and the ceremony was called Rasme Mehndi. Trays laden with fruits, flowers, clothes, shoes and Jewells were sent for the groom. The most important item sent in the tray was henna which was applied on the hands and feet of the groom. Later, on the day of the marriage, Rasme Sehra Bandi was celebrated in the groom's house. Here, flowers were tied in threads and were then tied to the groom's forehead. The Sehra was tied to the groom's forehead by a respected old man or a married woman. The dressed up groom then headed for the brides house along with his relatives, and friends towards the girls house. The procession or the Baraat was accompanied by different kinds of musicians, dancers, singers etc. who performed in front of the Baraat. There was lightening arrangements also and torches were carried by bearers to show the path. Everybody was dressed up in their new and best clothes. There also used to be Aatishbaazi or fireworks all along the way.

The Baraat was received with great respect and was entertained with articles of food and cool drinks or Sherbets. The bride was usually dressed up in a yellow dress called Manjha and the Mushatas were called for the make-up of the bride. They applied Mehendi on the hands and feet, and beautified the brides face with several creams and pastes. Then seven to eight married woman or Suhagans applied oil to the bride's hair and combed it. The hair was plaited and the head-parting was decorated with jewel made of pearls.

Later on, a moon-shaped pendant was fixed on her forehead. Collyrium and antimony was used these to the brides eyes.[429]

Finally the Nikaah or the marriage took palce. A Qazi or the judicial head generally performed the Nikaah after ascertaining the acceptance of the alliance by both the girl and the boy. The Qazi caused the bridegroom to repeat after him in Arabic first, a form of deprecation, then the 109th, 112th, 113th & 114th chapters of the Koran, the five creeds, the articles of belief and lastly a thanks giving

---

[429] Mohammad Quli Qutb Shah, Kulliyat.

was read and repeated. After this the groom repeated the marriage contract. The Qazi finally blessed them and offered a supplication that they may be as loving as Adam & Eve, Abraham & Sarah and others. A plateful of sugar candy and dates were scattered over the heads of those present who rushed forward to collect it.

The ceremony called Jalwa has been beautifully described by Muhammad Quli in his collection of verses. It was a ceremony that made the bride and the groom look at each other for the first time. A fixed number of old married ladies held a mirror in their hands and then asked the girl and the boy to look into the mirror and have a first look at each other. The bride used to be very shy while looking at her husband. The newly wedded drank Sherbet and ate betel from each other's hands.

After the Nikaah was finalized, the bride had to leave for her husband's house. This ceremony has been described as Ruksati or the departure. After remaining for four days in her husband's place, the bride returned to her father's place. On the occasion of Rasme Chauthi or as the 4th day after marriage was called, a grand dinner was hosted by the bride's father. Trays of gifts and food were sent to the groom's place through the servants to the groom's house. Another important festivity was Rasme Hiljam when food was distributed amongst the people. On the first five Fridays or Jummas Jumagi was performed.

On these 5 Fridays dinners were hosted by the relatives of the bride and several Nazr and Nazrana or gifts were given to each other and the poor. On the first Jumagi the bride's mother hosted the dinner and on the next, it was the term of the brother of the bride. The last or the fifth Jumangi was hosted by the groom's father and mother. There was a lot of revelry and fun. Professional singers called Mirasins were called to perform during the dinner. The guests greatly enjoyed the food and the accompanying music and dance.

The office of the Sadarat-ul-Auliya which was created during the period of the Asaf Jah I attended to the ecclesiastical matters besides judicial duties. The Sadarat-ul-Auliya made appointments of Qazis who were the Muslim religious functionaries. The Qazis besides their other duties, supervised the marriage ceremony of Muslims, administered marriage deeds, prepared, and attested marriage certificates called Siyaha-i-Nikah. [430]The Siyaha from the Qazis of the district of the Nizam's dominions commenced from the year 1771 A.D. The Siyahas of the earlier period contain the following particulars:-

1. Seal of the Qazi
2. Place and date of Nikah(Marriage)
3. Name of Nikah (Bride groom).
4. Name of Mankoha(Bride).
5. Name of Wakil (Legal Council).

---

[430] Asaf Jahi Records, Daftar-i-Darul Insha.

6. Name of Shahidan (witness).
7. Mihr (the consideration for marriage to be necessarily given by the husband to his wife in cash or kind.)

The example of an old Sujaha is given below:

"Sujaha-I-Nikah dated 17th Zilhijja 1194 H/ 14th Dec. 1780 AD. Of the marriage of Jumatatunnisa Begum, daughter of Asaf Jah I with Kawaja Badiuddin Khan S/o. Musa Khan under the wikalit of Qamaruddin Daula Bahadur Mansur Jung, before the witness of Nawazish Ali Khan Bahadur and Hakim Muhammad Jafar Khan. Mihr Rs. 100,000, camels 100 and Horses 100".

The common man could not give too many parties during the marriage. However, he tried his best to do as much as he could, and not give any discomfort to his new relatives who were also his daughter's new in-laws.

The Muslim men could have as many as far wives at a time. This was legalized by their religion. However, the poor Muslims preferred to have one wife only. This was mainly due to the poor living conditions of the people. It was difficult to look after one wife and her children and one could not afford to have more than one wife. The royalty and the nobility had many wives, sometimes even more than four. In addition to his, their Harem, consisted of several concubines too. In fact, the greater the number of concubines, the greater was the prestige of the man, as it showed his economic prosperity. There was no taboo attached to the keeping of concubines. The women being many in the house the atmosphere was not always congenial. On the order hand, there was always some plot being hatched by one wife against the other. The wives were jealous of one another and tries to belittle the other in front of the husband. If one succeeded in making him happy then her importance increased in the harem. However, all were not bad and there were wives who considered their husbands as their Gods and were always loyal to them.[431]

EUROPEAN MARRIAGE.

The European women got married to men of their choice. The European marriages were not settled by the parents but by groom and the bride themselves. There was no apprehension in marrying either widows or divorcees amongst the Europeans. Both male and females enjoyed similar opportunities and rights in marriage, divorce and re-marriages of widows and divorces. The marriage took place in the religious places called Church. They were married by the chaplain or the priest of the church. The couple were married according to the rituals of the sect that they belonged to. The Protestants were married according to the Protestant rituals and the Catholics according to their

---

[431] Mulla Wajhi, Sabras, pp. 97.98.

customs. During the early days of their arrival, when the Catholic priests were very few in the region, the Protestants got married in Catholic churches by the Catholic priests. This was resented by the higher authorities who were advocators of their own sect and did not like their men to have anything to do with the other sect and with the women of other countries. Sometimes the groom and the clergy were punished for disobeying the orders.[432] The companies, kept passing orders regarding this and also ordered them to marry the women of their own countries.

Some of the European also married Indian women but they could not fully satisfy them and these men always longed for women of their own country who would understand them fully. Whenever such an opportunity arose they would abandon the Indian women and marry the Europeans. The respective companies sent women from their country, for the servants working in India. A French clergyman saw a ship full of English woman who had come down to the Andhra Desa to marry and settle down. Many had found partners in Masulipatnam and Madras and had settled down. While the others were taken to the other English settlements at Surat, Bengal, Bombay etc.[433]

Sometimes the girls who could not find good companies and good life in their country tried their luck in India. When they came here their standing in the social ladder

---

[432] The Diaries of Streynsham Master, p. 106
[433] Abbe Carre p.685

automatically moved up. To a young girl India was a last resort and nearly all welcomed an offer from some indulgent relative to send them there with as little enthusiasm as Sophia Fowke who wrote to her brother in the year 1787 A. D. that, "As I look upon my fate at best to be a very poor one, India, even on the terms you represent it situated as I am, I prefer to anything England will afford me; it is the only alternative, and I will embrace it with joy."[434] The arrival of such girls and their marriage in India, led to the formation of a new class of people called as Anglo Indians. Though they stayed and died in India, and their children were born and brought up here, the loyalty of this class was always with the mother country, i.e. Britain.

DIVORCE.

The system of separation from ones wife before the death of either the husband or the wife was absent in the high Hindu society. The marriage ceremony and tying of the Thali suggested that a man and his wife were inseparable in their lifetime. They could be separated from each other only by natural calamities. If a girl was married to a man she remained married to him for life. There was no way in which she could come out of the wedlock. If the husband married a second time or went to concubines, she had to bear up with all the insults. The right to remarry was given

---

[434] Holden Furber, John Company At Work, p 339

only to Hindu men of higher castes and not to the higher caste and not to the higher caste Hindu women. If a wife died, man could take a second wife. The system of divorced was absent as far as the high Hindu society was concerned.

However, in some Sudra castes, the system of divorce was legalized. In the caste of the Kapus the system of divorce was prevalent.[435] A man could divorce his wife and remarry another woman. The divorced wife also possessed the right to marry another man. There was equality amongst men and women in the land owning class so far as divorce was concerned. Amongst the untouchables, divorce took place on trifle matters. It was very quickly decided upon.

In the tribal society of Andhra Desa, divorce was common. The husband and the wife had equal rights of separation. The divorce proceedings could be initiated by either of two concerned parties. The right to second marriage was also given to the tribal men and tribal women. In tribes such as Lambadas or Sugalis, as they were also called, divorce was very common.[436] When the divorce was granted, if the wife was found to be at fault then she had to return the bride price or the Mumloo back to her previous husband. Mamloo was the bride price paid by grooms to the bride's father at the time of marriage. However, if the husband was at fault, then the wife need not return the

---

[435] W. Francis, <u>Madras District Gazetters, Vizagapatnam</u>, pp.77-78

[436] G. Bhadru, <u>Role of the Lambadas in Telangana Armed sruggle in Janagaon Taluq, 1945-1951</u>.A.D, M. Phil. Dissertation, Kakatiya University.

Mamloo. If a wife was unable to return the Mamloo, then she did not become eligible for re-marriage. The man and women had equal rights in divorce and re-marriages after separation. However, as the Mamloo was given to the girl father at the time of marriage, the bride's had very less or no control over the money. It became almost impossible to repay the Mamloo as the amount would already be spent by her father on drinking and merry making.

In tribes like Yanadies, Yerukalas, and the Chenchus etc. the marriage tie was very loose.[437] it was very easy to divorce the estranged couple. In the Koya tribe, widows and divorced woman could remarry.[438] In the caste of Godagula who were basically Hindus, divorce was allowed. A man could divorce his wife and could remarry.

The procedure for divorce in the Muslim society was very simple. It was known as Talaq. The Muslim society had legalized the system of divorce. The Qazi granted the divorce. It was a system where a man could break away from a marriage. A man could remarry after giving divorce to his wife. The Muslim women also had the right to divorce their husbands. Though the Muslim women could remarry after the divorce, it was seldom that they married again. However, it was very difficult for a divorce to find another life partner.

---

[437] Nellore Manual, p.148
[438] Godavary Manual, p.65

The European women too had the right to divorce. They separated from their husbands if they could not adjust with them or if they faced any difficulty from them.

WIDOWHOOD.

When the husband of a Hindu woman died, the entire atmosphere of the house changed towards her. Her life became miserable. As the girls were married young and in case their husbands were of an older age than them, then it was natural that the men pre-deceased their wives. There are instances of old man men buying young girls from their parents and then marrying them. The old men soon died, leaving behind a young widow. An old man from the Kistna district had and young girl from her parents. He married her. But she escaped from his house on the first night itself and committed suicide by jumping into a well.[439]

The marriage presented a very comical sight as the husband appeared to be the father or even the grandfather of his own wife. The difference in age of the couples often led to confusion regarding the relationship of a man and his wife. When the difference in age was large, then the young brides became widow's very early life. Sometimes, they became widows even in a week. Once a widow, she remained so throughout her life. The custom of re-marriage of widows did not exist in the high caste Hindu society.

---

[439] Abbe J. A. Dubois, p. 217

Once married to a man, she remained only his wife till death took her away. She was not allowed to remarry. "It is great disgrace for women to marry again, and they are regarded as no better than prostitutes, but men may marry again at any time."[440]

Sometimes, it so happened that when a marriage alliance had been fixed and if the boy died before actual marriage ceremonies could be performed, then too a girl was declared a widow. A contemporary French priest wrote that such a women could never marry again. It was not acceptable to the society. He has written that a youth from the Gollavaru caste, died before his marriage could be solemnized. Only the marriage proposal had been accepted and no ritual had been performed. The bride's father married his daughter to another boy of the same caste. This created a great tension in the Golla community. The girl's relatives and even the persons, who had attended the marriage ceremonies, were expelled from the caste. Later on all of them had to face a lot of difficulties because of this excommunication from the caste.[441]

In the Hindu society, there was no place for a widow. The woman who was the mistress of the entire house, on the death of her husband became a slave.[442] The attitude of her family towards her became intolerable. Her own sons

---

[440] <u>Anonymous Relation</u>, pp. 72-73
[441] Abbe Dubois, p.40
[442] Travernier, pp. 406-407

started to hate her. They no longer wanted her in the house. The close relatives also would not give a hand to support her. Her presence in the house itself was thought to be an ill omen. They preferred her to leave the house as soon as possible. There was no place for her to live. Her own house could no longer give a shelter to her. She was a burden on her own near and dear ones. She had to bear the hatred and scorn of all. No respect was shown to her. A widow, had to shave off her hair, discard all the clothes, jewelleries and eat only once in a day. She was given a white cloth to cover her body. The cloth would also be old and torn. She had to spend her entire day in serving the inmates of the house. All the menial works were left for her.

If there was no work then she had to retire to the Puja room and do penance. There was nobody to talk to her or to ask her about her health. All physical discomforts had to be borne by her without any complaint.

The widow was not allowed to go anywhere outside. She could not take part in any ceremony. The family was always suspicious of a widow. They felt that she might fall in bad company and bring a bad name for them. Hence, she was always imprisoned inside the house. There was no entertainment for her. She was never allowed to wear anything nice on a festive day. The others behaved as if they were doing her a great favor in allowing her to stay in the house. The condition of the widows became pathetic when some male member started casting his bad eyes on her.

In spite of being faultless, all the blames and insults were heaped upon her. In some houses, the widows became an object of lust for the male members of the family. Soon she became a loathsome person for the ladies of the house and they started hatching plots to do away with her. At other instances the torturing life forced a woman to kill herself.

The young girls became fed up of their dreadful lives and left their house. As the girls knew no occupation and were not educated, the easiest way to earn their livelihood was to sell themselves. They began to lead an immoral life. "It is no wonder that many of this class [Hindu widows] should betake themselves to an immoral course of life, and that the term 'widow' should be almost synonymous with 'prostitute'. And here is a fruitful source of crime... the family avoid disgrace by getting rid of the widow, it may be by directly foul means, or by harshness and cruelty and taunts that drive her commit suicide".[443]

The Muslim widows did not have any such custom to follow. When their husbands died the Muslim women were free to marry another man if they chose to. Similarly, the European women could marry another man on the death of their husbands. The wife of Joseph Hynmers, Catherine Hynmers married Elihu Yale after the death of her first

---

[443] Nellore District Manual, p.250

husband.[444] Similarly, the widow of John Tivill married George Ramsden.[445]

SATI SAHAGAMANA.

On the other hand the women, who could not bear the loss of their husbands, ended their lives after the death of their husband's. It was the prevailing custom in the 17th and 18th centuries in Andhra Desa that a widow should burn herself along with her husband. The willing and the unwilling had to submit to this social cruelty. They had no other way. However, the custom of Sati or Sahagamana prevailed mostly amongst the higher castes of the Hindu society. The lower castes and tribes did not adhere to this inhuman practice. However, we come across instances of Kapu women etc. resorting to Sati after the death of their husband. While the Muslim literature is silent in this custom of the Hindus, the European literature is full of the instances of Sati. The British, French and the Dutch travelers of contemporary Andhra Desa have left behind vivid account of this horrible custom. They have described in details about the dress and mood of the widow and also the behavior of the onlookers.

The custom of Sahagamana was in fact encouraged by the upholders of Hinduism. The Brahmins who were

---

[444] The Diaries of S. Master, pp. 189-190
[445] ibid, p. 198

said to be the guardian of Hindu religion were the greatest advocates of Sati. The women themselves also felt that by committing sati, they were doing a great religious work and that they would become a legend in their native place after performing the act. The Hindu rulers also felt that by commemorating Sati hood they were doing a great duty towards the society by upholding Dharma in their respective kingdoms. A large number of women from royal household would commit Sati on the death of their husbands. In fact the Hindu concubines of the native rulers burnt themselves to death along with the legally wedded wives of the Raja. "On the 25th came news of the death of Wenkatadrapa, King of Velur, after fifty years region, and that ties three wives (of whom Obiamma Queen of Paleakate, was one) had burned themselves with the corpse."[446]

Another incident of the nobility performing the voluntary Sati hood has been discovered in the writings of Abbe Carre. He says that Mandala Naik, the Golconda army general had gone to St. Thome leading the army against the French of St. Thome. He was killed by a musket shot. "Finally the memory of the general was solemnized cum sonitu (sic.) to the sound of thousands of instruments and by the light of an enormous fire lit on a pyre composed of everything combustible. In this they burnt the corpse of this Hindu prince, with four of his wives, who had the courage to throw themselves, alive on the folames; the latter

---

[446] Journal of Mr. Peter Williamson Floris, p. 443

consumed their bodies, but sent their souls to other eternal fires, much hotter than those terrestrial ones. "[447]

When the royals performed any ritual, it becomes the fashion of the time. The common women tried to follow the examples set forth by the Queens and the ladies of the Nobles. They became more fascinated with the ritual of Sati and tried to imitate them. Even, when asked and sometimes ordered not to indulge in the act, they did not adhere to the orders and tried to perform sati. A woman who burnt herself on the funeral pyre of her dead husband attained a sort of sainthood. She was held in great reverence by all the people of the village. Temples were constructed in her name in her native village and people prayed there. In the year 1820 A. D., for one Sati Veeramma in Chintalapudi village a temple was constructed.[448] Every year on the day of her sati hood Puja was performed at her temple. People came in large numbers and great fair was organized there. The women who committed Sati were termed as Perentalu. The village bards and minstrels composed songs on their bravery and faithfulness.

They sang these songs while roaming about the village, begging for alms. The people would flock around them to hear them sing stories of the brave ladies. The Perentalus became folklore of the village.[449]

---

[447] Abbe Carre, p. 507.
[448] Mc. Ms., West Godavari Dist. Ed. Rajendra Prasad, p.16
[449] ibid., p. 17

"Patipaluku Satulaku Varamartha Mani Yunchi
Hitavutoda Patini Eechchaginchi
Dharinini Yolanaga Tanuvu Daptamu Jesi
Varamu Jedakanatti Prabahu Vema"

The Woman who holds her husband's words as the truth and who loves her lord with affection shall by burning her body fully inherit heaven.[450] Vemana was the first social reformer of the Andhra country. He has glorified the horrifying custom of widow burning. He says that a woman, who followed her husband blindly while he was alive, should also follow him in his death. By becoming a Sati she would attain heavenly abode. It was very unfortunate that Vemana, who has spoken against the evils of the caste system and other evils of the society, should fully appreciate and idolize sati hood.

"Yet there are few left, that in pure love to their deceased husbands die voluntarily in solemnizing their funerals, believing their souls shall keep company in their transmigrations".[451] Most of the times the women who became widows did not want to live any longer. They were afraid of the life which they had to lead after the death of their husbands. They felt it better to end their lives along with the funeral of their husbands. Some could have been much agonized at the loss of their life partner and would

---

[450] C.P. Brown, <u>Verses of Vemana</u>, p.288.
[451] Methwold's Relations, pp. 25-26.

have lost the love of life. The women who had made up their mind to commit sati were no longer afraid of death. Having once decided they finished their task without hesitation. They were never sad. In fact they felt very happy in doing this great religious act. One can also draw the inference, that the life of the widows being very hard and sorrowful they felt it better to end their lives along with their husbands. They were respected and treated well as long as their men were alive. After his death, they had no life worth to lead. Hence, they put an end to their sorrows ending their lives. When a woman committed Sahagamana, not only was they defied, but the entire family was held in a high position in the entire village. There was nothing to lose but the life of a desperate woman.

Accordingly, women allowed themselves to be misled into committing Sahagamana. The method of committing the practice differed with the religious sect followed by the dead man. If the dead man belonged to the sect that believed in burning the dead bodies, then the women had to enter the funeral pyre along with the body of her husband. On the other hand if the husband was from the sect who buried their dead then the women was buried alive in the sand along with the dead body. Both such practices have been described by the European travelers to the Andhra Desa. The Europeans have given a long description of the method adopted to commit sati. "The other was a Campowaroes wife, and she, after the same solemn preparation, fetching her run and crying all the way Bama Narina, Bama Narina, leapt into the pit where her husband lay burning, upon whom her by standing friends threw so many logs that she felt not so much fire for the fewell. "[452] Another, account gives us the other way of committing the act. It says "Gentus are not buried, but thrown into fire and burned; then come their wives with joyful countenance, and jump into the fire beside their husbands". [453] Big holes were dug in areas which hand sandy soil. The dead body and the widow were made to sit inside. The relatives and friends, then poured mud and sand over them and jumped and danced over it for shifting the women inside. Tavernier, the French traveler of the 17th century also witnessed the burning of a widow. He says that a joyous atmosphere prevailed everywhere. The widow was dressed as bride and was dancing with betel leaves in her mouth. The relatives and her friends accompanied her with a lot of musicians that included drummers, flutists and others. After going round the pyre three times, she was pushed into it by the Brahmins. Her relatives and the friends threw combustible items into the pyre "to make it burn more vehemently, that the bodies may be sooner consumed".[454] However, all women are not same. There were several women in the region who did not want to burn themselves with their husbands. However, they were

---

[452] Methwold's Relations, pp. 28-29
[453] Schorer's Relations, p.58.
[454] Tavernier, pp.411-412

forced to emulate themselves in the funeral pyres of their husbands. The relatives of the dead man may have their vested interests in her death. With her death the custody of the minor children would be given to some relatives. They would naturally be in charge of the wealth also, that was left behind by her dead husband. As such they did not hesitate to do away with her. The other reason could also be that they would have to feed extra mouths, in case the dead husband did not leave much property behind. In both the circumstances it would be beneficial for the relatives to put the widow to death. The fear of the widows going astray and degrading the family name and honor was another reason. The widow, at the time of entering the fire, gave away all her jewelry to her relatives and the Brahmin priest who performed the rituals. The woman was dressed up as a bride and was wearing her bridal dress and ornaments. The Brahmins were very anxious to accumulate wealth and this was very easy way to become rich. Hence, the priestly class lost no moment in exhorting the ignorant ladies to commit Sati.

"Some of the women they burn at the fiery flames of their deceased Husbands are not very willing thereto, notwithstanding all the wicked devices practiced by those wretches…….. One I saw very unnaturally handled by the Brahmans and their associates, for, repenting of such an intended act, they laid violent hands on her and threw her into the fire which was not thoroughly inflamed, and there pressed the poore creature donwe with a long powle until she was consumed."[455] Some of the women who committed Sahagamana did not do it voluntarily. The ideals associated with the practice made them willing to commit the ghastly act but at the precise moment many wanted to back away. The fire and the great congregation made them to realize the situation and they did not want to enter the flames. However, the Brahmins and her relatives did not allow her to change her mind. They felt that it would present a bad example to other women and also lower the prestige of the family in the village. An old woman of fifty years of age, has been described as willing to come out of the fire, but was prevented by the people. The harsh reality of the physical pain had forced the woman to come out of the fire but she was not allowed to come out and was pushed back. [456] The Brahmins who accompanied her, and the huge procession that followed behind, always exhorted her and spoke loudly so that others could hear of her constancy and courage. The European travelers believed that to make the woman out of her sense, the priest mixed some intoxicant in the betel that the widow was given to chew. While some said that they were fed an intoxicating flower called Dhutry, others have said that she was given an intoxicating beverage. The woman and her action would be constantly praised by the following processionists who sang songs of her courage and

---

[455] Thomas Bowrey, pp. 35-40.
[456] Annonymous Relations, pp.74.

faithfulness. When she finally jumped into the fire, the music became quit deafening so as to not allow the public to hear her cries of terror and pain. The fire of the funeral pyre was burnt with more ferocity by adding extra Ghee, Oil, large blocks of fire wood, and other combustible items so that the widow would perish soon without much pain and trouble.

PREVENTION OF SATI.

A remarkable thing happened with the establishment of the Qutub Shahi rule over the Andhra country. The practice of Sahagamana that was held in the higest esteem by the Hindu royalty did not find any support during the rule of the Golconda Kings. The Muslim rulers viewed the committing of Sati as suicide by the Hindu women.

"This (Sati) is not permitted in where Moslems are numerous, being against their rule; and I have myself seen on two occasions that it was prevented when the woman were practically ready to jump into the fire. I have also been told several times that they administer something good, which makes the women more inclined to be burnt."[457]

The religion of Islam asks its followers to stop all types of suicide as it is considered a sin to take away one's life which is a gift of God. Though there was no official communiqué with regard to the stoppage of Sati, yet the officials of the

---

[457] Annonymous Relations, pp.75.

King used their authority in curtailing it. The officials of the Kingdom tried in their own way to put a stop to this heinous practice. The contemporary records mention the activities of the Muslim Governor of Golconda kingdom in this regard. The Governor passed an order which made it necessary for a wife, to seek permission for burning the dead body of her husband. One can draw the inference that the rule was passed mainly to check the custom of burning of widows along with the dead body. However, as the burning could not be stopped forcibly but only through persuasions, some of the widows succeeded in getting the permission. But the widows who had little children to take care of never got the permission to burn themselves. They were denied the permission on the ground that they had to live in order to take care of the children to bring them up.[458] The widows who survived in order to take care of their children tried their best to lead a life of austerity and goodness. Some spent their time in worshiping the various Hindu Gods, while others were involved in doing some charitable work. Some could be seen providing drinking water to travelers on the road, while come others sold a type of lentil soup to the tired and hungry people. The widows were also forced to sell liquor to the travelers in order to sustain themselves and their children. The local liquor was called Tari which was got from the plan tree. It was in great demand in Golconda territory. To sustain themselves some of the poor widows

---

[458] Tavernier's Travels, pp.406-407

provided light for the tobacco of the people. They always kept a fire burning next to them for the light, so as to earn a little money.

The Muslim officers could not forcibly stop a woman from committing Sati. They feared the feared the wrath of the Brahmins who were considered as the sole authority on the Hindu religion. The religious tax paid by the Hindus gave them the freedom of religion and this being the religious act, nothing much could be done. The Golconda rulers never passed any law to stop it. Some of them readily agreed to give the permission after receiving a handsome bride. Some other promised the young and beautiful widows stay in their own Harem. Once when the Cotawal of Masulipatanam was visiting the English factory, a woman from the goldsmith's caste, came asking permission for self immolation. It was refused. The Cotwal pleaded with her and promised to help her and asked her to stay at his own house. However, the adamant woman went and hanged herself to death.[459]

The number of cases of Sati came down reasonably under the Muslim rulers. However, it was to the credit of the British who passed laws prohibiting it. Even when they were mere traders on the Andhra soil, they tried their best to best friend the woman and ask her to stop this act of self immolation. They were very rarely successful as the woman never heeded to their advice. "At Visakhapatnam, the English Deputy Governor

---

[459] Methwold's Relations, p. 29.

Holcombe refused permission for the burning of a woman. He threatened and bribed the Brahmins for asking the woman to desist from such an act."[460] It can be seen from the study of several instances of Sati hood that the Brahmins, if wanted to, could stop this so called religious act. But they only remained the patrons of such horrible acts. The public had full faith in the priestly class, who only exploited the ignorant people instead of enlightening them. The Britishers also used force to stop this crime. Bowrey mentions the rescue of a 10 year old girl by a group of English seamen. The rescuers did not face any resitence from the onlookers. The girl was taken to the factory at Masulipatanam and baptized to Christianity. [461]

When the Northern Circars passed into the hands of the British, then it become easy for them to regulate this practice in the regions under their command. "In 1789 A. D., the old Zamindar of Nuzvidu, Narasimha died. His eldest wife Pedda Venkamma wanted to commit Sati along with an image of her deceased husband, but this was prevented by the officer commanding the station."[462] Though no law was passed by them which prohibited Sati, yet in their personal capacity the Englishmen tried to limit the burning of widows. Sometimes, they used force and at the other used

---

[460] Niccolo manucci, Storio Do Mogor, vol. III.

[461] Thomas Bowrey, pp. 35-40

[462] Gordon Mackenzie, A Manual of the Kistna District, 1883

persuasion and bribery to stop the woman from committing suicide. There was also a change witnessed in the phsycology of the women of Andhra. When the Brahmin owning the Srotiyam of Kokkaravapalle committed suicide, due to unknown reasons, his wife did not burn herself to death. On the other hand, she continued to enjoy the "Yajamanavrathi and the income left over after the payment of Srotriyam".[463] Another instance of a woman refusing to commit Sati has been given by Abbe Dubois. At Kangeddy in Chitoorpalem, a woman belonging to the ruling class did not adhere to the entreaties or to the force applied by the relatives of her dead husband. She flatly refused to commit Sati even though she came from a family well renowned for producing women who have been always committing Sati. The woman stubbornly refused to burn herself with the dead body of her husband. Dubois also writes that the practice of burning of widows was slowly being given up by the Brahmins. The Sudra class which always looked up to the Brahmins in any act of religion followed suit. However, the people belonging to the "tribe of the Rajas" i.e. the ruling class continued to burn their women.[464]

In the nineteenth century, the government Records mention some of the cases of Sati. In 1816 A.D., nearly six widows died the cruel death in Vizagapatam. In between the years 1816 & 1819 A. D., two Brahmin women, one Razu

---

[463] T. V. Mahalingam, pp. 248-249.
[464] Abbe Dubois, p.237

woman, and six Sudra women were burnt in the funeral pyres of their husbands at Rajahmundry.[465] In the year 1819, in the Godavary District, the woman committed Sati even before the news could reach the Magistrate. She was the wife of the Dewan of Venkatgiri.[466] However, in the same year when a woman of the Sudra caste belonging to the Naidu clan, wanted to commit Sati, she was prevented by the Collector who scared the gathering away by saying that "there were trying to cause the death of the women" which was punishable under the law. However, as far as the law prohibiting Sati was concerned, in the year 1819 AD, it said, that "The act of immolation is always perfectly voluntary on the party of the Widow."[467] As such there was no legal ban on the practice of Sati.

It was only in the year 1821, when a law was passed by the govt. of the Nizam at Hyderabad, to prohibit Sati completely. "After 1821 A.D., Siraj-ul-Mulk, the Diwan of Hyderabad, passed reforms which called for the Abolition of Sati by the wives of the Hindu subjects." [468] The passage of this act legally made the burning of widows an action against the law of the land. It became illegal even to "promote" the cause of Sati.[469] the British Collector of Cuddapah, reported

[465] K.K. Datta, <u>A Social History of Modern India</u>, 1868, pp 245-246.
[466] Godavary District Records, 1770-1835, p.129
[467] ibid. p. 128.
[468] Dr. M.A. Muttallib, pp. 52-54
[469] Godavary District Records, 1770-1835, pp. 84-87.

to his superiors in his letters dated 9-3-1822, that he was trying his best to put a stop to the practice of Suttee.[470] with the passage of the Act for Abolition of Sati, the heinous crime came to be curtailed. The woman became free of the religious dogmas and became conscious of their right to live and walked into the modern period.

DEVADASIS AND PUBLIC WOMEN.

During the Vijayanagara period, three types of public women existed. They never married. Their man profession was singing and dancing. The three classes of public women were the Devadasis, the courtesans and the prostitutes. Of the three, utmost importance and respect was given to the Devadasis. As the name itself suggest the Deva-Dasis were the servants of God. They dedicated themselves to the deity in temple. Their main job was to look after and please the Gods. At a fixed period of time, they would come, all dressed up, to the temple and offer their services to the Lord in the form of dance. These women were well versed in dance, music and songs. They were respectable women. They were patronized by the state and the public. Some of them lived a luxurious life and were very rich. They were well adept in Indian classical dances like Kuchipudi and Bharat Natyam. William Methwold, British traveler, saw the dances of these women and was full of praise. During

---

[470] ibid. p. 317

the great Hindu festival like Mahanavami, they would dance before the chariots of the Gods which was being pulled by the devotees.[471] The Gods were put in the chariot and taken all around the city or villages. The huge procession that followed it was preceded by the Devadasis. They continued to dance for all the eight days of celebration of these festivals. Other festivals also saw large numbers of these dancing girls bedecked with ornaments and good clothes, dancing in front of the Gods. However, the European travelers of the contemporary period say that these women would also prostitute themselves to gain wealth and fame.[472]

On the other hand, the courtesans were the woman who mainly acted as entertainers of the highest authorities in the kingdom. They were also highly accomplished in the art of music and dance. They presented themselves to the King for his pleasure and also acted as mistresses of great officers of the Vijayanagara Empire. They were much respected and were high demand. They also enjoyed certain privileges that were high in demand. They also enjoyed certain privileges that were not allowed to anyone. They could visit the Queen herself directly, without any obstacles. They chewed betel leaves in front of the King himself. This was a privilege enjoyed exclusively by the courtesans.[473] Some of them possessed a lot of wealth and land property which they

[471] Sewell, p. 262
[472] Samuel Purchas, pp.220-221
[473] Sewell, pp. 242-269

donated to the state, after their death if legal successor was absent. The last category of public women prostituted to the common men of the kingdom. They paid a professional tax to the State.[474]

In the 17th and 18th centuries, when the country of Andhra came under the Qutb Shahi Kings, a lot of changes took place in the position of the public women. The three divisions of public women continued to exist but there was a shift in the importance of the Devadasis. The Devadasis, who danced in the temples for pleasing the gods continued to do so. However, their number and position was largely depleted. They continued to dance still in the temples of villages and were patronized by the people. They continued to dance and sing in front of the temple deity. They tried to please the Gods and simultaneously entertained the on looking public. However, not all were happy with this distinction and honor enjoyed by the Devadasis. The Shataka literature of contemporary Andhra speak against the existing rule. Chowdappa (1600-1630 A. D.), a Brahmin Karnam of Cuddapah, deplored the employment of dancing girls in all the functions of the society.[475] His verses are full of irony when he says that no religious and social function seems to be complete without the notch girls in the country called Andhra. Their presence and importance has been acknowledged even by the contemporary European travelers

---

[474] Elliot, <u>History of India</u>, p.112
[475] Sarojani Regani, p. 41

of the region. "In the Gentu country, they (prostitutes) have to come regularly twice a day to dance in the temples, in return for which they receive some annual (?) gratificationn".[476] While describing, the dancing girls, they mention the performances given by them in early morning and in the evening at the temples. It was their daily duty to please the deity twice daily with their dancing and singing. The villagers would be present in large numbers. In fact one could say that it was a very good way of entertaining the entire village. People from different parts of the village, belonging to various castes and profession would have come to appreciate them.

The girls dedicated to the services of the Gods came from different castes and class of people. The girls from the Kaikkolam caste were dedicated to those temples where the Brahmins were the Pujaris or the priest. In the Kaikkolam caste, a girl from each family was dedicated to the village deity and she had to offer herself to the temple service. Most of these girls acted as prostitutes to the Brahimn priests of the temple. It can be said that all the Brahmin priests had a Kaikkolam girl attached to themselves. These girls had good manners and were well read. They were enchanting and pretty. The art of dancing and singing were imparted to them in childhood itself and such they were well versed in them. They were in great demand as concubines from all the communities irrespective of the castes. When the

---

[476] Annonymous Relation, p.72.

Muslims came to power these girls were sought after by them as well. Slowly, the girls attached themselves to the Muslim officers in power and continued to enjoy the gifts of life. Similarly, when the English East India Company came to power, the Kaikkolam girls went over to the British officers, who could not retain unaffected by the charms of these girls. However, the association of these girls with the foreigners was not allowed by the Hindu law. "The prostitutes who dance regularly in the pagodas are forbidden to associate with Christians, Moslems, Pariahs, or other foreigners, under penalty of great disgrace".[477] This shows the shrewdness of the priestly class in being over jealous of their concubines. However, once the power slipped from hands of the Brahmins, these dancing girls left them for the more prosperous and powerful either Muslim or English administrative officers.

On the other hand, the girls from the Lingayat caste were dedicated to the temples where the Jangama or the Lingayat priest was the head of the temple.[478] They were known as Basavis. The castes such as the Sanis, the Devadasis, and others who also dedicated their daughters to the service of the temple. The Deavadasis were the only caste whose women were given the rights of adopting female children. A single woman in the Devadasi clan could adopt a girl as her own daughter and when she grew up she too was

---

[477] ibid.,p.71.
[478] Edgar Thurston.

dedicated to the service of the temple. However, though said to belong to the temple, these women's actual profession was to prostitute themselves.[479]

It can be said that though in the legal sense, these girls were said to be serving the Gods yet in the reality they were only the mistress of various important people of the villages or towns. Women whose children died at birth often took oaths to dedicate their girl child "to the God as a prostitute".[480]

It was a great privilege for a family to dedicate their daughters to the village deity. The family came to be respected in the village. The profession of serving the Gods was hereditary. The daughters took the profession of their mothers. When any donations were made to the temple, a part of the income was given to the dancing girls of the temple. An inscription of the year 1626 A. D. at Amravati says the cows donated by the donor Handrikam Peddappa were meant for supplying ghee for lamps and the male calves for plugging the fields of god Amaresvara. It also mentions that of the produce of the temples lands, one-fourth share or Chikukapalu should be given to the Sanis of the temple. It also refers to the shares allotted to the temple servants from the endowment made to the temple. It states that the people engaged in priestly functions were given higher shares than the

---

[479] Gordon Mackenzie
[480] <u>Annonymous Relation</u>, p.76.

rest of the temple functionaries.[481] The people appreciated the dancing and they were held in great esteem and respect. Some of these of women, by acquiring wealth grew very rich and they themselves gave large amount in donations for charitable works in the village.[482] The Dasis of the Coromandel Coast have been described as the "walking flesh-trees bearing golden fruits" by a Sanskrit poet.[483] The great wealth possessed by the Deva Dasis must have influenced the poet for describing them as bearing golden fruits.

However, with the coming in of the Muslims to power, in the region, the position of the deva Dasis was reduced. The rules no longer patronized the temples and were no longer interested in the dance of the Deva Dasis. "In the country of the Moslems, who do not accept this practice, there is no custom of dancing in the pagodas..."[484] The special position that these women enjoyed under the vijaynagar Empire was lost. In some places, the local people tried to maintain the old custom of Devadasis in the templates. But it became difficult to meet the huge expenditure. The loss of eminent position by the Hindus in administration was another cause for the lapse of the Devadasi system. These women found it hard to maintain their high living standard and became no more than the other dancing girls. They took to prostitution in order to live. The celebrations of Hindu festivities were not

[481] M. Krishna Kumari, <u>Pancharamas in Medieval Andhra Desa</u>.
[482] Edgar Thurston.
[483] Travancore Census Report, 1901.
[484] Annonymous relations, p.71.

as grand as in the past. During this period very few temples were built. In fact, the maintenance of the old temples had become very difficult. The forces of the King sometimes demolished temples to control the application. All these incidents must have surely affected the lives of the Deva Dasis. We find the European travelers of the period making no distinction between the dancing girls of the temples and the common dancing girls. The main reason could be the fact that these Devadasis were forced to live the life of a common courtesan and had lost the age old distinction of serving the Lord. Later on it was made mandatory for all the dancing girls of the Kingdom to go the King's court every year and present their dances to him. This degraded the Devadasis' position who were equaled with the rest of the dancing girls and had to dance before the King and his courtiers. This had never happened before.

The courtesans were the dancing girls who lived in the King's court. They were well versed in singing, dancing and in playing the different musical instruments. The main difference between the Devadasis and the courtesans was that while the former only danced in the temples the latter danced in the court of the King and front of his officers.

However, this difference was lost when the Muslims occupied the throne of Andhra Desa. The kings and the nobles were attracted towards these girls and enjoyed their accomplishments. During the region of the Golconda kings the dancing girls called Taramati, Premavati and Bhagamati were famous courtesans and they stayed in palaces built by the king. They entertained him with their songs and dances every evening. It is believed that they danced at a distance far from the fort of Golconda and the king used to see them through a telescope. "The dancing girls are most accomplished women among the Hindus. They read, write, sing, and play as well as dance."[485] Nobody could keep himself aloof from the enchantment of these girls. The dancing girl's calld Luliyan and Kanchanis, came from different parts of Telangana, Bihar, Ahmadabad, Lahore, and Kabul to present their songs and dances at the celebration of the birthday of king Abdullah Qutb Shah.[486] They were said to be very fair and beautiful and some were also dusk colored. They played the Mandal Nawaz, a musical instrument and entertained the royalty and the nobility. They used flowers in their heads and a lot of perfumes on their bodies. They were invited by the officers to the palaces even during the celebrations of the Birthday of Paigambar Mohammad. The dances were held in the evening and the dancers numbering more than one thousand danced in a circle. However, these girls were the courtesans who lived in the court of the kings for entertaining him and his guests with their songs and dances. They maintained their moral limitations and only on important occasions. They were the state's property and were maintained by it. In the year 1791 A. D., the dancing girls were called for entertained,

---

[485]   Rev. M. Phillips, <u>Evolution of Hinduism</u>, 1903
[486]   Mirza Nizamuddin Ahmed Saidi, <u>Hadiqatus Salatin</u>, pp. 34-40

when the Nabob of Carnatic and the governor of Madras dined together.[487] Sometimes big Zamindars or local Rajas, maintained dancing girls and trained them in the traditional art of music and dance. They provided them with good teachers and later on when the education was over, these girls were presented before an audience.[488] They were trained according to the principals laid down in treatises of traditional learning viz. the Bharata Sastra and Sangeeta Ratnakara.

During the rule of the Asaf Jahi kings, a number of courtesans lived in the city of Hyderabad. However, the most famous courtesans were Chanda Bibi. She was a courtesan during the period of the second and the third Nizams of Hyderabad. She was good dancer, singer, musician and an equally good poetess. She was great attraction in Hyderabad during her lifetime. She was given the title of Maha Laqa Bai by the Second Nizam, Mir Nizam Ali Khan, Asaf Jah II, in 1217 H. or in 1799 A. D. A great Jashna was held and she also received a Naubat and Ghariyal from the King.[489] She was a versatile personality. She was very beautiful and clever and was well versed in Urdu and Persian languages. She was always well dressed and was a trend- setter of fashion during her days. She had also learned the tactics of war. At first she was in the music staff of the Nizam. But with the help of her intelligence and hard work, she gained in position

---

[487] J. T. Wheeler, Madras in Olden Times.
[488] Enugula Veeraswamy, Kasiyatra Charitralu, p.204
[489] Ghulam Samadani Khan Gougher, Hayathe Mahalaqa, 1906

and became his courtesan. She was very close to him and often advised him in administrative works. She was a regular feature in the court of the Nizam II and the Nobels bowed to her. Mir Alam, the Prime Minister of the Nizam found pleasure in teaching her. Her contributed a Masanavi in her honor. Chandu Lal, one of the most influential Ministers of the Nizam, wrote verses in praise of her beauty and talents.[490] The lists of her admire and patrons included the mane of the Third Nizam, who came close to her after the death of the Nizam II. She owned huge Jagirs which were given to her by her admires. She even arranged massive get together on the Bund of Hussain Sagar. The British and the French too look pleasure in her company. She was the first Deccani poetess and her first volume of verses was presented to Captian Malcolm, the then British Resident of Hyderabad. In spite of being a courtesan, she was very religious and also very generous. She died very rich and issues less. Her intension was to open educational institutions in Hyderabad, especially for girls. When she died her property included palaces and gardens and several jagirs. The hard cash alone came to about rupees one crorer. Her properties worth crores were acquired by the Third Nizam after her death. She attended the Maula Ali Urs every year for all the four days. The Mahalaqa Urs at Maula Ali is celebrated till this day.

The third types of public women were the prostitutes. During the period under study, one can visualize the

---

[490] G. Krishna, The story of Telugus and their Culuture, pp. 192-195

important position of the Nautch girls in the social Strata of the people. These girls were very large in numbers. The fact that only this profession was open to all types of needy women must be a major reason for it. Tavernier, the French traveler says "There are so great a number of common women as well in the city as in the suburbs, and in the fortress, which is like another city, that there are generally above twenty thousand set down in the Deroga's book; without which license, it is not lawful for any woman to profess the trade".[491] The dancing girls protected by the kingdom of Golconda and were allowed to practice their profession without any fear or hindrance. They would stand the doors of their houses as soon as it was evening. They dressed up beautifully and kept their houses alighted in the night so as to welcome the visitors. They would themselves very often invite the passersby to come and spend their evenings in their houses. No taboo was attached to people visiting these girls. Anyone was free to spend his nights with them. This system helped in controlling adultery. Several of such women were maintained as regular concubines of certain rich and powerful personalities. As concubines they enjoyed the riches of their masters and led a carefree life. Sometimes they interfered in the official jobs of their masters. The contemporary Shataka literature condemns the petty chieftains for wasting their riches on the dancing girls. The other Telugu works of the period also speak in

---

[491] Tavernier, pp. 128-129

ill terms regarding the influence these women had on the ruling and powerful elite of the region.[492]In the Bhadyatha Meedapadedaka, the mixing of the sons of high level Ministers with dancing girls was deplored by none other than the king. In Jaggakavi's Chandrarekha Vilaapam, written in the Prabhandha style, a contemporary powerful man's affair with a prostitute girl named Chandrarekha was described.[493] The Muslim gentleman provided their sons with concubines as soon as they were big enough. This was done to make their sons stay at homes and not to bring bad name to the family. The dances and songs of the nautch girls had became a part and parcel of every festivity. When a man returned from his trip outside then his welcome party would be inadequate without a nautch dance. Every religious festival witnessed the dance of the Devadasis. Every marriage whether Hindu or Muslim was celebrated with a dance performance by the prostitutes.[494] The birth of Muslim children and the circumcision also featured their dances and songs. The nautch dance was known as Mejuvani at Masulipatnam in the Nineteenth century.[495]

However, it seems that the condition of these public women was not always very good, as their houses have been

---

[492] S. Krishna, The Vastavai Family of Peddapuram, 1550-1850, Ph. D. thesis, Andhra University, 1986

[493] C. Ramalakshmi, Literary conditions in Northern Circars under East India Company, PAPHC, verses 28-35

[494] Tabee, <u>Behram and Gulandan</u>.

[495] Enugula Veeraswamy, p. 218

referred to as huts. In the region under study, there were certain castes that never allowed their women to marry. They were all given up as prostitutes. The girls of the Adapapa caste served as the attendants of the ladies belonging to the Zamindaras and were never allowed to marry.[496] Similarly, in the Jakkulas caste, each family gave up one of their daughters for prostitution. Amongst the Dommaras and some sub castes of the Madigas, the woman prostituted themselves with the consent of their communities. Some of the Dommara women were well versed in vocal and instrumental music and acted as dancers and singers. In the Madiga caste, women became Basavis that denotes the term prostitute. In the Jogi caste, the widows were allowed to follow this profession and earn their living. In the small caste of the Sanis the girls danced and prostituted. A woman adopting this profession was first married to a sword after attaining maturity. A caste called as the Boga Waru has been mentioned in the travelogue of a contemporary European. The women of this tribe comprised of two types namely, "One that will prostitute themselves to any better tribe than themselves, but to none worse" and the other of plain looking girls who married and continued the tribe.[497] If the daughters of these married women where good looking then they were brought back into the profession. Another reference is also to be found regarding this caste. Bogam

---

[496] Edgar Thurston.
[497] Methwold's Relations, p. 17

Vandlu were the dancing girl caste who obtained their livelihood by prostitution. The daughters in this caste were not married. However, contrary to the custom when two sisters, were married off, by a father, the marriage proved unhappy and did not survive. The people are afraid of making any further attempt for fear of similar results.[498] These dancing girls were taught to dance and sing from a very early age. The bodies of the children being tender and nimble, they could perform various postures of dance.

The prostitutes did not pay any taxes to the state. Unlike the Vijaynagar Kingdom where they paid taxes to the king and had their profession legalized, in the Golconda Kingdom the profession was not a legal one. These women were not given respect in the Andhra country. "Ganjam onwards, nautch girls, when they come on to the stage with Tanpura and Veena, except when they sing, they should not sit. Without any compunction they will be made to stand for hours together"[499] However, they were also a powerful community and in most places they had hereditary rights over their property. In places of importance they lived in large numbers so that they would be in an advantageous position. At Srikakulam, their houses equaled the number of houses of the Vaishnavite priests.[500]

---

[498] Narhahari Gopalakristnamah Chetty, <u>A Manual of the Kurnool District</u>, Madras, 1886

[499] Enugula Veeraswamy, p. 219

[500] ibid. p.204.

Chapter V

MATERIAL CONDITIONS

In this chapter, the material conditions that prevailed the 17th and 18th century Andhra Desa, has been covered. The different aspects covered under the topic, Material Conditions are, the mode of the housing system that existed during those times, the furniture and the decoration of the houses. The food habits of the local Telugu people. The Muslims and the Europeans are also dealt with. The mutual influence on each others' food habits and the adoption of the eating style of each other has been traced. The introduction of some new fruits and vegetables, in the Telugu-speaking region, by the Muslims and the Europeans has also been mentioned.

The topic also deals with the apparels that were worn by the people. The rich and the powerful wore the finest quality of dresses while the poor had cloth just enough to cover the vital pats of his body. The adoption of the Muslim dressing style by the rich and powerful Hindus was witnessed in the 17th century. Similarly, in the 18th century, the Hindus and the Muslims, both tried to adopt the Anglican dress. The Hindu and the Muslim men put on a number of jewelry. They put rings, ear-rings and other ornaments. The Muslim were keen in using the cosmetic also. While some used certain natural herbs like henna to colour their hair, the others put Surma in their eyes.

In the dressing style of the women, both Hindu and Muslim women preferred to put on Sarees. The Muslim women also wore a type of dress which resembled the modern Salwar Kurta. They loved to wear jewelry. A number of different ornaments for the different parts of the body were being made and worn by the women. The dress and the jewelry of the bride were different from the daily costumes. The material for the manufacture of the jewelry was different and depended on the economic status of the people. While the rich wore ornaments of gold, silver and precious stones and pearls, the lower caste the tribes wore ornaments made of copper and the bones of the animals. The women loved to put flowers in their hair and put on different kinds of cosmetic inorder to enhance their beauty.

HOUSING

The seventeenth century saw the emergence of Persian style of architecture in the Andhra Desa. The Muslim rulers were very keen that this style should be reflected in all the buildings that were built by them. The buildings built for private use and for public purposes bore the replica of this style. Before the advent of the Nuslims, the style of building houses in Andhra Desa was very simple. Though the palaces of the Hindu Kings were as magnificent as the palaces of the Muslim Kings, the common man, lived in houses that even lacked the basic structure like windows.[501] On the other hand the Muslim houses had both windows and balconies. The Hindus adopted this from the Muslims and started constructing windows in their houses. The Hindu officials who worked under the Muslim rulers were influenced by the Muslim culture and living styles. As such during the eighteenth century, the Hindu Kayastha officials of the Nizam, built their residential houses on the Islamic pattern.[502] they construted separate living quarters for men and women, as a result of the Parda system, which was as important feature of the Muslim culture. In 1797 A. D., James Achilles was the British Resident at Hyderabad. He married a local lady belonging to the Muslim nobility.

---

[501] Mulla Wajhi, Qutb Mushtari, v.1314.
[502] Karen Leonard, The Kayasthas of Hyderabad. Ph.D. thsis, University of Wisconsin.

When he got the new Residency constructed, he built separate Zenana quarters for the ladies of his house, based on the Muslim culture of Parda.[503] While the northern front of the Residency had an English look, the southern front was quite oriental in appearance. The building was constructed to suit both the Europeans and the Muslims.

In the period under study, the European style was still in its infancy stage. But, the following century i.e. the nineteenth century saw the impact of this style over the buildings constructed in Andhra. However, in the late eighteenth century, the style aroused the interests of some Muslim nobles who wanted to make their houses in the European pattern of architecture. They wanted to decorate their inner rooms with the costly fancy items from the different countries of the world/ as such there used to be a sort of competition among the rich Hyderabad for acquiring such goods.[504] The demand by Persian higher ups, for items such as large looking glasses, globes, Japanese writing desk, perfume bottles, a multiplying glass, the portrait of the English King in the Parliament robes, etc. was always high. The upper strata of the society, stated copying the European style in the decoration of their houses.[505] The

[503] Bilkiz Alladin, <u>Cultural Exchange Between The Residency And Hyderabad, in Helen B, Butt's The Composite Nature Of Hyderabad</u>, p.50.

[504] Records of Fort St. George, Letters To Fort St. George for 1693-94.

[505] W. H. Moreland, From Akbar to Aurangzeb-A Case Study In Indian Economic History, pp. 70-71.

Hindu Nayakas were always after any "English toys" that might be available. Even animals like the Irish greyhounds, the English mastiffs, water spaniels, hawks, apes, parrots, etc. were asked to be brought from outside. Later on, when the Zamindars became important, they too adopted the European manners and style.[506]

However, with the rise of new styles of construction, the native Hindu pattern did not suffer in the least. The style first adapted itself to the Persian architecture and got intermingled with it. The intermingling of the native style and the Islamic style gave rise to a new unique style of construction. The mosques built by the Kadiri nobles show the Islamic style on the exteriors and the Hindu style on the interior.[507] In the smaller towns and the villages the Hindu people built their homes on the styles of the olden times. They preferred to build their houses in the traditional style only. The temples that were built in this period were if traditional types only. Likewise, When the Muslim higher class adopted the European style, the Islamic style did not fade away. The secular buildings adopted the foreign style but had separate quarters for their ladies. The religious buildings were all of the Islamic style of architecture.

---

[506] Vishakapatnam Manual.

[507] Syed Basha Biyabani, <u>Impact of Early Saints (Sufis) of Khuttagulla, Kadiri Taluq, Anantpur District, 16th Century A. D.</u>, in PAPHC, vol. XV, pp.99-104.

CAPITAL CITY

After the occupation of the Andhra country, the Qutb Shahis invited the architects from Iran to design the capital city of their newly acquired kingdom. As such all the royal palaces and the residential houses of the rich and powerful Muslims were based in the Persian style. The Kings made it a point build even the public buildings like the mosques, Ashur Khanas, hospitals, and the educational institutions in their kingdom, on the Persian style of construction. The city of Hyderabad itself was designed on the Persian style with its building having the domes and the arches.[508] The Alam was adopted as the symbol in every building constructed by the Qutb Shahs.

One of the most famous Persian architects, who came over to the Golconda Kingdom from Iran, was Allama Meer Muhammad Momin Astrabadi. He helped in the construction of the famous buildings of Hyderabad. He drew the first plan of the city of Hyderabad. While drawing the plan he had the Isfahan, the city of Iran, in his mind and hence after the completion of the work, he called the new city as Isfhan-e-Nou.[509] he also built the first building of Hyderabad, and the world famous Charminar. It was constructed in the middle of the city.[510] Eventually, the

---

[508] Dr. Sadiq naqvi, The Iran-Deccan Relations, p.62.
[509] Mohiuddin Qadri Zore, Hyat-e-Meer Momin, p.50.
[510] K. S. S Sheshan, Hyderabad, as seen by the French Traveler Count Modave, in Hyderabad-400,

structure came to be in surrounded by shops of different kinds. Of every evening, large quantity of merchandise was spread out on the streets at the Chowk or the crossroad at Charminar. Thevenot said that the Charminar was surrounded by "ugly shops made of wood, and coverd with the straw, where they sell fruit...".[511] There were a number of shops around the structure which were very rudimentary in their construction style and hence spoilt the look and the beauty of the Charminar.

Meer Momin also contributed to the construction of the religious building called the Badshahi Ashur Khana. It was built just after the completion of the Charminar. It was under his direction that the foundation of the Mecca Masjid in the city opposite the famous Charminar was laid down. The other Ahur Khanas in the city that were built in the Persian style were the Ashur Khana-e-Hussaini Alam, Ahur Khana-e-Maulla Ali, Allava-e-Sartooq, Ahur khana-Rasool, and the others. Though there was no set pattern for the construction of the Ashur Khanas, yet in most buildings the Persian characteristics are evident. One distinct feature of the building of those times was that five arches or gateways for the entry into the building. The immigrants from Iran decorated the different buildings with geometrical designs. One of the famous calligraphers was Muhammad Fakhar Shirazi.

---

[511] Thevenot, p.133.

Bernier, the Frenchman, who visited Andhra Desa in-between the years 1656 and 1668 A. D. found Hyderabad, one of the most beautiful cities of the east. Another traveler from France, Louins Laurent De Federabe, Count of Mondave, visited Hyderabad thrice in-between 1757 and 1777. He was impressed by the city of Hyderabad and said that it was very beautiful.[512] However, he was disillusioned by the fort of Golconda and wrote. "This place, so celebrated in the world appears to me to merit little of its reputation". The reason could be that constant use and the lack of repair would have spoilt the outside look of the massive fort. The Asaf Jahis might not be paying much attention to the old Qutb Shahi fort.

During the Qutb Shahi rule the city was divided into quadrants and each quadrant was set apart for a particular social class of the people.[513] The north west quadrant was occupied by royal palaces and the state offices. The north east quadrant was reserved for the nobles, and the southern quadrants were occupied by Jagirdars and other important officials. This pattern changed during the Asaf Jahi rule. Thought there was no strict division of housing in the term of social class, one finds that the palaces of the rulers and the houses of the Paigah nobles were situated in the southern west quadrant. Mostly the people settled down in areas in

---

[512] K. S. S Sheshan, op. cit.
[513] Ratna Naidu, <u>Old Cities, New Predicaments, A study of Hyderabad</u>.

relation to their profession. And slowly each quarter came to be occupied by a particular caste and sect of social status.

The Europeans too stayed there and the Portuguese had been given the permission to have their church there too.[514] In the Seventeenth century, references of French, Dutch, and the English at Golconda, have been made in the contemporary travelogues. One could locate there, the magnificent houses of the rich and the simple houses of the common inhabitant. The city of Hyderabad had long streets. However, these streets were not paved properly and were very dusty.[515] Later on, under the Asaf Jahi rule, the English had built a permanent Residency at the capital city.

THE PALACE

The palace of the Qutb Shahi Kings was made of stones and had many windows.[516] Nobody was allowed inside the palace without the royal permission. The royal palaces had pipes that led water unto the highest apartments. The water served in keeping the palace cool during the hot summer months. The city also had magnificent gardens where the King and his wives came to enjoyed nature.[517] The gardens were kept very clean and had a variety of fruit trees and flower trees that lined side by side a very clean pathway

[514] Abbe Dubois, <u>Hindu Manners, Customs, and Tradition</u>.
[515] Tavernier, p.123.
[516] Thevenot, p.133.
[517] Tavernier, p.122.

where one could walk.[518] However, unlike the gardens of Europe, the gardens had neither bed of flowers nor any water fountains. They only had water ponds. The other famous architectural feat was the tombs of the Qutb Shahi Kings and Queens. These tombs were also built in the Perian style of architecture. They were very nicely maintained. The tombs of the famous nobles and the tombs of the favourite eunuchs of the Kings were also constructed along with their patrons'.

RICH PERSIANS

The houses of the well to do were all two storied and were built in the Persian style. These homes were all made of wood. The houses of Persons of Quality were very good.[519] In the city, there was a square Meidan or ground where the people i.e. the noble had built their houses. The houses were very strong and well built. Such houses had separate quarters for men and women attached to each other within the same area or compound. Sometimes they were also linked through a corridor. The houses were constructed with a courtyard in the center and rooms around it. As the women stayed indoors most of the time, due to the existence of the Purdah system, the houses were built so as to allow them to enjoy the evening and fresh air within the premises of their

---

[518] Thevenot, p.132.
[519] Thevenot, p.132.

own homes. Thus the main portion of the house took one side of the square and was approached a porch or portico.[520]

There were arches at the high door or gate through which an elephant could easily pass. Adjacent to the entrance was small rooms or apartments for watchmen or other servants to live. No outsider could straightaway enter the main building unnoticed.

The main hall i.e. the Dalan was entered through a large verandah or PEshdalan. It was also entered through a corridor, which had rooms on either side. On both sides of the large halls there were rooms with high ceilings and large windows and overhead ventilators. On the other side of the courtyard were large and small rooms for different purposes and connected with doors, each leading to the other room. At the extreme end connected by the corridors were the kitchens, toilets, store rooms, stairs and small quarters for the maids.

The basements for all houses were high and were reached by steps. The walls and doors were coloured and in many case floral and stuccowork was made on them. The courtyards had lawns, trees, and small fountains of water. The terraces were used in summer and in evening for Cool breeze.

Both male and female servants were in attendance always within the homes of the rich people. The number

---

[520] Dr. M. A. Nayeem, <u>The Splendour of Hyderabad, Last Phase of an Oriental Culture, 1591-1594 A.D, pp.107-108.</u>

of servants depended on the persons' income and status. They were meant for different purposes and were employed in large numbers. They did all types of domestic work and accompanied the master on outside trips also.

Many of Qutb Shahi localities and landmarks survived and retained their name their names under the rule of the Asaf Jahi dynasty. It has been often recorded that when Aurangabad, the Mughal Emperor, entered the city of Haiderabad and saw the palaces he was awestruck by their magnificence and great size. Some of the Nizams' nobles continued to reside in the Qutb Shahi nobles' localities. They lived in two- storied wooden houses, built in the Persian style and enclosed by high walls on all four sides. Inside the walls, were attractive courtyards and fountains, full of different varities of trees bearing fruits and flowers. But the narrow lanes that existed between the residences of different nobles were unprepossessing and often very dirty.[521]

The visitors to the Andhra Desa during the rule of the Nizams' say that the importance of the capital city was on the decline. All have spoken about the decay of Hyderabad, as the second ruler of the dynasty, Nizam Ali Khan, was more interested in staying at Aurangabad than at Hyderabad. However, when the government was shifted

---

[521] Frenchman de Modave, Lt. Col. John Upton who visited the city in 1777 and a French officer of de Burry's army who visited in 1750: J Sarkar, <u>Hyderabad and Golconda in 1750 as seen through French eyes</u>, Islamic culture, vol. XX, 1936.

to the city of Hyderabad them it once again became very famous and hospitable.

MIDDLE CLASS

The house of the average Muslims were similar to that of the Hindus.[522] The homes of average middle class people were proportionately smaller than of the rich people. There were only a few rooms and they had a smaller or no courtyard at all. However, the average or middle class Muslims had only one house for both men and women.[523] They could not afford to construct separate quarters.

The Hindu middle class, generally, made only one story house. They were very particular about the cleanliness of their houses. The floor was daily swept clean and then it was plastered with cow dung.[524] The doors and the outside area were also plastered with cow dung every day. In the open they planted the holy plant of Tulce i.e. the plant of calaminth, and worshipped it every morning and tended it with diligence. In one and the same house lived the family alongwith the relatives and their Gods. The cattle was also brought inside when it rained outside. Even the middle class had servants at their homes for attending to the household

---

[522] Ghawwasi, <u>Saif ul Mulk</u>, V. 328.

[523] M. A. Nayeem, op. cit.

[524] A. Venkateswara rao, <u>History of the Kalamkari industry of Masulioatnam during the 17th and 18th centuries</u>, 1990, Ph. D. Thesis, Osmania University.

work.[525] They helped the ladies in the house. There were workers even to help in looking after the cattle.[526] They were looked after well by their employees and were given food as the day's work came to a close.

POOR

The ordinary houses "are not above two Fathom high; they raise them no higher, that they may have the fresh Air during the heats, and most part of them are only of Earth".[527] The houses of the common man in the city of Hyderabad, were very badly constructed. It was built only of mud. The ceilings were very low and there were no windows. During summer it would be very hot inside. During there rainy season, the houses must have been washed out. While describing the capital city of in the Golconda Kingdom, Thevenot says that the houses on the suburbs of the city were built only of mud and the roof was thatched with straw. He called them huts. The houses of the poor within the city and on the outskirts resembled each other. They were enough to just give shade to their inhabitants. It shows that they must have been very tiny in structure. There was glaring differences in the riches and possessions of the population of Andhra Desa in the 17th and the 18th century.

---

[525] M. A. Nayeem, op.cit.

[526] S. S.

[527] M. Thevennot, p.132.

TOWNS

In the other towns of the region, palmyra leaves, teak timbers, Chunam and bricks were for the construction of the houses. In the towns, houses of two storeys were also built.[528] At Rajahmundry, the good houses of the prosperous people were on each side of the main street. They were generally of one story and were built of mud and the roof was tiled. In the narrow lanes the middle and lower classes built their houses which were small and good-looking. They were also built of mud and the roofs were tiled. At few places in the towns, large and spacious houses with upper stories existed and they belonged to the Zamindars or landholders of the nearby areas. Some were also inhabited by wealthy traders principally the Brahmins.

The Muslims were all urban oriented and occupied an important place there. They constructed a number of mosques in the places where they resided.[529] They formed the majority of people living at the port towns. At the port city of Masulipatnam, the houses were describe as being large and commodious. They were built of brick and lime mortar. The roofs were almost all tiled. Most of these houses had double stories. The residence were all prosperous, as the main profession there was mercantilism. In order towns

---

[528] John A. C. Boswell, <u>Manual of the Nellore District of the Presidency of Madras</u>, p.213.

[529] E. Thornton, <u>Gazetters of territories under E. I. Co</u>., pp. 253-254.

too, tiles were used for the roofs. The walls were generally made of brick and stone. A prosperous townsman, generally, inhabited a rather larger house than the peasant did.[530] At Masulipatnam, there was a boom in the construction of buildings, for living purpose, in the second half of the 17th century.[531] The main reason was the demand for such houses by the foreigners who came there for trading purposes. The building were dark from front but inside they were done very nicely. They used to be richly decorated and were full of all the comforts of life.

However at some places like Venkatagiri, the houses were much inferiors to those in the Tamil villages.[532] They were built of mud with thatched roofs. They did not surround a square court; nor did they have any verandah to keep off the sun or rain. The houses in Cumbum or the Eastern Division were generally thatched houses, the roof consisting of either hill grass or cumbum stalks. In the inland areas, the houses were flat-roofed, the roof consisting of brushwood covered with mud.

VILLAGES

The Telugu villages were not closely crowded together, but were, but were built with plenty of room between each

---

[530] Godavary Manual.

[531] S. Arasrathnam, Masulipatnam and Cambay, A History of Two Port Towns, 1500-1800.

[532] Francis Buchanan, A journey from Madras through the countries of Mysore, Canara, and Malabar, 1807, p.30.

house. Even in respect of housing the caste prejudices were followed in the village. The lowest castes or the untouchable reside outside the villages in separate quarters. The Brahmins lived side by side with Sudras in the village and did not have their own distinct streets.[533] The Villagers built their houses on the basis of the Vastu Satra.[534] The Brahmins were expert in such knowledge and were generally consulted by the people before building their houses they could predict were one could find water on digging etc. the practice of keeping time was present at some of the villages. At the Nandikum village of the Godavary district, time keeping was present.

Generally, the houses were of two types- the Chavadi Illu or the hall house and the Manduva Illu or the courtyard houses. The diference between the two houses was that the former had a broad hall that stretched from the front to the back of the house. The rooms were at the sides. In the latter type of houses a narrow passage ran from one side of the house to the other. The courtyard was in the center and two verandahs surrounded it. The rooms opened into the verandahs. The rich and higher castes built the Chavadi illu with the kitchen always in the west portion of the house. The front of the houses was decorate with lime Muggu, every morning. The lower parts of the doors gave a pleasing

---

[533] Godavari Manual, p.53.
[534] H. V.

yellow and red look, as they were decorate with the yellow saffron turmeric and red Kumkumam.[535]

The houses of the Brahmins and Komatis were generally the best in every village.[536] The outlook of the houses of the Brahmins gave the look of prosperity.[537] Generally, their houses had large doors. The rich had cattle sheds in the house enclosures it self. In the Muslim houses of rich people, separate apartments were provided for the women. Some of the houses of the well to do Hindus were ornamented with carved work and ornamental devices on the walls. Some of such houses had represented the Hindu Gods and their consorts.

All the houses in the village were thatched with palmyra leaves. Under the roof the people who could afford it made a ceiling of mud. It served as a storehouse and protected the house itself, if the roof got on fire.[538] It was a very common sight to see the thatched roofs catching fire during the hot summer days. Often the walls were made of mud. Some times the walls were made of split bamboo, smeared with mud. The roof was tiled and the houses had windows and open courtyards. The walls were, sometimes, built with stone and mud and plastered over with a mixture of clay and cowdung. The wood was utilized in the making of beams, posts,

---

[535] <u>Godavari Gazeette</u>, pp. 43-44.
[536] John A. C. <u>Boswell, Manual of the Nellore District of the Presidency of Madras</u>, p. 213.
[537] <u>S. S.</u>
[538] <u>Godavary Gazeette</u>, op. cit.

and bamboo. The use of egitimber for dwelling houses was prohibited in the houses of the Cumbum area.[539] the cattle were kept out doors in poorer households. Only during the rainy season they were brought indoors.

However, the Ryots or the Kapus were beginning to build for themselves houses with brick and Chunam. As a result of prosperous, as they were the land owing class they built better houses. A prosperous man built a larger house than the common peasant did. His house consisted, perhaps, of three or four rooms, with a courtyard in the center.[540] In front of their houses they built a big platform.[541] These platforms were called Arugu and they were made for people to sit down on.[542] These platforms were decorated with white and red stripes of Chunam or lime. It was built on each side of the entrance of the house. The owner sat in the cool of the evening to hear the gossip of the day and to chat with his friends. The house was surrounded with a compound wall all around.[543] They had separate sheds within their compounds for their cattle both for agricultural and for milking purposes.[544] There were stacks of hay and fodder for the cattle near the main building and everything about the house suggested a state of prosperity. Their houses

[539] Narahari Gopalakristamah.
[540] Godavary Gazeette.
[541] S. S.
[542] Godavary Gazeette.
[543] H. V.
[544] S S.

were full of all the things required for a healthy and wealthy life. It was full of sustenance.

Sometimes the dwellings of an average person meant three or four detached huts. One hut served as a sleeping room for the family, another for a working room and kitchen, and a third for a storeroom for goods. The huts were circular in shape. The walls were made of mud and the roof was pointed in the center and was thatched.[545] The Hindus, whether rich or poor, were conscious of cleanliness and always kept their clean. As they had to work and cook in the same room it was essential for them to keep their houses very neat.[546]

However all of the persons concerned with agriculture were not prosperous. In the early 19th century the condition of the farmers was not very good. Bad housing, bad sanitation, insufficient food and impoverished life characterized the economic life of the average ryot.[547] As such one can infer that the situation of the ryots had started to decline in the late half of the 18 th century itself. They survived on the bare minimum. A ryot's house had generally two rooms with a hall in between. The houses were generally built on a raised Pyal.[548] As a rule there was no separate sleeping apartment

---

[545] John A.C Boswell, op. cit.

[546] Edward Thornton, <u>A Gazetter of the territories under the Government of the E. I.Co. and the Native states on the continent of India</u>, p.431.

[547] A. Jagannadhan, <u>Some Aspects of Socio-Economic Conditions in the Ceded District, 1800-1810</u>, in Itihass, vol. IV, 1976.

[548] Narahari Gopalakristamah, op. cit.

in most houses. As a consequence all the members of the family slept in one single room only.

Every village was having a temple.[549] The religious places had their roofs made of slate stone or brick in Chunam.[550] The secular buildings were prohibited from using these materials in their construction.

The travelers and the pilgrims stayed in, Choultries or rest houses. Most of choultries were nothing but places but places surrounded by mud walls, 12 feet high, thatched with straw, about 16 feet long from 10 to 12 broad. In walls were holes for putting an earthen vessel that served as a lamp in the night. The servants of the travelers, and the palanquin boys that accomapanied their their masters, also slept in choultries along with the master. All ate rice and curry.[551] During summer months, the provision of water to travelers was done through the temporary construction of water houses or the "Sali Vendras".[552] The Queen and the person of quality often constructed rest houses for the pilgrims and travelers. It was seen as a work of piety that would earn them some good merits in life. The stay was free in such Sarais or the rest houses. They were built generally next to the mosques but were open to all people irrespective of their castes and creed.

---

[549] Dr. Heynes Journey, <u>Observations made on a tour from Samulcottah to Hyderabad, 1798.</u>

[550] Narahari Gopalakristamah, op. cit.

[551] Dr. Heynes Journey, op. cit.

[552] H. V., poem no. 160.

TRIBAL DWELLINGS

The tribe had their own housing system. They lived in villages far from the dwelling of the upper caste people. While some tribe had settled down in villages of their own, other were still of a nomadic nature.

The Koya tribe lived in small villages. Solely people of the tribe usally inhabited the village, any outsiders had to live in a separate quarter. The Koyas made their houses with bamboo and the roof was made with a thatch of gross or palmyra.[553]

Another tribe called the Dommaras were of a nomadic nature.[554] As the main profession of these people was acrobatics, they moved from one place to another to earn a living. The Dommaras, pitched their camp usually on the outskirts of a village or a town which they used to visit to perform earn a living. They lived in small portable huts called Gudise. The materials for their temporary dwellings consisted of bamboo and date leaf mats to spread over them. When on the move, they carried all their belonging on the on the backs of donkeys which they reared. They also reared pigs, which followed them when on march. They earned their living by demonstrating their acrobatics feats to villagers and the townsmen.

---

[553] <u>Godavary Gazeette</u>, p.67.

[554] Dr. R. Soma Reddy, <u>The life of Dommaras as Reflected in the Literature and Epigraphs of Medical Telugu Country</u>, A. P. History Congres, Kakinada, 1984, p.33.

The tribe of the Chenchus lived in small communities called Gudems.[555] The Chenchus had abandoned the nomadic life and had started to lead a settled life. The Gudems were generally placed near the plains and villages and were never shifted from place to place. Their huts were in the shape of beehives. The Chenchus were very particular about hygiene and always kept their dwellings cleanly swept. The walls were of wicker work, about 3ft. high, with conical roofs of straw, with a sort of screen thrown in front of the low entrance. Their main profession was during the harvest seasons when they worked as labourers, on the agricultural fields, and gathered the different types of grains produced. They also hunted the wild animals for their food, in the jungles.

EUROPEAN DWELLINGS

The Europeans came to Andhra Desa as traders. Generally, they settled down at the port town as it was convenient for keep an eye on their workforce. However, some of the men also stayed in the capital city to look after their interests in the royal court. In the early days of their arrival, the foreigners were allowed to build houses of their own. The Qutb Shahi officials were suspicious of all foreigners and did not allow them to construct building either for living purpose or for their mercantile activities. As

---

[555] Narahari Gopalakristnamah, p.159.

such, they lived in houses built by locals and paid the rent for the house. These houses were small and cramped and could accommodate only a few people. In the early years of their arrival, the English house had only 8 to 9 persons staying.

At Masulipatnam, it was only in the late eighteenth century, that the permission for the construction of their own buildings was given to them. The Europeans made it a rule for all their staff to stay in houses that belonged to the companies. However, in the earlier days when they stayed in the rented houses, the officials of the English Company stayed outside the official residence in two storyed houses. The main reason was that the houses were all one storyed high and it was not healthy for them or their family to stay there. The ground was always wet and moist because of the salt water.

As such, when permission to build houses was received, they always constructed two storied houses, so that they could stay on top and not develop any disease. This was mainly true for the port cities. Over a period of time, in the port city of Masulipatnam, the areas that they stayed in, came to be know according to their nationalities, such as Frenchpeta, English Palem, Volanda Palem or Holland Palem, etc.

The Dutch were better located at Masulipatnam than the English.[556] At Masulipatnam, the Dutch had a plot of

---

[556] William Foster, <u>The English factories in India, 1622-1623</u>, p. 70.

land given to them by the rulers, where they built residences to which officials retired for amusement and recreation. As it was on high ground it also served as a place of refuge when the port town were flooded with salt water. The Dutch women and children also stayed in the factory along with their men at Masulipatnam. The men conducted their business from the very same palce.[557] They also built houses in the hinterland of the port where they would retire for amusements and rest. In a village at Palakollu, the Dutch had built a large building of stone. It housed 8 to 10 Dutch officials and 70 Indian labourers.[558]

The English at the port of Masulipatnam, had a double storyed house built for health reasons.[559] The ground floor was always wet and soggy as a result of the salt water from the sea. Inside the place of their stay they constructed rooms even for their workers. They had the washers or the Dhobi staying inside their precincts. They had had built a house for the washers' of the clothes and also separate rooms for the cook inside their factory.[560] A garden and a dove-house were also put up inside the campus. From time to time they also repaired dwellings and constructed new buildings to stay in as and when the time required.

---

[557] India in the 17ᵗʰ century-Memoirs of Francois Martin, 1670-74, vol. I Tr. Lotika Varadrajan.

[558] Sinnappah Arasaratnam, p.68

[559] The Diaries of Streynsham Master, p.384.

[560] William Foster, English Factories in India, 1630-1633, p.263.

FURNITURE

The use of furniture on a large scale was introduce during these times.[561] The Telugu were frugal in the utilization of furniture. The furniture in a normal Telugu household, consisted only of the cot or the Charpoy. The increase of the family prosperity was chiefly seen in the better quality of the clothes worn, in the superior kind of food eaten, and especially in the greater number of the jewels worn both by the men and women, particularly on the Hindu feasts day.[562] Inspite of an increase in the family fortunes they hesitated to spend more on the furniture.

The Muslims brought in the use of wooden Divans and the carpets into the region. The English started the use of furniture on a large scale in the day to day activities. They utilized furniture in work and in leisure times. These new ways brought about a distinct change in the living style of the people of Andhra. The Muslim nobles and later on the Hindu high officials copied the living style of the English. The English too were not left to themselves and adopted many lifestyles of the Muslim nobility.[563] Some of the rich

---

[561] W. H. Moreland, op. cit.
[562] Godavary Manual.
[563] Bilkiz Alladin, <u>Cultural Exchange Between The Residency And Hyderabad</u>, in Helen B. Butt ed. <u>The Composite Nature of Hyderabad –An Extension Seminar</u>.

Hindus as a result of the influence of European manners, had started using chairs in their houses.[564]

During the early period of Muslim rule, there were no tables and chairs in Hyderabad. The Muslim high society used the Islamic style of furniture only. There were low wooden platforms or Takhats, and low beds or Palangris, which were placed on the Takhats.[565] The beds of the rich were woven of canvas tape called Niver. The Takhats were covered with cotton mats called Daris, or with cotton cushions called Gadahs. Over it bed sheets were spread. On Takhats sometimes carpets were also spread for elegance and comfort. At the other end of the Takhats were placed large barrel shaped cushions or Gautakiyas to recline comfortably. The every day Gautakiyas had white coverings. On the eve of important function the cushions were draped with costly covers made of either silk or velvet cloth and also had gold or silver embroidered work done on the covers.

The well to do Muslims enjoyed their evenings with their family in the courtyards. There, they sat on wooden Tipay or stool made of rush frass and cane. The outer verandahs or Peshdalans were hung with screen i.e. Chilman. They were convertible and could be folded when not in use. At the doors, curtains of cloth or Pusdah were hung. They were in single piece or in two piecec.

---

[564] <u>Govadary Gazeette</u>.
[565] M. A. Nayeem, op. cit.

The demand for European furniture and articles of internal decoration, from the Kings, the Muslim nobles and the Hindu Nayakas was very high. The European merchants either presented it to them or they ordered for them and made payments for it. Some of the widely demanded articles were "fair large looking glasses," Japanese writing desk, and "any English toys may be available".[566] The portrait of the English King "in Parliament robes" was also presented to the King of Golconda. The animals like the Irish greyhounds, English mastiffs, water spaniels, hawks, apes, parrots etc. were also asked to be brought.

Due to the affect of Muslim culture, some richer Hindu ryots and merchants had started using tape cots and mattresses and cushions also. Nulaka or rope was used for native cots. It was made of epifibre. Some wealthy people also used grass mats and carpets. Similarly, as a result of Muslim influence, woolen and cotton carpets were also beginning to be more freely used though mats were most common. The articles of furniture in a prosperous Hindu household were generally limited to a few wooden cots, the bottoms of which were made of laced rope or tape, a few stools and boxes and one or two large jars for storing grains. The utensils consisted of a few brass or tin earthen pots, and dishes for culinary purposes.[567] They also had wooden

---

[566] W. H. Moreland, <u>From Akbar to Aurangzeb, A Study In Indian Economic History</u>, pp. 70-71.

[567] Jonn A.C. Boswell, op. cit.

boxes to contain the family jewels and a few palmyra leaf books.[568] All the vessels were kept scrupulously bright and clean. Some even had cups mad of silver.

The furniture in an average ryot's house consisted of Charpoy or wooden cots woven with epifibre or roselle fibre. The utensils consisted of mud pots and a few brass pots. The beds of poor and middle class were made of rope woven rush grass, ban, etc.[569] The utensils in the house of a rich farmer were very similar to those in an ordinary ryot's house. They were only of a better quality and more numerous.[570] There was less of utensils in a Hindu household as they ate in leaves and not on plates etc.

Chairs, Tables, Couches used by English and by the other Europeans. Some Englishmen making profit by selling the stuff to the factory.[571] In course of time the rich Andhra people adopted this. By the nineteenth century the European furniture had replaced the local furniture. The chandeliers, furniture, Irish linen and cottons were all imported from foreign countries on the demand of the rich Muslims.[572]

In the house of the tribes extremely poor household items could be found. Some of the utensils and the bedding

---

[568] Godavary Manual.

[569] M. A. Nayeem, op. cit.

[570] Godavary Manual.

[571] Records of Fort St. George, Masulipatnam Consultation Book of 1682-83,p.2.

[572] Bikeez Alladin, p.51.

items were the following: the wooden or stone sockets in which the grain was pounded, wooden pestle for pounding grain, flat basket over with their bamboo stripes in which articles were exposed to the sun, old earthen post for cooking, gunny bags, tattered quilts, mats of straw etc.[573]

FOOD

The Hindus were very particular about their food habits. They would have their bath before eating their food. They took their food only on leaf plates. The "caste prejudice requires that any earthen vessel which has been used for eating be broken and never used a second time for the same purposes" The food was cooked in earthen pots. They never used any porcelain crockery for eating purposes. The Hindus, in particular the Brahmins, had a fixed time for taking their food. They were vegetarians and only took the dairy products such as milk and Ghee. "They have a due command of their Appetite both as to Time and the Matter they feed on, to wit, Roots, Herbs, Rice, and Cutchery, all manner of Fruits, but nothing that had Life, or likely to produce Vital Heat, as Eggs, which they will not eat; but they will drink Milk and boil'd Butter, which they call Ghe".[574] The Brahmins and the Baniyans did not add any living thing in their diet. They were strict vegetarians. The

---

[573] Dr. R.S. Reddy, op.cit
[574] John Fryer,p.94.

Sudra caste ate the meat of other animals but not of the cows and calves.[575] They revered the cows and believed that their souls go into the calves and cows. Hewer, the fifth caste that consisted of the Untouchables ate the flash of cows. They also ate the flesh of the dead animals.[576] Some of the tribes the Dommaras reared pigs.

The Kapus who were the Royots of Andhra Desa grew different crope in the region.[577] The Jonna, rice, hay and the paddy seeds have been mentioned in the contemporary literature. The different varieties of the paddy seeds are even mentioned. They also grew a number of vegetables in their lands. The Gazettes of the early half of the 19th century give us a lot of information on the types of vegetables that were grown in the region. A there could not have been major change in the dietary habits of the population in fifty years only, we have taken it as a source material for the information on vegetables.

Some of the vegetables that were consumed by the people of the higher castes were tomato, bottlegourd or Anapakayalu.[578] Thses were also used as a diet for the sick. Squash gourd i.e.Gummadi Kaylu was much used by the Brahmins. Some of the vegetables such as Coccinea India or Donda Kayalu and Lab lab Cullratus or Chikkudikayalu was much used by Brahmins, but seldom cultivated by ryots

[575] William Foster, <u>The English Factories</u>, 1656-1600 p.261.
[576] Anonymous Relations, p. 70.
[577] <u>H.V.</u>
[578] John A.C. Boswell, pp.374-417

in their fields. As such they were grown by the Brahmins themselves. The Brahmins had a small garden in the backyard of their house and they grew a few fruit trees and vegetables there.[579] Brinjals and luffa gourds or Birakaya were highly prized vegetables. Colocasie was such a vegetable whose leaf, stalk and roots were all used for curry.[580]

Some of the other favorite vegetables were ladyfinger, snake gourd, cucumber, squash gourds, bottle ground, and the green leafy vegetables, such as, Totakura, sorrel or Sukkakura, Gongura, spinach, fenugreek or Mentikura were all grown in a very little quantity. Humans and animals ate the leaves of the Gongura plan. Drum stick or Munagakayalu long pods were used as vegetable.[581] Radish or Mullangi, coconut, tamarind fruit, sugar cane and cane jiggery, date jiggery etc. were also consumed. The dried cucumber was used during wet seasons for curry. Its seeds were dried and oil taken out for domestic purposes or it was bruised and cooked with rice. Onion formed an important part of daily food of the people of Andhra Desa.

The condiments such as coriander, ginger, chiles, garlic, and mustard seed were used to bring out a better flavor in the food. The merchants did business in different spices and condiments, which were very good smelling.[582] They sold the spices of South India to the different parts of the

---

[579] S.S.
[580] John A.C. Boswell
[581] Vizag Munual, p. 147
[582] H.V.

country. The leaves and the seeds of coriander or Kottimiri were used. The coriander seeds were grinded and used as spice in the food.

Paddy, sorghum, gingelly seeds, hemp, spiked millet, red gram, green gram, raggi, great millet, horse gram, black gram, Bengal gram were some of the crope grown and consumed by the locals. In Nagala Dimre Kaifiyat, we have details of crops like Jawar, Bajra, Redgram, castor seeds, Bengal gram grown in small quantities in sandy soil along with betel leave, bananas, lemon, coconut, mango, citrus, sugarcane, orange and vegetable and cucumber which were also grown.[583] Oil of castor, linseed, Kusuma, gingelly was pressed and taken out. The Tila Ghataka took out the oil from the different varieties of seeds.

Tobacco was a foreign product that was brought into the Andhra Desa in-between the years 1600-1650 AD by the Portuguese.[584] The red chilly was also brought from South America. At first it was seldom used in the food preparations. Only in the 17th century the production and the use of chilly in Andhra Desa increased. Timmayya Singhraju, a contemporary of Gaudaraya of Vijayanagara said that chilly was brought from foreign lands. After coming in of the Europeans some seeds etc. were brought from London and Bangalore to the areas of Andhra, but climate was not found

---

[583] M. Krishnamurthy, Mackenzie Manuscript As a sourse of Comprenhensive Historiography, PAPHC, p.99.
[584] S. Pratap Reddy, Andhraula Sanghika Charitra, p.298.

to be suitable etc.[585] The brought a capital kind of orange from Batavia, and planted it at Placadole. The oranges there still retain the name of Batai Naringa Pandu or the Batavian orange.[586]

Some of the food preparations mentioned in the contemporary literature, were Pulihora, Junnu curd, pickles, Atukulu, Dossi, Arisalu, Roti, Gadalu, Chakarah, Booralu, Pooris, Kudumus etc. Another popular dish was vada.[587] Mango and Oosirikaya pickles were very palatable and people enjoyed eating them.[588] Vemana, the social reformer of the 17th centure, said that, food without ghee and curry was considered as dogs' food. The general items of food was rice, dal, curd and buttermilk, tamarind, ghee, and vegetable.[589] The spices like pepper powder, tamarind, dried pieces of mangoes, also find mention. While travelling the people carried their food with themselves. All the dry items were taken on journeys. The food was carried on the shoulders in a Kavadi. A long stick was placed on the shoulders and on both ends pots were tied. In it were kept the eatable. Any liquid food was carried in the hollow of a

---

[585] John A.C. Boswell, pp.374-417.

[586] Henry Morris, op.cit.

[587] Tallapaka, <u>Venkateshwara Shataka</u>, in Vidwan Vedam Venkatakrishna Sharma, <u>Shataka Vangmaya Sarvaswamu</u>, Part I, p.89.

[588] <u>H.V.</u>

[589] <u>Godavary Manual.</u>

dried up long gourd.[590] Different types of food was prepared from the fruits like pudding etc.[591]

The food taken by the poor was just enough for sustenance. Food was not cheap.[592] Meat was very costly and so was sugar and Ghee. However, the price of poultry was cheaper. It was very difficult to afford a decent meal. Their food consisted of ".. very coarse rice and water and some times a little dryed fish to relish it".[593] The leaves of Totakura, and the Anapakaya vegetable was consumed much by the poorer classes.[594] The agricultural worker would eat from 24-30 oz. of rice per day together with meat very occasionally, and some vegetable oil and spices. Most of them suffered from deficiency, and some vegetable oil and spices. Most of them suffered from deficiency diseases and malnutrition. The food of the common man, sometimes consisted of Khichdi.[595] It was made of pulse with rice and eaten hot with a little Ghee in the evening. During the day they made a little parched pulse or other gram with which they satisfied their lean stomach. They took Ambally, a more or less thick gruel of rice or of Bajra etc. It was eaten with a little oil and red chilly if possible. The Cholam food like

---

[590] S.S.
[591] H.V.
[592] Marie Delphine Roger, Cookery during the Qutb Shahi period, unpublished paper, Oriental Manuscripts Library, Hyderabad.
[593] Thomas Bowrey,p.97.
[594] Vizag Manual.
[595] Marie Delphine Roger, op.cit.

Jowar was also boiled like rice and was eaten or rather drunk with Majjiga or buttermilk.[596]

The people also smoked leaves of tobacco. The tobacco was being sold to the Lambasies by the ryots. They rolled the leaf, lit it at one end and went on smoking till it warned the lips, and then it was thrown away. The poor people did not know the bad effects of tobacco and allowed their small children to take it too. "The children of three or four years of age frequently take it and it is made as frequently them as meat and drinke."[597] Some people also ate the tobacco leaves in betel.[598] It was considered as a pleasure that men intensely enjoyed.

The tribes like the Boyas were hunters by profession. They killed the birds in the jungles and ate them.[599] The chenchus ate millets, bajra, rice, salt, chilly and tamarind. Hunting provided them with food. They rosted the flesh of various animals like deer, sheep, monkey, bear, variety of cats and birds like hen, peacock, pigeon, eagle, etc.[600] A kind of tuber called Chenchu Gaddalu was roasted and eaten after coating it with honey.

The rich Muslims ate Roti, Kabab and Achar from time to time. During Moharram only vegetarian food was

---

[596] S.S.

[597] Thomas Bowrey, p. 79.

[598] Chowdappa's Shataka, in Vedam Vekatakrishna Sharma's Vangmaya Sarvasyamu, Part I, p.170.

[599] H. V.

[600] Bukkarayapatnam Kaifiyat, vol. 99. 129.

made. The food of the aristocratic people was very rich and was full of meat, fat and sugar.[601] Fried food, Murabbah, Firni, Falooda, Halwa, Malinda, Sheer O Nabat was eaten. The rice dishes included Khuska, Qubuli, Pulao, Biryani, Khichdi, Yakhni Pulao with Burani or sauce. The snacks include the Samosa, Kabad with Paneer and Sirka. Meatballs and Doppiaza were the mouthwatering recipies. The sweets include Mazafer, Rataloo ki kheer, Shakkar pare, Jaleebis, Falooda and etc. Muhammad Quli has mentioned Idd-e-Puris, Sheer Khurma etc.[602] Shir Khurma was drink made of creamy milk and ghee garnered with dates, pistachios, almonds and other condiments and finally mixed with sugar. It was offered to the guests on their arrival at a person's house.

Sheereni or sweets was distributed to the people on a victory and on alliances being formed during the rule of the Nizam.[603] Camel and chicken was served to soldiers after a victory.[604] Harees, Nahari, full of oil, Doppiaza of liver and heart, big Roti, and Baigan was sometimes given to the soldiers by the Kings. They were also served sliced onions, ginger, radishes. They were mixed together and eaten raw.

The demand for porcelain was great in the royal and the noble households of Golconda. The English merchants

[601] Marie Delphahine Roger, op.cit.
[602] Muhammad Quli Qutb Shah, Kulliyat.
[603] Henry George Briggs, <u>The Nizam his History and Relations with the British Government</u>
[604] Marie Delphine Roger, op.cit.

brought it from China. T he Persian merchants at Petapoli had a great liking for the Chinese porcelain.[605] The English tried to bring in the porcelain from Staffordshire, England, but the demand was very low "since the Muhammadans are the only class of native population who use crockery"

The King and the nobles had perfect and elaborate table manners. During the parties the host received the guest with Pan or betel and flowers.[606] The hands were washed with rose water before meals. The food was served on a Dastarkhan or a cloth spread on the floor. It was generally white in colour. Sometimes, red colour cloth was used during festivities. It would be covered with Zari work. The people sat in rows on both sides of the Dastarkhanas. The dishes were placed in the center. The food was taken in silence. If a guest could not make it to the party, the food was sent through a servant. According to Tavernier, the nobility of Golconda took their dinner at 10 O' clock in the night.

FRUITS

The Qutb Shahi kings loved the fruits of Iran. The fruits were imported from as far as Samarkand. The dry fruits of Iran was also very famous amongst the royalty and nobility of Golconda.[607] The Europeans made it a rule to

---

[605] William Foster, <u>English factories in India</u>, 1629-1633, p.235.
[606] Marie Delphine Roger, op.cit.
[607] <u>Farmans and other Documents of the Deccan Sultans, 1406-1687 A.D.</u>

always present the King with the dry fruits of Iran. Raisins were brought and presented to the Sultan. The grapes of Golconda were very famous. The Qutb Shahi kings were knows to have developed a very big type of high quality grape, called Inab-e-Shahi.[608] A part of the grapes were pressed to make a fairly good white wine. Some of the other fruits that grew in the region were watermelon, betel vine, plantain, sweet potatoes or yams etc. oranges and pineapples were also grown in abundance.[609]

The English stored at their factory wheat, butter, oil, arrack, sugar, etc. The Dutch stored even water in their factories for themselves and for their Indian servants. It was done so that they would be well stocked with the provisions in times of famines, which was very common in the region.[610] While the Indians felt that the prices of food items was very high in the region, the English have left behind staring that the food rates were very low in the region. "The country is a very cheap place of residence,.." and "All provisions are extreme cheap". The region was very rich in the number of goats and sheep and hens, which could be bought "from 6d.to 10d. a piece and the hens 2d.".[611]

The major changes in the food could be seen in the higher ups only. The common man continued to eat his old diet. However, the English official and the rich Muslims

---

[608] Marie Delphine Roger, op.cit.
[609] Henry Morries, p.67.
[610] William Foster, <u>E.F.I., 1656-1600</u>, p.261.
[611] ibid.

started enjoying each other's food and eating habits. The European quickly picked up the dietary habits of the East. As their cook were the local people, the local food soon became palatable to them. They became used to the use of spies and the other condiments in their food. They had started enjoying the hot and spicy food of the Andhra Desa. The tropical fruits like bananas and the papaya became their favourites for the morning bed tea.[612] The other fruits that they ate during the day were the sweet limes, oranges, custard apple, mango, pineapple, etc. The Englishmen had also started taking rice and curries for their food. The Mulligatawny soup that was made from the different kinds of pulses was their favourite. They had even started smoking Hookahs and took Paan or beetle leaves during the day. On the other hand, the Hyderabadi nobleman along with his family, adopted the English breakfast. It consisted of porridge, marmalade, cakes, pastry, plum puddings and plum cakes etc. Over a period of time the tea parties were also introduced in the speaking region, and the ballroom dancing became the style of the day. The birth of clubs was taking place and the participation of ladies in these celebrations was another great landmark of the times.

The temples were surrounded with garden all around them.[613] Native flowers were grown in gardens attached

---

[612] Bilkiz Alladin, op. cit.
[613] <u>H. V.</u>

as Inam lands to Pagodas or temples.[614] They were used
for presentation on festival days and for decorating the
images of the temple Gods and for adorning the hair of
the dancing girls. Some of the famous flowers were Dasari
puva or Hibiscus rosa Sineusis, Mallipuva or Jasmine, and
Crandumalli, which was another kind of jasmine etc. Ippa
oil was used only in the temple for lighting the torches in
the night.

DRINKS

The Kings, nobles and the common of Andhra Desa
were much interested in drinking the intoxicating drinks.
The famous drinks were Toddy, Sendhi and Bhang.[615] The
drinks of Europe were specially brought as presents for
the King and his nobles or taken by the Europeans. They
include different kinds of wine, Brandy, Mum etc.

People were also used to takings of Bhang an
intoxicant.[616] Large plantations of palmyra trees and date
palms could be found in the region. Tavernier, the French
traveler, recounts as having seen several trees around the
capital city of the Kingdom.[617] Several horses loaded with
the intoxicating drinks "Today" daily went towards the
city to sell the stuff. It was a very common drink that was

---

[614] John A. C. Boswell, op. cit.
[615] Mohammad Quli Shah, Kulliyat.
[616] Koochi Manchi Timmanna, Kukkuteshwara Shataka.
[617] Tavernier, pp.128-129.

consumed and enjoyed by all.[618] Vemana's verses also reveal that the local people consumed toddy on a large scale.[619] English drank a type of liquor called "Panch". It was derived from "Panch" in Hindustani as it was a mixture of five items.[620] Another liquor available was Arrack which was a kind of spirit. It was made by distilling rice and jaggery together.[621] The locals and the Europeans took it.

Some of the non-intoxicating drinks that were taken tea, Sherbet, fruit juice etc. The Dutch enjoyed drinking tea in the afternoon. They also drank a mixture of water and sugar that was boiled.[622] The unadulterated fruit juice of Jamun was described as very sweet and tasty by the Dutch writer of the contemporary period.[623]

DRESS

The Kapu grew cotton in his fields and looked after their growth himself.[624] It can be said with certainty that this would have been the same in the period under study. Every process from the picking of the cotton from the tree to the manufacture of his eyes. He only allowed the cleaning of the cotton by the Dudekula caste of professional cotton

---

[618] Thevenot, p.136.
[619] C. P. Brown, <u>The Verses of Vemana</u>, Book I. verse 7.
[620] William Foster, <u>English Factories in India, 1630-33</u>, p.230.
[621] Thomas Bowrey, p.77.
[622] <u>Godavary Gazeette</u>, p. 199.
[623] <u>Anonymous Relations, p.</u> 22.
[624] C. F. Brackenbury, <u>Cuddapah District Gazetteers</u>, p. 129.

cleaners. The ginning on which the Kapu womenfolk were employed, was performed by propelling stone rollers over the cotton up and down the verandah of their house. The men spin the yarn at the house itself and supply it to weavers to make up into such clothes as he and his family required.

The Malas manufactured black cotton for the women. Sometimes the clothes were coloured in white with red or black border. The thread for these cloths was already dyed. The Mala women spun the thread from the local cotton and the men wove the cloth for themselves and for the other untouchables. The cotton woven for other Sudra caste, was not their cotton but those provided by the Kapus. The men and women paid regular wages for spinning and weaving the cloth.[625] The Togatas and the Sales made softer fabrics out of the imported yarn. The dyeing of clothes was done by the caste people Maddivandlu, Rangarazus and Balijas.[626] Ravikas with silk borders were manufactured for export. Cotton carpets and turbans were made by the Musalman weavers. Woolen blankets and cotton tapes for cots were generally made by the Muslim women. The Gadaba women wore fibre clothing that was made by them.[627]

The raw silk, silk thread, silk cloth, velvet damasks, and gold thread were imported from China and Far East. These were used for wearing apparel by the nobility and for their

---

[625] Edgar Thurston, op, cit., vol IV.
[626] Narahari Gopalakistamha, op. cit.
[627] Edgar Thurston, op.cit.

tents and tapestries.[628] Moonga silk from Bengal was used by both men and women for their clothes. It was also used for carpet making. It was an imitation of the gold thread. Woolen cloths green, pale blue, and other colours were the chief imports from England. The cloths were required for garments, to cover palanquins and for use on saddles. The cloth of red colour was used for servant cloths.

When one looks at the style of dressing of the Hindus and the Muslims of the period under study, one finds that there was very less difference. "Muslamans often dressed up like Hindus…."[629] The only difference was the caste mark that was put on the forehead by the Hindus. The dress of the people was simple and unchanged for centuries. The men's dress consisted of three pieces, viz. an upper cloth, under cloth and a turban. On the feet sandals were usually worn.[630] Turbans were generally, white in colour. The Karnams, the Reddys, and others all put on turbans.[631] Turbans were of two types a plain Rumal woven round the head or a twisted fine cloth.[632] A small number of men wore Angis over their Dhotis. These Angis had four knots. The knots of the Angi were called Bara Bandhi. The common people went about with a coarse Chaddar thrown around their shoulders to cover the upper part of their body, while the rich men wore

---

[628] P. M. Joshi, <u>Textile Industry and Trade in Golkonda</u>, p. 137.
[629] W. Francis, <u>Anantpur District Gazetteer.</u>
[630] Narahari Gopalakristamah, op.cit.
[631] <u>S. S.</u>
[632] C. P. Brown, op. cit

silk shawls. The upper garments for men were sometimes coloured.[633]

In the villages, the Reddys formed the most prominent sectin of the village community of the Rayalseema, South coastal Andhra and the Telangana areas. The men wore striped turbans, black stirped cloak on their shoulders, and sandals on their feet.[634] The Rajus or the Kshatriyas wore Angis and Dhoti tucked tightly around the legs.[635] Sometimes they also put on Pyjamas. The lesser Rajus put on turbans, Chadar, and carried handkerchiefs.

During the rule of the Qutb Shahs the Kulah and Caba were the common dress for the men. The Kuleh or the cap was put on the head. However, as the days passed the Kings dressed themselves up in the local fashion. The Sultan of Golconda, Muhammad Quli Qutb Shah, dressed up like a Telgu King.[636] Tavernier says that the Deccani Omarhs rejected the old Turkish style of dressing and adopted a new style. The king and the Omrahs kept an Angarakhs on the shoulders and put on the Chaubandh. On the head they put a Pagri like the Deccani people. On the feet they put Chappals called Apashahi which were a little bent in the front.

---

[633] C.F. Brackenbury, op. cit.

[634] H. K. Sherwani, op.cit.

[635] <u>Venugopala Shataka.</u>

[636] Mohammad Quli Qutb Shah, Kulliyat, p.132.

During Asaf Jahs, both Hindus and Muslims were dressed up in the Mughal fashion of dressing. Sherwani and Turkish cap or Dastaar of Asaf Jahs were worn in big cities.

During the two centuries under study, the women of Andhra Desa, both Hindu and Muslim, continued to wear the same dress i.e. the Saree. It consisted of a single cloth varying in length from 12 to 16 cubits and in breadth from one to one and a half yards. The Sarees were dyed of various bright colours, and tied in different ways to distinguish caste. The Sarees that were worn daily were of fast and different colours. The Sarees' end was tied to the waist. The women wore special sarees and red blouses only on festivals. They took it out on other days. The Erukula women tied up their Kongus or the free corner of their sarees in such a way that their children were protected from the sun.

The saree was worn over a bodice or o Ravika with half sleeves. Red was the prevailing colour of the Sarees and Ravikas.[637] Young girls and prostitute wore a half jacket. But custom prohibited widows and all elderly women from wearing any such ravika under the sarees. The Erukula women wore colourful blouses.

The Muslim ladies also wore an alternative dress, the Dopatta, which was possibly borrowed from the northern parts of India. It was 4 & ½ yards long, and its one end was tucked into the Paijama or trousers. The Paijama was embroidered and was kept in check by a girdle that was

---

[637] C.F. Brackenbury, op. cit.

also embroidered at the ends.[638] For brids, yellow dress or Manjha were made.[639] The Muslim women always covered their heads with the loose end of the Sari or the Dopatta because of the Parda system.[640]

The common people of Andhra Desa were very scantily dressed. They utilized their clothing to cover their private parts only. They had "...a small clout just to cover their privities."[641] The common man among the Hindus wore a Dhoti with the upper part of the body bare. When at work they contented themselves with a small loincloth.[642] The Muslim men wore Lungis. The poorer classes and the tribes did not tie a turban on their head but tied a single cloth round the waist. It served as a turban under the hot sun. The shepherds covered themselves with coarse blankets when they took their flocks of sheep and goat out to graze.[643] They did so to protect themselves from the heat of the glaring sun.

The different tribes dressed up in colourful garments. The dress varied from tribe to tribe. In the tribe of the Chenchus, men were nearly in a state of nudity, having only a piece of cloth, round their loins. Caps made of leaves of trees or of cloth was also worn by them. [644] They put

---

[638] H. K. Sherwani, History of the Qutb Shahi Dynasty, p.521.

[639] H. K. Sherwani, Nizam Ihdn Khutubat, Lecture at Delhi University, 1971.

[640] H. K. Sherwani, op. cit., p.521

[641] Thomas Bowrey, p. 97.

[642] H. K Sherwani, op. cit., pp. 521-522.

[643] S. S

[644] Narahari Gopalakistamha.

peacock feather in their heads and loved to put red flowers in their hair.[645] The Pedakanti women were not allowed to wear Ravikas or blouses.[646] The Lambadi women wore Langa made of the Karwar cloth, which was of red or green colour.[647] It was embroidered. The bodice called Chola or Choli was also embroidered in the front and on the shoulders. It was fastened with the help of cords at the back. A piece of cloth was fastened at the waist and thrown over the head.

The children of all classes were left naked till the age of three or four. They played in the mud all day and when they got dirty, the mothers put several most of water on their heads and gave them a bath to clean them up.[648] It was on festivals only that they put on any kind of dress. The richer class also left their children without any clothes on. However, on festivals their children would be dressed in rich and good clothes.

ORNAMENTS

The ornaments of the Hindu higher classes were made of gold and silver metals. Sometimes these jewels were set with precious stones and pearls. The men wore pearl and gold earring and diamond studs.[649] They also put on waist

---

[645] Yayaticharitramu.

[646] Narahari Gopalakistamha.

[647] Edgar Thurston.

[648] Methwold's Relations, p.26

[649] C. P. Brown, The verses of Vemana, p. 55-56.

girdle of gold or silver wire. They put rings in the fingers. Bracelets and necklaces were also wore by the gentleman. They also wore ear studs with diamonds set in them. Some times, the upper lobe of the ear was also performed and tiny ear rings with rubies and pearl hangings was worn. Gold or silver Kadas and armlets were worn by the men according to their status.

The Hindu women wore circular and half-moon ornaments of gold on the top of their heads. The diamond Merugudi was also worn on the head.[650] At the back of the head, the Ragidi was wore. The Kuppa, Chamanti Puvvu, and Saralu and Choodamani were dome of the ornaments worn on the hair. The Addiga or bracelet of red coral was worn by most of the married women. The marriage Thali or the Mangalasutra was another important ornament wore by all married women. Nose ornaments were also worn of rubies or diamonds, or of a curve of pearls called Nathu. The women put 6 to 8 earrings in their ears. On the legs were worn anklets of silver or brass and toe of silver.[651]

The ornaments worn by a Kapu women has been described in the contemporary literature. She wore a Mala or necklace made of beads and pearls. A round thick necklace, in the shape of a ring, was also worn by them. It was called Kante. A Mala of black beads was also worn. Other ornaments included the nose ring, toe rings, finger rings

---

[650] Chengala Raya Kavi, <u>Madana Gopala Shatakamu.</u>
[651] Nellore Manual, p. 214.

and bracelets.[652] The ornament used for the head, which was worn in the center parting, has also been mentioned. The gold smith was employed for making new ornaments or polishing the old ones.

Bangles were made of glass and worn by all native women except the widows.[653] Golden bangles called Kangan were worn by the rich women. The rich people wore earrings studded with pearls, and rings in fingers. The local name of the jewelry were as follows. "BIbbilikayali, Mattelu or toe ornaments, Maninupuramulu, Sandi Dandelu or Armlets, Bahupurulu i.e. ornaments worn around the arms, Tallapaka etc.[654]

The women wore necklace and long chains called Haras. Necklets were made in single line, with or without a pendant. Sometimes they were also made in two or multiple bands. Precious stones of different size and shapes were embedded in the Haras. Generally, the necklaces were made in "V" or "U" shape.[655] On the waist, a simple cord like or pearl stringed "Yajnapavita" was worn. On the waist, girdles of pearls called Kanchi was worn. Some times they were made of gold also. The shoulder ornaments consisted of a simple pearl string or round pieces of precious metal made into a small chain with a large piece of pearl pendant.

---

[652] S.S.

[653] Narahari Gopalakistamaha, op. cit.

[654] Venateshwara Shataka.

[655] A. Kamalavasini and B. Sreepadma, <u>Jewellery in Sri Kumarmam Temple Sculpture</u>, PAPHC XII, pp. 99-101.

Sometimes they were also of 3 pearl bands. On upper arm below shoulder line, tight bands of ornamentation could be seen. On forearm and on the backside of the palm also jewels were worn. In the legs, plain rings, anklets, tubular anklets etc. were made and worn with great pride.

The ornaments worn and received as gifts by the Muslim bridegroom were Sarpanch, Sarpatti, Zigha, Turra, Kalgi, Kanthi, Chanderhaar, Bajubandh, Bighbandh, Navrattan, Dastbandhm Sumran.[656] Some of the other ornaments were one pair of Yakut, Sarpatti, Almas, Tazbi-Zammarudh, gold Pandaan with precious stones emedded on it, Chaugarh Hookah, gold Thali, small Dabbiyan.

The jewelry of the Muslim ladies were sarpatti. Morassa, almas, diamond Har, diamond Bij Bandh, Baju Bandh, Dast Bandh, Nawrattan Dhuglhuki, Aassi, Kada, Sisphul, Chnad, Finger rings Angistari of precious stones, Natta or nose rings of gold, Hadli, Jaimarugh.

The people of the lower order wore jewels made of brass or bell metal set with glass or pebbles. Copper jewelry also was in vogue by the poor people. The Chenchu women wore decent ornaments, which were made of silver and copper.[657] In the tribe of the Lambadis, the women were much attached to the ornaments made of bones and ivory. Bracelets to the elbow on either arm made of brass or horn,

---

[656] Raja Girdhari Prasad, Shahi Shadi, 1892.
[657] Narahari Gopalakistamha.

Hasali or necklace, anklets, cowries, silver pendant, nose ornaments etc. were worn.[658]

HAIR STYLE AND COSMETIC

The Hindu men and women had their daily baths once or twice.[659] After doing t heir duties, the women of the village, had their bath and dressed up in clean clothes.[660] In the Hamsa Vimshti it has been mentioned that the people used a kind of soap to clean their body and hair. Every fortnightly the hairs were applied with oil so as to free it from dirt and other things. The rich people used scented oil for their hair. Both men and women had long hair which was cleaned daily with the help of a comb. The Hindu men used to tie up their hair behind their heads. The hair of the women was usually worn long. It was put up in a knot at the side of the head and was bulged out with an artificial chignon of wool or hair. Sometimes, the hair was also worn in plaits. The length and size of the plaits was increased by artificial plaits, which were inter woven.[661] In the tribes of the Lambadi, the women tied their hair in a knot at the top of the head.[662]

---

[658] Edgar Thurston, vol. IV.
[659] Anonymous Relations, p.78.
[660] S.S.
[661] Nellore Manual,pp. 213-214.
[662] Edgar Thurston, op. cit.

The married Hindu women rubbed turmeric over their bodies to give themselves a yellow complexion. The fair colour was much admired by the native people of Andhra Desa. They used betel leaves and nuts to colour their lips red. They also applied Katuka to their eyes. They put sweet scented flowers in their hairs to look beautiful.

The tribal women too applied different methods to beautify themselves. The Chenchu women smeared their faces with the oil they extracted from Sarapappu and Kamigapappu to beautify themselves. The Lambadi women tattooed themselves. They made elaborate patterns on the backs of the hands and a tattooed dot on the left side of the nose.

The Muslim ladies used sandalwood paste all over their bodies to beautify themselves. They applied collorium in the eyes and also used perfumes on their bodies. Henna was applied on the hands, feet and on their too. The men too used Henna for their hair.

Chapter VI

EDUCATION, RECREATION & MEDICINE

In this chapter, the prevailing mode of education and medical treatment available to the people of Andhra in the 17th and the 18th century has been discussed. The pervasion of education was limited to the upper casts only and the lower castes were still devoid of its usefulness. However, it was during this period that the lower castes had started to understand its importance. The instances show that they had started learning to read and write. The field of medicine benefitted a lot with the arrival of the Muslims and the Europeans. They brought with themselves new methods of treatment. The recreational activities that the people enjoyed taking part in, have also been mentioned. The different games that were played and the different drama and puppet shows that were watched by the masses have been mentioned in this chapter.

EDUCATION

In the seventeenth century, the education system was not available to all the people. Infect, it was available to only the fifty percent of the total population as the women were kept out of the learning field. It was a male dominated society. A very few women were education as in the earlier period of the Vijayanagar period. However, even the male percentage of literate was very low as the writing and reading were thought to be the profession of the higher castes only. The existing system has been Muslims and the Europeans have been looked into.

HINDU SCHOOLS

Amongst the Hindus, the Brahmins were the caste that was concerned with the art of writing and reading. It was said that they knew 64 Vidyas.[663] they were masters of different languages and were good poets. They were well versed in the Hindu scriptures like the Vedas. They worked as teachers and imparted education to the children at the

---

[663] H. V.

village schools. The school was held under a tree in the open air. The sources of a later date provide us with the information regarding the curriculum of schools. In the absence of the contemporary source one has to take the help of the later sources. Five subjects were always taught at the Hindu schools. They were reading, grammar, writing, arithmetic and memoriter exercise in high dialect and Sanskrit.[664] Some of the other things taught were matters connected with religion, ceremonies, the calendar festivals, lucks and unlucky days and etc. in higher education, the medium of instruction was in Sanskrit and the subjects taught were Vedas, Upanishads, logic, philosophy, Panini's grammar, rhetoric, Ramayana and the other epics, Kalidasa's dramas, Hindu law, both temporal and spiritual etc.

The student learnt the alphabets by writing them on the sand mud.[665] When they finally learnt to write, they were provide with leaves of the Asristolochia Indica to write on. Sometimes they also wrote either with a reed on paper or with a kind of pencil on the palaca or haligey, which were used as slates. The writing could be effaced with a wet cloth. The pupil copied the next day's lesson on their slates and learnt it by heart in their houses. The next day, they repeated the same in front of the teacher. In this way they not only mastered the writing and reading but also improved their

---

[664] C. D. Manual, of the Administration of the Madras Presidency, pp.591-592.

[665] Chanrasekhara Sataka.

memory. The boys obtained thorough knowledge of 4 or 5 great classics of their mother tongue, and became perfectly able to read their vernacular.

The teacher gave harsh punishments to the naughty children. He beat them with came and tied them to a pole, bent like a bow.[666] Some of the children were onto some prank, and often tied the Shikha of the teacher to something or the other whenever he slept during the school hours.

The lower casts gave their children training in their traditional profession. However, it has been mentioned that some of the Hindus first let their children learn the reading and writing and only after that, they were taught the family profession.[667] As they learnt the traditional art from a very early age, they became experts in their field of vocation. Some of the Banias or the Komatis of Andhra Desa initiated their children into the diamond trade from a very early age.[668] They were first taught to verify the purity of the diamond. Later on they were asked to verify the pureness themselves and also to price stones correctly on the basis of their purity. If the assessment was found to be correct, then the child was rewarded with a quarter percentage of the profit derived from the sale of the stone. Similarly in the Mangala caste, when the boys were eight years old, they were taught their traditional art of shaving. They were first

---

[666] H. V.
[667] H. K. Sherwani, p.522
[668] Tavernier's Travels.

asked to shave an earthen pot which was turned upside down and was smeared with damp earth. When the mud dried, the boy was asked to scrap it off, under the direction of an experienced barber.[669] Similarly, the weaver caste also let their children to paint the clothes with pencils from a very early age.[670] This practice not only initiated the little boys into the profession but over a period of time also made them independent and specialists in field of work.

MUSLIM SCHOOLS

With the arrival of the Muslims, the method of education saw a change. The Muslim children were education in schools called Madara's. these schools were generally attached to a mosque. The Muslim parents were more interested in providing the knowledge of reading and writing to their children than professional education. The Muslim government made it compulsory for all Muslims to send their children to school. All the Muslim children were to compulsorily attend these mosque-schools daily and study under the teacher known as Mullas.[671] The basic curriculum of all such mosque-schools was religious. The Kings and the nobles, during the Qutb Shahi period, were very interested in the education of their people. Hence the Kings opened

---

[669] Edgar Thurston and K. Rangachari, vol.IV.
[670] John Fryer, p.90.
[671] M. A. Muid Khan, <u>Arabian Poets of Golconda</u>, p.27.

several schools and appointed teachers at the cost of the state machinery. They were the lovers of the company of scholars and were great patrons of Scholarship. The scholars from Persia and Arabia were invited to the Kingdom. The Kings organized big libraries also for the benefit of scholars. Kings Mohammad Quli Qutb Shah, Muhammad Qutb Shah, and Abdullah Qutb Shah constructed several mosques and Madrasas or schools for imparting education to their subjects. [672] We do not find any reference of Hindus sending their children to such schools.

The Muslim schools were mostly government sponsored. Primary and secondary education was provided with teachers called Mullahs. [673] The contemporary literature Tarikhe Zafran, Tarikhe Qutb Shahi, Tarikhe Hadiqatul Alam, and Hadiqatus Salatin, speak of several schools, baths, and mosques that were built during the region of the Qutb Shahs. The Tarikhe Zafran States that about 7,00,000 Huns were used for building mosques, Madrasas, the Charminar, Khanqahs, Baghs etc. Infact, originally the Charminar, was also used as a college. The Tarikhe Hadiqatul Alam says that in Charminar, rooms were constructed for teaching. The minarets of the Charminar contained apartments for the use of the teachers and the students of the college residing

---

[672] ibid., p.26.

[673] Nasiruddin Hashmi, Ahde Asafi Ki Kadeem Taleem, 1336H.-1385H.

there.[674] The Darys Shifa was built for imparting medical education to the children. The Jami Masjid built on the north east of Charminar, by Mohammad Quli Qutb Shah in 1597 AD, had a school attached to it.[675] According to the <u>Mahanamah</u>, this school served the needs both the Hindus and Muslmans.[676] Similarly Sherwani, while describing the Sayedabad mosque built in 1605 AD, states "we also know that every mosque of any pretensions had a school attached to it; and the rooms all around the might well have served as a kind of boarding school where both teachers and pupils lived together.[677] Similarly, the Sufi Khanqahs were very important centers of learning. They served as schools and colleges where both secular and religious education was imparted.[678] That the study of the local languages like Telugu and Sanskrit, was cultivated in the Khanqahs in Andhra Des, is know from the Telugu work entitled Sringara-Manjari. The authorship of this work in Telugu as will as in Sanskrit is ascribed to Akbar Shah, the son of Syed Shah Raju II, the pontiff of a Sufi Khanqah at Hyderabad. The book is said to have been written during the period of

---

[674] Syed Naimatullah, <u>Deeni Madarsas of Hyderabad</u>, M. Phil. Dissertation, p.10.

[675] Anonymous, <u>Tuzuk-e-Qutb Shahi</u>, p.6.

[676] ibid. f.no.iii.

[677] H. K. Sherwani, pp.316-317.

[678] R. Soma Reddy, <u>History of Religious Institutions in Andhra Desa from A.D. 1300 to 1600</u>, Ph.D. thesis, Osmania University, 1980.

the last Qutb Shahi King, Abul Hasan Tanesha.[679] This is a clear proof of the fact that, the ascetics of the Khanqahs endeavoured to learn the language of the local people in order to converse with them freely on the mysteries of the Sufi Philosophy.

The curriculum of the Muslim schools was mainly religious.[680] In higher education the subjects taught were Hadis, Fiqa, the Holy Quran, Tafseer, Mantikh or philosophy etc. at the primary level, early knowledge of the above mentioned subjects were taught. The learning began with the ceremony of Bismillah by the Mulla or the teacher. At first the students were taught the rudimentary of the Arabic language and then he was to study the Quran.[681] Persian was also taught in advanced schools. The students also learnt Hindostani too. However, no education was given in history, geography or in arithmetic.

There was a flow of immigrant scholars to Golconda from Iran. Some of the scholars of the Qutb Shahi period were Syed Kamaluddin Mazundarani, Mir Qutbuddin, Naimutullah, Mir Murtaza, Mir Muhammd etc.[682] Several books were written by these scholars. Some of the books written were Burhame Qate or the dictionary by Mir Momin, the Hadiquatus Salatin by Nizammuddin, Allah Ibon Khatun translated the books Kitab-ul-Irshaad and

---

[679] H. K. Sherwani, p.605.
[680] Syed Naimtillah, op. cit.
[681] C. D. Maclean.
[682] Syed Naimatullah, op. cit.

Jahne Abbasi. The noble of the King were very learned people. Some of the learned nobles them were Allah Ibne Khatum, Mujiduddin, Mir Syed Muhammad Safrani, Maulana Raunaki, Qazi Ahsan, Qazi Zahiruddin, Hakim Abdul Jabbar Gilani, etc. They taught the poor students on their own, either in their own houses or in the mosques or in the Sufi Khankhahs.

Under the Asaf Jahi, two types of schools flourished. One was sponsored and maintained by the government and the King and the Prime Minister appointed their teachers. The other type was maintained by the Omrahs, on their own where they themselves imparted knowledge. The Ulemas too maintained school at their houses, mosques or in the Sufi Khankahs. The Govt. provided grants in aid to such school. In 1744 AD, at the Madarsa at Hyderabad the salary of senior and junior teachers was Rs.30 and Rs.20, respectively. The department called Susur-us-Sudur looked after the salary etc. of the teachers. During the region of the second Nizam, schools were founded in the district and the Qasbas. A teacher was posted ther and an allowance of a few Annas was given to him.

MISSIONARY EDUCATION

The missionary Fathers were the pioneers in European method of education in Andhra Desa. The Jesuit Father opened schools for the converts to Christianity. However, they were not very successful in their efforts. The schools were also utilized for the proselytizing purpose. With the decline of the Jesuits by the year 1759, a new era began. The Evangelists and the other opened a number of schools, seminaries and printing presses in various places in South India. They took it upon themselves to first teach the Indians and then convert them.[683] The first such school was opened in Vishakapatnam in 1805 AD and the other followed very soon after.

EDUCATION OF WOMEN

As far as the education of the Hindu women is concerned one does not come across and historical data. The contemporary books are all silent in this regard. The girls were normally taught all the household chores like cooking, pounding rice and etc. They were taught to behave respectfully towards all elders, to serve their in-laws, to look after the younger ones and etc.[684] All over India it is enough for a woman to know how to cook, pound rice and give birth to children......."[685]

No historical evidence of the school education of ladies is found. However, the upper strata of the Muslim ladies received education if they wanted to. There was no prohibition

---

[683] Kenneth Ingham, <u>Reformers in India, 1793-1833</u>, p.48.
[684] <u>H. V.</u>
[685] Abbe J. A. Dubois, p. 94.

as far as learning was concerned. Due the existence of the Parda system, the women could not go out to educate themselves. As such, the nobles and other high –ranking officials, used to themselves teach the womenfolk of their family, in the house itself. Sometimes aged men also were appointed to impart knowledge to the ladies. Khaireeyat-un-Nissa Begum, the daughter of Mohammad Qutb Shah, built a mosque at Khairatabad for her teacher, Mullah Abdul Malik. It shows that the Qutb Shahi Princesses were educated.[686] The girls usually got their education from their father, brother, elder sisters etc. Sometime, the lucky ones got some taught domestic chores. The lower classes seldom received any education.

The Queens and the other ladies from high-ranking families donated or built schools for imparting education to the poor students. Hayat Bakshi Begum built a residential school that had 125 rooms.[687] This school was free of cost for all the students coming ther to gain knowledge. The daughter of Hayat Bakshi Begum, Khatija Sultana, was a learned lady who patronized literature and art.[688] Another learned ladyof the Qutb Shahi period was Khaireeyat-un-nissa Begum. She was the daughter of King Muhammad Qutb Shah. She had built a mosque at Khairatabad for her

---

[686] Rafat-e-Rizwana, Qutb Shahi Ahat Ki Begamat, A. P. Research Journal, vol.7, 1990.
[687] Nasiruddin Hashimi,.
[688] Rafat-e-Rizwana.

teacher, Mullah Abdul Malik which clearly proofs that she was tutored by an eminent scholar.

The courtesans and the dancers were also well educated. They were witty and charming. Chanda Bibi was a famous courtesan during the period of the second Nizam.[689] She was well educated and much talented in the art of music and dance. She could hold discussion with scholars on poetry collections in Persian and Hindi. She has written beautiful Urdu couplets, which she collected in a book and presented it to the British Resident of Hyderabad. She was able to win over several high-ranking nobles and European officials because of her wit and humour. She enjoyed so much power and popularity that she sat in the court of the Nizam every day. When she died she left behind a property worth crores of rupees. The Telugu contemporary records say that the prostitutes were well versed in the texts concerning the physical relationships.

RECREATION

The people of Andhra Desa had past time activities. The coming in of the Muslims and the Europeans increased the number of such activities. The boys and girls had number of games and amusements. "These are often curiously similar to those of the children of western nations."[690] Some of the

---

[689] Dr. Sadiq Naqvi, <u>Mahalakha Chanda</u>.
[690] W. Francis, p.41.

games that the boys of Andhra Desa played, were similar to the ones played by the boys of the English nation.

The little boys played with marbles and tops.[691] The boys also played hide and seek by tying the eyes of a boy with a cloth and he caught the rest of them, they also played Gonibilla, Banthulu, etc. the British brought in the game of cricket, and the boys played with a brick for a wicket. The boys also flew kites.[692]

Some of the games played by the girls of the Andhra Desa were, hide and seek, games played with cowries, and the Kolattam. The girls also played with dolls. Doll's weddings were frequently celebrated. Dancing was the main active amusement. Singing and dancing with clasped hands, jumping and skipping were the other favourite pastimes. A game peculiar to the Deccan was called Phokdi Phu and it was a favourite past time activity of the girls.[693] The other game mentioned was Dhan Dhanki. The ladies liked listening to music, to play Maddela, Veena, Tambura, and cymbals, they also loved to swing.

Chaugan or polo and Kabaddi were the game, which was enjoyed by the Kings and the public.[694] Infact, the game of Polo was brought to Andhra by the Muslims. Chess was

---

691 H.V. and W. Francis.
692 C.F. Brackenbury, p.74.
693 Mohammad Quli Qutb Shah, Kulliyat.
694 ibid.

a prevalent game. Local Rajahs patronized it.[695] The royalty and nobility went on hunting and excursions to various places in the kingdom.[696] The royal ladies accompanied the King on his hunting expeditions and hunted the birds with their pet hawks. Abdullah Qutb Shah visited the port city of Masulipatnam in the year along with the members of his family.[697] He is said to have visited the quarters of the European merchants and the Dhobi Ghat. There he witnessed how the fisherman caught fish. The Kings also loved to go for sight seeing during the rainy season. The King and his party went nearby places for a week or so.[698] The King accompanied by his nobles went on hunting expedition in the rainy season. At Hyderabad eagles were sported as birds of game and hawking was extensively prevalent. As such crows were very few in the city.[699] Another popular game that the royals enjoyed watching was wrestling.

The Royals of Andhra Desa were also interested in dance and songs. All the Kings patronized dancers of his choice and granted large sums of money and gift to his favourites. History has recorded that the Qutub Shahi kings of Golconda patronized Kuchipudi dancers. The Bhamakalapam and Gollakalapam of the Ku8chipudi

[695] Dr. S. Krishan, <u>The Vastavai Family of Peddapuram, 1550-1850</u>, Ph. D, Thesis, Andhra University, 1986.
[696] Mirza Nizamuddin Ahmed Saidi, <u>Hadiqatus Salatin</u>, ed. Ali Ashgar Bilgrami.
[697] Mirza Mizamuddin Ahmed Saidi, p.224.
[698] ibid., pp.31-33.
[699] Enugula Veeraswamy, <u>Kasiyatra Charitra</u>, p. 29.

dance are said to be composed by Siddhendra Jogi of the 17ᵗʰ century.[700] In order to direct and purify the art of dancing from the prostitutes he initiated and trained a whole clan of Brahmin boys into the art of dancing. The King made a perpetual grant of the village Kuchipudi to the Brahmin troupe who performed the dance drama in that village situated between Vijayawadaand Masulipatam in 1678 A. D., the King Abul Hasan Tanashah, was on a tour accompanied by Madanna, his Prime Minister. At night they heard the sound of Ghungarus or anklets. On inquiry it was found out that the sounds were from a temple where the Brahmin boys were dancing. On witnessing the dance, the King was greatly affected and he gave away the entire village as Inam to the Brahmin families engaged in the art of dancing. King Muhammad Quli Qutb Shah mentions several Ragas in the Lavazinate Shahi of his book.[701] the mentioned in the book are Mugat, dhansari, Shankara Bharan, Sri Raga, Malhara and Ramkari. In another couplet he mentions the insrtrument Tabla that was played by the musicians. It is believed that some of his poems were set to music and were sung by the professional singers. He composed poems even on the beauty of the dancers. He fancied them in their colourful dresses. His couplet is given below:

---

[700] B. Ramaraju, <u>Folk Arts of Andhra Pradesh</u> in <u>South Indian studies</u>, ed. H. M. Nayak & B. R. Gopal.

[701] Muhammad Quli Qutb Shah.

"Haidar Mahal Muhabbat wa Ishq Ka Jalwa Gaye,
Aur Yazdani Nagme Bajaye".
The other couplet goes along thus:
"Haidar Mahal Men Dayam Haidar Ka Jalwa Gao
Ars Asman Dharat Par Nusrat Tabal Bajao"

One of the favourite recreations of the Kings was to watch the ladies singing and dancing.[702] As such on almost all occasions the dancing girls were present. On King's birthday, the Luliyan danced and played the instrument called Mandal Nawaz.[703] on the Birthdday of the Paigambar Mohammad, on the arrival of some dignitry, on the occasion of marriage, on other festivals, the dancing girls were invited. The famous nautch girls under the Qutb Shahis were Tramati, Bhagamati, and Premamati.[704] The vocal music was very much in existence as they are shown teaching their disciples. They were all Hindu converts to Islam. These girls also taught their art to their girl disciples. "The royal palace had a portico where the musicians come several times a day to play upon their instruments for the King".[705] The Kings loved to be entertained by the musicians who played both vocally and instrumental music. It is said

---

[702] Mirza Nizamuddin, op.cit.

[703] ibid., p.34-40.

[704] S. Dasarathi, <u>Bhagamati, Taraamti, and Premamati in Miniatures of A.P. State Museum</u>, unpublished paper, Oriental Manuscripts Library.

[705] Thevenot, p.132.

that a particular Qutb Shahi King could not go to sleep without hearing these.[706]

During the reign of Nizam II of the Asaf Jahi family, Chanda Bibi was the most famous courtesan. She was an accomplished dancer and singer. She also wrote beautiful couplets in Urdu, which she complied in a book and presented it to the British Resident. The king did not only patronize her but several nobles were her fans. Even the British Resident was said to be enraptured by her beauty and drains. When she died, she lift behind Crores in cash, jewelry, and lands.[707] similarly, the source of a later date gives ud the region by extending patronization to the artists. The kings of Vijayanagaram were patrons of fine art and literature.[708] So they got some dancing girls trained according to the principles laid down in <u>Bharata Sastra</u> (the art of theatrical learning) and <u>Sangeeta Ratnakara</u> (the treatise dealing with music). These girls would give performances on festivities and whenever any guests paid a visit to the ruler. The important nobles too were very fond of music and dance and spent their leisure time in music and dance. Raju Chundoo Lal, was the Pesher of the second Nizam. His major recreation too was music and literature. "At about midnight his business is closed, and he is them attended by singers and musicians, and by a number of

---

[706] Niccolo Manucci, <u>Storia Do Mogor</u>, vol.III.

[707] Gulam Samadani Khan Gauhar, <u>Hayathe Mahalaqa</u>, 1324H.

[708] Enugula Veerasamy, p.204.

persons who are eminent for their learning, their skill in poetry, or for any other polite attainment, with whom he converses for about hour, and then retires to rest".[709]

The lower class of men played games of cards and gambled a lot. The upper caste also played cards but for small stakes only.[710] The mea of all classes indulged in cockfighting.[711] The people would keep petcocks, fed them nicely to fight and ultimately get killed. Sometimes, the cock race was also organized. During the festival of Sankranthi, or on certain special days variety of cocks in different colours could be seen.

Another popular game of the common masses was wrestling. It was equally popular amongst the royals and the common people. It was known as Kustipattalu and Dandapatalu in the local language.[712] The wrestlers adopted different tricks during the fight. The Telugu New Year's Day was the great occasion for driving pig. It was organized by the Boya caste.[713] It aroused great excitement in the young and the old. The other recreation of adults was the Pulijudam.[714] It was played with stones on any surface marked out with a diagram. It was a game of two players. Ramfight, buffalo

---

[709] Henry George Briggs, <u>The Nizam his relations with the British Government</u>, vol. I, London, 1861.

[710] W. Francis.

[711] <u>H. V.</u>

[712] ibid.

[713] W. Francis, op.cit.

[714] C. F. Brackenbury, p.74.

fight, puppet show, magic show, and monkey game were the other entertainment.[715]

During festivals the Hindus went to fairs in large numbers. There they enjoyed watching "the puppet players and tumblers with their exquisite tricks".[716] The dancing girls performed at the temples whenever a festival took place. "Others bring charmed snakes and vipers in baskets, which they let loose, and with their hands put in again, piping unto them, and receiving their attention".[717] the acrobats with their fine action humorous dialogues captivated the audience.[718] Their stature used be us this and erect as an arrow. When they walked slow and smooth as water, while marching fast they resembled the fast blowing wind. Their movements were such that not only humans but also even angles loved to behold them. Women who had very nimble and agile body performed the acrobatic feats. The foreigners were very much bewildered by their show of agility and excellence.[719] A record of 17th century tells about the tragic death of a female acrobat Vellakka, who while performing some feat on a pole fell and died on the spot and hero stone was set up in her memory.[720]

---

[715] Anirudha Ray, <u>4 cities of Deccan, 1776</u>, <u>Itihaas</u>, vol. XII, 1984.
[716] <u>Methwolds Relations</u>, p.20.
[717] ibid.
[718] Muhammad Quli Qutb Shah.
[719] John Fryer, p. 89.
[720] Aniruddha Ray, op. cit.

A favourite amusement was to attend the shows given by the nomadic artists. Bommalatam a marionette display was very common.[721] A cotton screen was erected, backed by lights, and dolls made of oiled paper were held up on sticks and moved about, while the action was explained or commented on by singers behind the screen. The people traveled round the villages and give a performance wherever they could secure sufficient patronage.[722] Contributions took the form of money or of oil for the foot-lights. Scenes from the 'Ramayana' and the 'Mahabharata' and the story of 'Desing Raja' of Gingee were the favourite plays. Sometimes the men and women of other settled castes, such as the Oddes, Kamsalas and Kammaras gave performance among themselves. The Dommaras also traveled round and gave gymnastic and acrobatic displays. The Jogs sang songs to the accompaniment of a drum and a tambourine. Another favourite play was Chenchunatakam, which related the amours of the God Obalapati, with a Chenchu girl. The plays were generally based on Hindu mythology, and are regarded as religious performance. They were acted at nights in the central street of a village. The spectators sitting round in a circle.[723]

The musical instruments of the people were drums, clarionets, cymbals, kettledrums, trumpets, flageolets,

---

[721] C. F. Brackenbury, op. cit.

[722] W. Francis, op. cit.

[723] John A, C Boswell, p. 215.

flutes, lutes, and violins with five strings, but all of rude description. The vocal music was sung by wandering men, in the form of Harikathas, Tolubommalats, Bhagavatams, and Tandanana stories. They were performed with the patronage of the temples. Most of these reveled in the purity of the Karnataka style of music, totally unaffected by the interaction in music that was going on in the royal courts. Yakshaganam was another popular item of song and dance among the masses.[724] Vidhinataka was a play, which was performed in the streets, the Saivite poets with missionary zeal introduce it.[725] The subject matter of the play was drawn mostly from the poets with missionary zeal. The village chief invited them to perform in the villages. After performance they went around the houses of the villagers and collected whatever was given. Pulivesham or Tiger Dance was a popular one-man dance performed during Dasara and Moharram festivals. Able-bodied men put on a modest cloth and had their whole body pained with stripes of a tiger. They also put on fabulous make up and put on a heavy tail. Burrakatha, puppet show and monkey show were some other favourite shows that the people flocked to watch and enjoy.[726]

---

[724] Dr. D. N. Verma, Music and Dance during the Qutb Shahi Rule.
[725] B. Ramaraju, op. cit.
[726] Aniruddha Ray, op. cit.

INTEGRATION OF CULTURE

An integration of Hindu and Muslim education could be visuailized in the caste of the Kayasthas. They attended the Madarsas wherethe Muslim population sent their children for learning. The Hindu migrants were from north India. They had become the resedents of Andhra Desa during the reign of the Asaf Jahs. Their children received education in Persian and Arabic. They were educated at the Madrasas by the Mullas. Like the Muslim children, they too had the ceremony of Bismillah before starting their learning. As they had their education like any other Muslim, they received government jobs very easily. They could talk fluently in Persian and Urdu. They also adopted the court manners very easily.[727]

The natives conversed with each other in Telugu. The Muslim migrants generally spoke the language of their native lands. But for conversation with the other Muslims they used Persian. However, it was not possible for everybody to be able to learn Persian, which was incidentally the court language. There was an urgent need for a lingua franca to be developed if conversation with each other and with the locals was to be done. The Qutb Shahi Kings would issue the Royal Farmans in both Telugu and Persian. Over a period, a language, which was a mixture of Persian and

---

[727] Karen B. Leonard, <u>The Kayasthas of Hyderabad</u>, Ph. D. thesis, University of Wisconsin.

Telugu, came into being. The development of 'Daccani' as a language is an example of the integration that had taken place amongst the people of Andhra Desa in the years 1600 AD and 1800 AD. It had its origin in the 14th century in the Bahamani Kingdom. However, it flourished in the Andhra Desa during the period of the Qutb Shahis who patronized the language. It became the lingua franca of the people of Andhra. Several Telugu words found a place in the Dekkani Urdu, as it slowly came to be known as. It was the link language of the common people. The Sultans patronized several Dekkani poets like Wajhi, Mulla Khiyali, Firoz, etc. They composed beautiful poems and mathnavis in Dakhni. It gained popularity with each dynasty and during Asaf Jahis it had become so popular that it was also spoken in the court. Several Urdu words also entered into the Telugu lexicon.

The Deccani language was made use of by the King Muhammad Quli Qutb Shah. He deliberately ignored the Persian words and used Deccani words in its place. For Khuda i.e. God, the words used by him were Swami, Miranjan, Jagat Ke Gosain etc. His poems are a treasure of such words. It shows that the Kings were very much interested in the common langyage i.e. Deccani Urdu.

MEDICINE

The Hindu form of treating the people of their ailments was through Ayurveda. The local medicine men used various herbs to treat the patients. With the arrival of the Muslims, a new treatment called Unani was brought in. the Europeans brought in the modern way of treating patients and were experts in operations.

One of the frequent diseases that occurred in the region was small pox.[728] A disease, which he called as "Akeron" generally, occurred in the small children. It inflamed the tongue and the month. The main cause for it was the great heat. The parents kept their children cool by giving them some herbs from time to time. Sometimes, it even affected the "guts" and the "fundament" and led to the death of the child. One major fatal disease was cholera or Moderchin.[729] It was treated by the cauterization of the feet or by binding the patient tightly.

In the verses of Vemana, we find the medicinal cure for some diseases. He says that the when a dog bites a man them lime juice should be applied on his head. It will cure him of the poisonous effects of the bite.[730] The use of herbs for the treatment of various ailments has been mentioned in the contemporary literature. The wives the help of the

---

[728] M. Thevnot, p. 147.
[729] ibid., p.151.
[730] S. Pratap Reddy, <u>Andhrula Sanghika Charitra</u>.

herbs for keeping their husbands under their control.[731] Similarly, the daughter in law used the medicine to stop the mother in law from talking. The men were said to be using some sort tonics for their physical vitality in order to visit a prostitute. The medicines used for making a man enslaved to a lady were described as being of green colour. The prostitutes mostly used it. When a lady was suffering labour pains, they were given the intoxicating drink Toddy so as to provide some relief to them from the insufferable pain. The wives of the barbers acted as mid wives and helped in the delivery of babies. The men performed the surgeries on the patients. Some had gained widespread popularity for their accomplishments in surgery.

When the Muslims came to the Telugu region, they brought the Unani form of medicinal treatment with themselves. The Hakims as the doctors were called utilized the medicinal properties of the various foods articles. The Unani medicine could be seen as a product of the culinary art.[732] The medicines mostly consisted of Halwa, Murrabah, rose or promegranate Sharnat, mint, apple or ginger preserve and etc. practitioners of the Unani medicines have suggested the classical association of Khichdi with Ghee and Achar. The Hakims said that it was good for the blood circulation.

---

[731] H. V.

[732] Marie Delphine Roger, Cookery during the Qutb Shahi period, unpublished paper, Oriental Manuscripts Library.

The Unani Hakims said that for the drugs to be effective, they must be taken with pleasure.

In a Unani treatise, certain combinations of food have been prohibited from consuming.[733] It also tells us the different kinds of heavy and light food, which were to be taken during which time. The book also deals with the that a person suffering from tuberculosis should eat. The composition of diets during seasons of the year is also described. The writer advised more curd and less of green leaves during the rainy season. During the winter months, he advised the people to eat red meat fried in ghee and lots of dry fruits. The properties of ready-made dishes are also dealt with. It gives us information the usefulness of one food to counter attack the allergy caused by the kind of food consumed. For example it says incases of the bad effects caused by taking quail soup, one will get relief if one eats Halwa.[734] Rhubarb or Rewand Chini and powdered common seed or Zira taken in limewater treated the looseness of the bowels.[735]

At the hospital cum medical college, called Darush Shifa, free treatment was given to all and sundry but nearly three hundred and fifty patients were lodged and fed at the expenses of the Government. At the cities the Hakims and the Vaids sat in some known places and gave potions

---

[733] S. bin Nooruddin, Zubdat-ul-Hukama.
[734] ibid.
[735] M. Thevnot, pp. 151-152.

and plaisters.[736] The state kept salaried Hakims and Vaids different towns at its expenses, and they were commanded not to charge the patients for treatment of the patients.[737] However, at the same time he says that in other places there were no physicians to treat the local public. The women would themselves treat the members of their family. They would collect the herbs that were known to them and would then give it to the patients.[738]

The allopathic treatment had come to Andhra Desa with the arrival of the European merchants. Some of the travelers like Bernier and Tavernier were doctors by profession. A surgeon named De Lann, Dutch by birth, was staying in Golconda.[739] He had almost become a family doctor for the royalty of Golconda. He treated the King, the Queen Mother and the Queen. He was handsomely awarded for his efforts. Later on, the Europeans started keeping doctors in their factories for treatment of their men. Andrew Munro and Robert Turing were the head surgeons, and James Munro was the surgeon at the English factory at Vizagapatam.[740] When the north coastal areas were ceded to the British, they started the inoculation programme there. During the year 1802 AD, in the Godavary district, Woodia

---

[736] Tavernier, pp. 231-232.

[737] ibid.

[738] ibid, p. 231.

[739] ibid, p.232.

[740] Henry Dodwell, Calender of the Madras Despatches, 1751-1752, p. 137

doctors were employed for the project.[741] Initially, only 7 persons were vaccinated for smallpox. The persons were given some money also as they would be unfit for work for someday. In 1801 AD, orders were passed requesting the Collectors to encourage few intelligent Brahmin doctors in each district to become practioners of inoculation. They were to be given rewards basing on the number of persons inoculated by each of them.[742]

---

[741] Godavari District Record, 1770-1835, pp. 373-392.
[742] Ibid.

CONCLUSION

The establishment of Muslim rule and the arrival of the Europeans on the soil of Andhra Desa brought about many Changes in the society of the region. The present study endeavours to find out the changes that occurred in the society due to the interactions of the Muslim culture, the European culture with the local traditions and culture in-between the years 1600 and 1800 AD in Andhra Desa.

The beginning of the 17th century marks the zenith of the Muslim power in Andhra country. The region was under Muhammad Quli Qutb Shah and its area coincided almost with the present boundary of the state of Andhra Pradesh. The seventeenth century also witnessed the arrival of the European trading companies from Denmark, England, Portugal, France and Netherlands who opened their trading centers called factories on the ports of the kingdom. The 18th century saw the consolidation of the English and the French companies in the trading and the political fields of the region. The century closed with the handing over of the coastal areas and the Ceded districts to the British by the Asaf Jahi ruler in the year 1800 AD.

The Andhra society in-between the years 1600-1800 AD consisted of three main type of people – the Hindus, the Muslims and the Europeans. The social stratification of the time was that the Hindus were divided into the traditional four castes which were further sub divided into a number of sub castes. There was the fifth caste of the untouchables and the sixth caste of the tribals that also lived in the Telugu speaking areas. The Sudra caste was further divided into a number of sub sects during the period under study. A number of new sub castes were also created as a result of the inter mingling of the locals with the foreigners.

One interesting feature of the Andhra society was that there were no major incidents of any class conflicts in the 17th and the 18th centuries, which was a common feature of the other South Indian states. I could find only stray references of the class conflicts. However, the land owning class of people were always treated as superior to the artisan groups. The trouble that broke out due to the distinction of the castes was often in the caste of the Untouchables. The Malas and the Madigas always resented any concession that was granted to either of the two, either by the social hierarchy or by the political authority.

Another important feature of the contemporary society was that there was social mobility witnessed amongst the people of Andhra Desa. There were migrations and immigrations on a large scale during the period under study. A lot of foreigners from the west Asian Muslim countries and from north India in the 17th century, and Hindu immigrants from north and west in the 18th century, came and settled down in the Andhra Desa. They were, infact, invited by the Kings of Andhra Desa to settle down in their kingdoms and after coming here they received patronage from the Kings. A lot of migration of the Telugu people also took place. With the establishment of the Muslim rule, there was a lack of opportunities for the Hindu population. They had become second grade citizens in their own region. As such, they shifted to further south to the Tamil lands, where the Hindu Nayakas received them with open hands. There was also the forced migrations of the Telugu speaking people as slaves to the far eastern countries of South east Asia. Sometimes they were kidnapped by the foreign traders or the circumstances forced them to sell themselves as slaves, to the traders.

There was a rise in the social consciousness of the people belonging to the lower castes in the Andhra Desa. The sub sects of the Sudra caste were trying to come up in the social ladder by becoming literate and by making inroads into the professions of the upper castes. As the lower castes tried to rise up in the society, a decline in the social standing of the upper castes was witnessed. The Hindu political authority who patronized the upper castes, especially the Brahmins, was to longer present. The lands granted to the Brahmins were confiscated by the Muslim government and granted to the religious men of Islam. While the condition of the Sudra caste increased, the upper castes were reduced to poverty. They were forced to take to the agricultural lands in order to make a living. Some of them had to take up employment as accountants under the Sudra headman of the village.

The remarkable feature of the years 1600-1800 AD was the growth of the social reform movements in Andhra Desa. Vemana and Swami Veerabrahmam became famous torch bearers of the oppressed communities. Both of them tried to uplift the downtrodden ones through their teachings. It can be said that their works mirrored the mood of the society. They criticized the blind superstitious practices of the people and also the upper castes and questioned their predominant position in the society. Vemana very categorically stated that by taking just taking birth in an upper caste family, one did not become a good man. It were the deeds of a man that made him either good or bad. Veerabrahmam was treated as Prophet by the members of the artisan communities especilly the Vishwabrahmins. He urged his followers to copy certain features of the Brahmins like applying of the religious mark on the head wearing of the sacred thread and come up. He laid great emphasis on the education of the lower castes and urged them to become literates.

Religion played a very important role in the life of the people of the Telugu speaking region. Widespread changes had crept up into the religious conditions of Andhra Desa in the 17th and the 18th centuries. The predominant position enjoyed by the Hindu religion was shaken. When the region was under the Hindu Kings, the Hindu religious institutions and the priests were in an enviable position. They were patronized by the state and they all lived a life of luxury and power. However, all this changed when the region passed into the hands of the Muslim King. Islam become the religion of the state. As such, Islam flourished enormously in Andhra Desa. It received patronization in both the centuries under study. While in the 17th century from the Qutb Shahi Kings and in the 18th century from the Asaf Jahi Kings. When the region become the Muslim Suba in 1686 AD, Islam received a tremendous boost. The Hindu were persecuted mercilessly and many of them migrated to the other Hindu regions.

With the powers of governance passing into the hands of the Muslim Kings, the religious men of Islam and the Islamic institutions occupied the most important position. Both received unrestrained help by the government for their maintenance and propogation. The region came to have many of their religious institutions like mosques, Khanqahs, Dargahs and the Ashurkhanas. The Islamic missionaries were supported by the rules in spreading the tenets of Islam amongst the non-believers and in getting converts to the religion. Many of the local Hindus were converted to Islam as a result of their religious zeal. Some of the conversions were also of a forced nature.

The Muslim constructed mosques in every village and town that had Muslim population. It has been found that some of such mosques were built on the grounds of the razed temples. It was considered a great religious act to build mosques and hence every Muslim officer and the army general constructed Mosques in the areas under him. The Mackenzie manuscripts are full of incidents that show the fanaticism of temples, Agraharas and the Mathas in some parts of the Andhra Desa. However, it was not a state policy to harass the followers of the other religions. The rules of the Qutb Shahi and the Asaf Jahis dynasties followed the policy of religious toleration. There was freedom of religion for all the inhabitants of the region. Even the foreign traders who came for mere trade and commerce purposes to Andhra Desa were allowed to bulid their churches. The region saw the construction of many Christian churches by the different communities of Europe. Due to this there was intermingling of different cultures. In the due course of time, Hindu population of the region started celebrating the Muslim the festivals. Similarly, the Muslims took part in the festivities of the Hindus.

The village deities had gained in the prominence and the major religious sects had lost the prominent position. Every village had a deity of its own and she was always a Goddess. Annul celebrations were held in her honour. The priests in the village goddess temple and in the annual celebrations were always from the lower order of the caste system. Sometimes even the untouchables were made the priests. The higher castes kept a distance from these celebrations. However, they could not deny the celebrations and afterwards had started participating in them.

The 17th and the 18th centuries also saw the entry of the Christian missionaries into Andhra Desa. Initially they were not very successful but during the period under study, they succeeded in getting converts from all the communities. Some of the forward castes like the Brahmins, Reddys and the Kammas, converted to this new religion. The French Jesuits were very successful in getting converts to their religion. The books on the Christian religion started coming out in Telugu and the Sidle was also translated into Telugu.

Women constitute a very important part of the social system. If their position in the society cannot be ascertained then the clear picture of the society is not visualized properly. During the period under study, women continued to be engrossed in their household chores. There was lack of education and professional equality was completely absent. The lower class women did help their men in the fields etc. yet, the freedom of profession was not [resent. In the higher classes the women never came out of the houses. Some of the upper caste Hindus kept their women under seclusion was not present in the Hindus society as a whole.

The Muslim kept their women under strict Parda or in seclusion. A Muslim house was divided into two different apartments, one was for the gentlemen and the other called Zenana was for the ladies. No outside was allowed inside the ladies' quarters. A young girl of 13 or 14 years of age was never allowed to venture outside and was to always stay indoors. In the higher Muslim societies, the lord of the house employed eunuchs to keep a guard over their womenfolk. A boy of an equal age was taken away from his mother from the zenana quarters and had to live with his fether and other male members of his family. Henceforth, he met his mother and sisters only on festivals or on other important days. However, amongst the lower classes of Muslim the system of Parda was not so strict.

In the Hindu and the Muslim communities the children were married at an young age. The arranged by the elders of the family. The marriage ceremonies in both the Hindu and the Muslim communities went on for several days. A lot of expenditure was incurred for keeping up the family name and prestige, which often in huge debts. Marriages involved a number of rituals. A Hindu marriage was solemnized with the tying of the Thali or the Mangalasutra. The higher castes Hindus, especially the Brahmins, gave dowry to their daughters which was known as Varakatnam.

However, amongst the Sudra and the Muslims bride price was paid. The Muslim called it Mehr and the fourth caste of Hindus called it as Kanyasulkam. Amongst the tribes there was neither the presence of dowry nor of bride price. Their marriage ceremonies were simple and did not involve huge expenditure. Marriage were conducted only after the mutual consent of the bride and the groom.

The Hindus as a rule were monogamous. However, in the absence of children, a man could marry a second or even a third time. However, he had to maintain all the wives. The Muslims were allowed by their religion to have four legal wives. However, this system was followed only by the as the poor could not afford to maintain four wives at the same time. The rich Muslims besides keeping a number of wives also kept concubines and visited the prostitutes too.

The system of divorce was present in the Muslim community. The husband and wife could separate from each other and remarry the person of their choice. The system of divorce, prevailed even in the Sudra caste of the Andhra Desa. However, the upper caste Hindus did not legalize the concept of divorce. Once married, the tie could not to broken. The tribal society also had the concept of legalized divorce. The men and women could remarry after the divorce.

The life of the Hindu windows was full of hardship. They were a neglected lot. Their position in the family, after becoming a widow, became worse than that of an animal.

Hence, most of them supported the system Sati Sahagamana wherein the widows were burnt alive in the funeral pyre of the husbands. However, the young girls who were afraid to immolate themselves, lived the life of a drudgery. They often ran away from homes and became prostitutes. However, in the Muslim society the widow could remarry if she wanted to. The European widows married without any inhibitions. The men in all the societies, including the Hindus, were allowed to marry if their wives had died. The tribal widow also had the right to remarry.

It has been found during the course of the study that the incidence of Sati Sahagamana or the burning of widow was large in Andhra Desa in-between the years 1600-1800 AD. All the contemporary writings of the Europeans report the prevalence of Sati and often cite the examples that they had seen with their own eyes. It was prevalent in all the castes of the Hindu society. However, the tribal society was free from this barbaric practice. The Muslim were against this system and wherever their was a Muslim Governor in the sub divisions of the Kingdom, the women were tried to be dissuaded from committing this act. But the Muslim authorities never passed any rule prohibiting the act as they did not want to interfere in the social customs of the Hindus. The traditional practice position in the society as the upholders of Hinduism was maintained and they also derived material benefits by conducting the rituals of Sati Sahagamana. With the coming in of the Europeans, the practice was condemned and they tried to put a stop to it. However, the act to stop the Sati system was passed only in the year 1822 AD.

Three type of public women existed in the Andhra Desa of the 17th and the 18th centuries. The courtesans and the Devadasis were the women who received utmost importance. These were the dancing girls. While the courtesans danced in the courts of the Kings, the Devadasis danced in the Hindu temple and royalty. They were respected in the society. There was also the ordinary prostitute who also danced but for the general public. There was no taboo attached to a man visiting a prostitute. Several rich men maintained concubines. Some of the rich Muslim men provided their young song with concubines so as to stop them from going astray. The importance of the Devadasis was reduced as a result of the decline of the temple. The King no longer gave grants to the temple which maintained them. The lack of funds forced many of them to take to prostitution. Some became the ordinary dancing girls so as to make a living. All celebrations whether public or private, religious or secular, was not deemed full if it was not accompanied by the dancing girls. The contemporary Telugu literature had condemned this practice.

The change witnessed in the material of the community of the Telugu speaking areas was in the fields of housing, furniture, food, dress and cosmetics. The foreigners brought with themselves the living style and culinary habits of their motherland. The Islamic style and the European style of architectures were added to the already existing Hindu style. The use of modern European furniture increased and locals tried to copy the living style of the Muslim and the Europeans and vice versa. The consumption of the betel leaves which was essentially a local custom was adopted by the Muslim and the English. The local intoxicant Toddy was enjoyed by the Hindus, the Muslims and the Europeans. Several new varieties of fruit and vegetables were brought into Andhra Desa by the Muslim and the European immigrants. While the rich ate grand meals the poor peasants' meals were enough just for his sustenance dress was adopted by the people who were associated with the court at the capital city of Haiderabad. In the rural areas there was no distinction in the dress style of the Muslims and the Hindus, and both were dressed up in the same way. The women of both sects were dressed up in Saree. However, the Europeans continued to dress up in their European style. It was only in the 19th century that the Indians picked up the European style and started dressing up like the English. While the men and women belonging to both the Hindu and the Muslim communities were much interested in the ornaments, the European men did not decorate themselves with any jewelry.

The education of the children was basically in the profession fields. The son taking up the family profession after his father was the practice of the day. Every father taught his art to his son. The knowledge of reading and writing was limited to the Brahmins. However, the period witnessed a tremendous change in the attitude in the people of the lower castes. They took to the art of learning and gaining knowledge. Many of them became well versed in reading and writing. They started to compete with the Brahmins and received patronage from the neo rich of the Sudra community. It has been found that the village had schools for children. However, there is no evidence of the education of the girls.

The Muslim provided education to their young children. The government took it upon itself to provide schools or Madarsas in every mosque, Khanqah and the other religious and public buildings. Several educational institutions were opened. The education provided was mostly free of cost. The teachers were appointed by the government and they received their salary from the government. The education provided in the Madarsas was mostly concerned with region. There were primary and secondary schools and also colleges in the Andhra Desa. The Muslim girls generally received their education at their homes from their family members only. The European missionaries opened the first modern school with English as the medium of instruction. The credit of opening the first schools for the girls also goes to them.

The recreational activities of the people were many. The children played with marbles and kites. The arrival of the

Europeans added the game of cricket to their recreation in the 19th century. Within a short period it became the most famous game. The elders played cards, took great pleasure in cock fighting, wrestling and in gambling. The game of polo was brought to Andhra Desa by the Muslim. The rich Muslims went excursions to the various parts of the kingdom. The Europeans took walks in the evenings. The concept of parties and clubs had started taking shape in the 18th century itself. The local royalty and the nobility started taking part in the European ways of amusements.

The girls played with dolls. They loved to swing and dance. Several games like Pokhari po and yo-yo were also played by them. The royal ladies took part in hunting expeditions along with their men. They also had trained birds of prey which stalked and killed the flying birds. After the European fashion, the ladies from the upper society, had also started partying.

In the medical field, the people of Andhra Desa followed the Ayurveda, Unani and the European style of medicines during the 17th and the 18th centuries. While the Unani way of medication was brought by the Muslims the modern Allopathic treatment was the contribution of the Europeans. In the 17th century itself the Europeans were treating the ailing population from several diseases. The Kings also employed them in treating them of their ailments. The government had opened treatment centers in the capital city and in the village and the towns. It has been found that the men of medicines i.e. Hakims and vaids were appointed in the village and the towns. They provided the people with advice and medicines for their ailments. The treatments were generally free of cost. The Vaids and the Hakims received their pay from the government. The most frequent diseases that frequently affected the people, were the upset of the stomachs, cholera and high fever. The children suffered from the diseases of the month.

Finally it can be said that these social it can be said that social changes reflect the changes that the traditional society of Andhra Desa, was under going in the 17th and 18th centuries, as a result of the exchange of ideas with the Muskim and the European immigrants. The medieval Andhra society was making way for the modern society during this period of time. The origin of the concept of religious toleration and secular state of the modern times can only be traced to the period under study. The social reformers of the 17th and the 18th centuries, paved the way social Reform Movements of the 19th century. An initiation was also made by the lower castes to come up in the society through the medium of education. An effort was made by them to try and uplift their position in the social hierarchy of the Andhra Desa.

A beginning was made during the period under study for the improvement in the condition of the women of the Andhra Desa. The first steps in the field of the girls' education and in the abolition of Sati were first initiated only in the 17th and 18th centuries.

At the same time the establishment of the British hegemony over the Telugu speaking areas was also made during this time. The establishment of the British Residency in 1786 AD gave them an open hand to meddle in the internal administration and the external relation of the Nizam of Hyderabad. The phase of the English rule over the parts of India had a initiation here.

While looking at the various fields, one can very definitely say that the medieval society of the Andhra Desa was slowly but surely walking towards the modern era of development and tranquility.

BIBLIOGRAPHY

PRIMARY SOURCES

INSCRIPTIONS

Andhra Pradesh Annual Reports on Epigraphy, 1965 onwards.

Annual Reports of the Archaeological Department of H.E.H the Nizam's Government, from 1914-1915 to 1940-1841.

Annual Reports in Indian Epigraphy.

Annual Reports of the Archaeogical Survey of India.

Annual Reports on South Indian Epigraphy.

Epigraphia Indica.

Epigraphia Indo-Moslemica.

Epigraphia Andhrica.

South Indian Inscriptions.

Inscriptions of Andhra Pradesh, Warangal District, ed. N. V.Ramanayya, 1974.

Inscriptions of Andhra Pradesh, Cuddapah District, P. V. P. Sastry, 1977-78

Cuddpah Inscriptions, ed. N. Venkataramanayya, Madras, 1972.

Topographical List of Inscription from the Madras Presidency, V. Rangacharya, Madras, 1915.

Andhra Pradesh Government Archaeological Series, ed. P. Sreenivasachari, P. B. Desai and N. Ramesan, Hyderabad, 1961.

LITERARY
PERSIAN

Anonymous, Tarikh-i-Golconda.

Anonymous, Tarikh-i-Qutbia.

Girdhari Lal Ahqar, Tarikh-e-Zafrah, Gorkhpur, 1927.

Mirza Nizamuddin Ahmed Saidi, <u>Hadiqatus Salatin</u>, 924 H.-1098 H.\1614-1644, ed. Syed Ali Asghar Bilgrami.

Mir Alam, <u>Hadiqat-ul-Alam</u>, 1800, Hyderabad.

Anonymous, <u>Tarikh-e-Muhammad Qutb Shahi</u>, Department of Archaeology, Hyderabad.

Raja Girdhari Prasad, <u>Shahi Shadi</u>, 1892.

Abdullah Qutb Shah, <u>Dewan-e- Abdullah Qutb Shah</u>.

Syed bin Nooruddin, <u>Zubdat-ul-Hukama.</u>

URDU

Muhammad Quli, <u>Diwan-e-Sultan Muhammad Quli Qutb Shah.</u>

Tabee, <u>Behram-o-Gulbadan.</u>

Ghawwasi, <u>Mina Satwant</u>.

Ghawwasi, <u>Saif ul Mulk</u>.

<u>Ghulam Samadani Khan Gougher, Hayathe Mahalaqa, 1906.</u>

Mulla Wajhi, <u>Qutb Mushtari.</u>

TELUGU

Ayyalaraju Narayanamatya, <u>Hamsavimshati</u>, Publ. Vavilla Ramaswamy Sastrulu & Sons, Madras, 1964.

Ponnaganti Telanganarya, <u>Yayaticharitramu</u>.

Palavekari Kadiripati, <u>Suka Saptati</u>.

Dittakavi Narayana Kavi, <u>Rangaraya Charitra</u>, 1790.

Enugula Veeraswamy, <u>Kasiyatra Charitra</u>, ed. P. Sitapati, Hyderab, 1973.

C. P. Brown, ed. <u>The Verses of Vemana</u>, 1892.

Venkatadhwari, <u>Viswagunadarshanamu,</u> Tr. Venkata Ramakrishna Kavulu,

SHATAKAS

Adidamu Surakavi, <u>Ramalingeshwar Shatakamu</u> in Nidadavolu Venkat Rao's <u>Shataka Samputi</u>.

<u>Chowdappa's Shataka</u>, in Vedam Venkatakrishna Sharma's Shataka <u>Vangmaya Sarvasyamu</u>.

Ganganapalli Syed Hussain Das, Ganganapalli Hussain's Shatakas in Vangoori Subba Rao's, Shataka Kavula Charitra.

Koochimanchi Timmanna, <u>Kukkuteshwara Shataka</u>, ed. Swami Shiva Sharaswami, <u>Shataka Samputi</u>.

Ramalingaraya, <u>Sri Giri Mallesa Satakamu</u>, Sataka Samuchchayamu, Andhra Sahitya Parishad, Kakinada, 1933.

Malampalli Mallikarjuna Panditaradhyulu, Sri Syamalamba Satakam, Sataka Samuchchayamu, Andhra Sahitya Parishad, Kakinada, 1933.

Vaddikasula Venkanna Kavi, <u>Shatru Samhara Venkatachala Shatakamu</u>.

Anonymous, <u>Venugopala Shataka.</u>

Bhalla Perakavi, <u>Bhadragiri Stakamu, Bhadrachalam</u>, 1750 A. D.

Chengala Raya Kavi, <u>Madana Gopala Shatakamu</u>.

Vemana, <u>Vemana Shatakamu</u>, S. Pratap Reddy, Social History of the Andhras.

Tallapaka Tirumalacharya, <u>Venkateshwara Shataka</u>, in Vidwan Vedam Venkatakrishna Sharma, <u>Shataka Vangmaya Sarvaswamu</u>.

KAIFIYATS

Colonel Gordoin Mackenzie, <u>Mackenzie Manuscripts.</u>

T. V Mahalingam, ed. <u>The Mackenzie Manuscripts, vols. I&II, Madra,</u> 1972 &1976.

TRAVOLOGUES

Abbe Carre, <u>The Travels of the Abbe Carre in India and the Near East, 1672-1674</u>. Tr. Lady Fawcett, ed. Charles Fawcett and Sir Richard Burn, New Delhi, 1990.

Abbe J.A Dubois, <u>Hindu Manners, Custom and Ceremonies</u>, ed. Henry K. Beauchamp, Oxford, 1897.

<u>The Voyage of Peter Floris</u>, ed. W. H. Moreland, Hakluyt Society, London, 1934.

John Fryer, <u>A New Account of East India and Persia being 9 years' Travels, 1672-1681</u>, ed. William Crooke, The Hakluyt Society, London, 1909.

<u>India in the 17th century- Memoirs of Francois Martin, 1670-74</u>, vols. I&II, Tr. Lotika Varadrajan.

<u>The Diaries of Streynsham Master, 1675-1680,</u> vols. I&II, ed. Sir Richard Carnac Temple, Indian Record series, London, 1911.

Samuel Purchas, <u>Purchas His Pilgrims</u>, vols. III-X, London, 1905.

<u>Voyage en Inde du Comte Modave, 1773-1776</u>, ed. J. Dolche, Paris, 1971.

<u>The Account of Antony Schorer</u>, ed. W.H. Moreland, <u>The Relations of Golconda</u>, Hakluyt Society, London, 1930.

<u>The Account of William Methwold</u>, ed. W.H. Moreland, <u>The Relations of Golconda</u>, Hakluyt Society, London, 1930.

<u>Annonymous Relations,</u> ed. W.H. Moreland, <u>The Relations of Golconda</u>, Hakluyt Society, London, 1930.

Dr. Heynes Journey, <u>Observations made on a toue from Samulcottah to Hyderabad, 1798</u>.

<u>The Travels of Thevenot and Carreri</u>, ed. Suredranath Sen, New Delhi, 1949.

<u>Tavernier's Travels in India</u>, ed. V. Ball, London, 1889.

<u>Bernier, Travels in Mogul Empire</u>, vols. I & II, 1916.

Thomas Bowery, <u>A Geographical Account of the Countries Around the Bay of Bengal, 1669-1679,</u> ed. Lt. Col. Sir Richard Temple, Hakluyt Society, London, 1905.

Francis Buchanan, <u>A Journey from Madras through the countries of Mysore, Canara, and Malabar in 1800.</u>

Niccolo Manucci, <u>Storio Do Mogor</u> vols. I-IV.

FARMANS AND SANADS

Yusuf Hussain Khan, <u>Farmans and Sanads of the Deccani Sultans</u>, Hyderabad, 1980.

Yusuf Hussain Khan, <u>Selected Waqai of the Deccan</u>, 1660-1671, Hyderabad, 1953.

<u>Newsletters, 1767-1799, Mawab Mir NIzam Ali Khan's Reign</u>, The Central Records Office, Hyderabad Govt., 1955.

<u>Framans and Sanadas of the Deccan Sultans, 1408-1687 A. D.</u>, State Archives, Govt. of A. P., Hyderabad, 1980.

EAST INDIA COMPANY ANY RECORDS

W. Foster and F. C. Danvers ed. <u>Letters Received by the East India Company from its Servants</u>, vols. I-VI, London, 1896-1902.

Charles Fawcett, ed. <u>The English Factories in India</u>, New Series, vols. I-IV, Oxford, 1935-1936.

William Foster, <u>The English factories in India</u>, vols. I-XIII, Oxford, 1906-1927.

Records of Fort St. George, <u>Masulipatnam Cosultation Book of 1682-83</u>, Madras, 1916.

Records of Fort St. George, <u>Letters To Fort St. George for 1693-94</u>, vol. V, Madras, 1920.

Records of Fort St. George, <u>Letters To Fort St. George for 1684-1685</u>, vol. III, Madras, 1917.

<u>Letters To Fort St. George for 1679-1765</u>, Madras, 1915.

<u>Letters To Fort St. George from subordinate factories in 1688</u>, Madras, 1915.

Henry Dodwell, <u>Calender of the Madras Despatches, 1744-1755</u>, Madras, 1920.

<u>Dispatches from England, 1670-1758</u>, Madras, 1911.

<u>Dispatches to England, 1694-1746</u>, Madras, 1915.

<u>Godavary District Records, 1770-1835</u>, Madras.

<u>Anantpur District Records.</u>

<u>Masulipatnam District Records.</u>

<u>Madras Census Report, 1871.</u>

<u>Madras Census Report, 1901.</u>

Madras Public Consultation, 1771, Madras, 1909.

The Diary and Consultation Book of Fort St. George, 1672-1766, Madras, 1910.

The Diary and Consultation Book of 1686, Madras, 1895.

The Diary and Consultation Book of Fort St. George, 1684, ed. Pringle, Madras, 1895.

J. T Wheeler, Early Records of British India, New Delhi, 1972.

TRANSLATIONS OF DUTCH RECORDS

Letters from India, 1600-1694, India Office, London.

Letters from Seventeen to India, 1614-1620, India Office, London.

Letters from the Governor General to various Factories, 1617-1699, India Office, London.

SECONDARY SOURCES

ENGLISH

Alexander Hamilton, A new Account of the East India's, 1690-93, London, 1811.

Abdul Majeed Siddiqi, <u>History of Golconda</u>, Hyderabad, 1956.

Syed Ali Asgher Bilgrami, <u>Land Marks of Deccan Hyderabad</u>, Hyderabad, 1927.

Syed Ali Asgher Bilgrami and C. Wilmott, <u>Historical and Descriptive Sketch of His Highness, the Nixam's Dominions</u>, Hyderabad, 1884.

C. Srinivas Reddy, <u>Structural Changes and the Declibe of Masulipatnam- A late 17th Century Question.</u>

C. Campbell, <u>Glimpses of the Nizam's Domonions</u>, U.S.A., 1898.

D. R. Pratap, <u>Festivals of Banjaras</u>.

David Ludden, <u>Peasant History in South India,</u> New Delhi, 1989.

Dennis Kincaid, <u>British Social Life in India, 1608-1937</u>, London, 1938.

Dharmender Prasad, <u>Social & Cultural Geography of Hyderabad City. A Historical Perspective.</u>

Dharmender Prasad, <u>Fairs, Festivals and Social Functions of Hyderabad</u>, 1984, Hyderabad.

Dr. M. A. Nayeem, The Splendour of Hyderabad, Last Phase of an Oriental Culture, 1591-1594 A. D.

Dr. Gangadham Appa Rao, Vemana and Sarvajna, Hyderabad, 1982.

Dr. Sadiq Naqvi, The Iran- Deccan Relations, Hyderabad, 1994.

Edgar Thurston and K. Rangachari, Castes and Tribes of Southern India, 1909.

Elliot and Dawson, History of India as told by her own Historians, London, 1871.

G. Krishna, The story of Telugus and their Culture.

G. S. Ghurye, Caste and Race in India, London, 1932.

H. K. Shrewani, The History of the Qutb Shahi Dynasty, New Delhi, 1974,.

Henry George Briggs, The Nizam his History and Relations with the British Government, vols. I & II, London, 1861.

Henry Heras, A Study of the Aravidu Dynasty of Vijayanagara, Madras, 1927.

Hilton Brown, The Sahibs – The life and ways of the British in India as Recorded by Themselves, London, 1948.

Holden Furber, <u>John Company At Work</u>, London, 1951.

H. D. Love, <u>Vestiges of Old Madras, 1600-1800</u>, London, 1913.

J. F. Richards, <u>Mughal Administration in Golconda</u>, Oxford, 1975.

J. T. Wheeler, <u>Madras in Olden Times</u>.

James Talboys Wheeler and Michael Machillan, <u>European Travellers in India</u>, 1956.

J. B. D. Gribble, <u>History of the Deccan</u>, vols. I & II, London, 1896.

Job Sudershan, <u>Great Cloud of Witnesses</u>. Narsapur, 1986.

Karen I. Leonard, <u>Social History of an Indian Caste: The Kayasths of Hyderabad,</u> California, 1978.

K A. NIzxami, <u>Some Aspects of Religion and Politics in India during the Thirteenth century.</u>

K. K Datta, <u>A Social History of Modern India</u>, 1868.

Kenneth Ingham, <u>Reformers in India, 1793-1833</u>, London, 1956.

K. Satyanarayana, <u>A Study of the History and Culture of the Andhras</u>, vol. I & II, New Delhi, 1983.

Om Prakash, <u>The Dutch Factories in India, 1617-1623</u>, New Delhi, 1984.

P. M. Joshi, <u>Textile Industry and Trade in Golkonda</u>.

P. Rama Raju, <u>Muharram folk songs in Telugu</u>, Hyderabad.

Khadavali Balendusekharam, <u>The Nayakas of Madura</u>, World Telugu Conference Publication.

Lester Hutchinson, <u>European Freebooters in Moghul India</u>, Bombay, 1964.

M. A. Muid Khan, <u>Arabian Poets of Golconda</u>.

M. M Ali Khan, <u>The Musings of a Mystic</u>, Hyderabad, 1966.

M. Pattabhirama Reddy, <u>Andhra Pradesh Historical Review</u>.

M. Krishna Kumari, <u>Pancharamas in Medieval Andhra Desa</u>.

Mazhar Husain, <u>List of Urses, Melas, Jatras etc. In H.E.H. the Nizam's Dominions</u>, 1349F., 1940 A.D., Govt. Central Press, Hyderabad,

Moore, Indian Appeal Cases, vols. I-III.

W. H. Moreland, From Akbar to Aurangzeb- A Case Study In Indian Economic History, New Delhi, 1994.

William Theodore De Bary, Sources of Indian Tradition.

Ratna Naidu, Old Cities, New Predicaments, A Study of Hyderabad.

Rev. M. Phillips, Evolution of Hinduism, 1903.

Rama Raju, Muhharam folk songs in Telugu, Hyderabad.

Robert Sewell, A Forgotten Empire, London, 1900.

S. Arasrathnam, Masulipatnam and Cambay, A History of Two Port Towns, 1500-1800.

S. K. T Veeraraghavacharya, History of Tirupati, 1978.

Radha Krishna Sharma, Temples of Telangana, Hyderabad, 1983.

S. Sakuntala, Diamond Mining in the Golconda and Bijapur Kingdoms during the 17th century.

Sha Rocco, Golconda and the Qutb Shahs, Lahore, 1920.

Sadiq Naqvi, Muslim Relgious Institutions and their role under the Qutb Shahs, Hyderabad, 1993.

Sadiq Naqvi, Qutb Shahi Ashurkhsnas of the Hyderabad City, Hyderabad, 1982.

Sinnappah Arasaratnam, Merchants, Companies & Commerce on the Coramandel Coast, 1650-1740, Oxford Press, Delhi, 1986.

Sir Thomas Munro, Summary of the Ceded Districts, 1807.

Siraj ul Hassan, The Castes and Tribes of H.E.H. The Nizam's Dominion, Bombay, 1920.

M. A. Vasunathi, Teligu literature in the Qutb Shahi Period, Hyderabad.

H. K. Sherwani and P.M. Joshi, History of Medieval Deccan, vols. I & II, Hyderabad, 1974.

H. K Sherwani, Muhammad Quli Qutb Shah, founder of Hyderabad, Bombay, 1967.

R. Soma Reddy, History of Religious Institutions of Andhra Pradesh, Hyderabad, 1986.

The Chronology of Modern Hyderabad, 1720-1890, pub. Central Records Office, Hyderabad, 1954.

Tapan Raychaudhari, Jan Company In Coromandel, 1605-1690, The Hague, 1962.

Thurston & Rangachary, <u>Castes and Tribes of Soouth India.</u>

T. V. Mahalingam, <u>Administration and Social Life under the Vijaynagara</u>, Madras, 1969.

V. Ramakrishna, <u>Reform Trends in Andhra: A Historical Survey</u>, Hyderabad.

Mohiuddin Qadri Zor, <u>Qutb Shahi Sultans and the Andhra Samaskarti</u>, Hyderabad, 1962.

V. Sudershan, G. Prakash Reddy, M. Sutyanarayana, ed. <u>Religion and Society in South India</u>, Hyderabad, 1987.

Ziauddin & Desai, <u>Mosques of India</u>, New Delhi, 1971.

URDU

Kamtar, <u>Dastaane Nabab Nizam Ali Khan</u>, 1221H.

H. K. Sherwani, <u>Nizam Ihdn Khutubat</u>, Lecture at Delhi University, 1971.

Mohammad Quli Qutb Shah, <u>Kulliyat</u>, ed. Dr. Sayeeda Zafar, pub. Trakki-e-Urdu Bureau, New Delhi.

Mohiuddin Qadri Zore, <u>Hyat-e-Meer Momin</u>, Hyderabad, 1941.

Zor, <u>Mukaddame Qulliyat-e-Sultan Muhammad Quli Qutb Shah</u>.

Nasir-ud-din Hashmi, <u>Ahde Asafi Ki Kadeem Taleem, 1336 H.-1385 H</u>., Hyderabad.

TELUGU

Arudra, <u>Samaghra Andhra Sahityam</u>, vols. VII-X, Vijayawada, 1990.

<u>Andhra Sahityamu Sanghika Jeevana Pratifalamu</u>.

A.Pathasarathi, <u>Balija Jananagada Samiksha in Vittarikrishna</u>.

N. Gangadharam, <u>Sri Pothuluri gari Jeevithamu Kaliyugatilakamu</u>., Rajamundry, 1950.

S, Pratap Reddy, <u>Andhrula Sanghika Charitra</u>, Hyderabad, 1949.

Dr. Masan Cennappa, <u>Prachina Kavyalu Gramina Jeevana Chitrna</u>.

T. Donappa, <u>Jana Pada Kala Sampada</u>, Vishalapatnam.

ARTICLES

A. R. Ramachandra Reddy, Historical Riddles of Venkatachala Vihara Shatakamu, <u>Itihaas</u>, vol. XVI, 1990.

Aniriddha Ray, <u>4 Cities of Deccan, 1776</u>, Itihaasm vol.XII, 1994.

A. Jagannadhan, Some Aspects of Socio- Economic Conditions in the Ceded District, 1800-1810, <u>Itihaas</u>, vol. IV, 1976.

A. Kamalavasini and B. Sreepadma, Jewellery in Sri Kumatmam Temple Sculpture, <u>Proceedings of Andhra Pradesh History Congress</u>, vol.XII, 1988.

B. Ramaraju, Folk Arts of Andhra Pradesh, <u>South Indian Studies</u>, ed. H. M. Nayak & B. R. Gopal.

Bilkiz Alladin, Cultural Exchange Between The Residency And Hyderabad, Helen B. Butt ed. <u>The Composite Nature of Hyderabad- An Extension Seminar</u>, Osmania University.

Dr. D. N. Verma, The Kalamkaris, Itihaas, vol.VIII, 1981.

Dr. M. A. Muttallib, Salient Features of the Judical Administration of the Asaf Jahis of Hyderabad, in V. K. Bawa, ed. Aspects of Deccan History, <u>Institute of Asian Studies,</u> Hyderabad.

Dr. R. Soma Reddy, Social Awakening Among Certain Oppressed Communities in Andhra during the Vijayanagar Period, <u>South Indian History Congress</u>, Proceedings of VIII Annual Conference, Quilon, 1988.

Dr. R. Soma Reddy, The life Dommaras as Reflected in the Literature and Epigraphs of Medieval Telugu Country, <u>A. P. History Congress</u>, Kakinada, 1984.

Dr. R. Soma Reddy, Revenue farming in Andhra 17th & 18th Centuries, <u>Proceedings of the National Seminar</u> on Agrarian Conditions in Andhra Desa, 17th and 18th Centuries, A.D., Dept. of History, Osmania University, Hyderabad, 1997.

Dr. R. Soma Reddy, Influence of Islam on Indian Culture, Bhakti and Sufi Movements, in <u>Indian Heritage and Culture (Telugu),</u> Telugu Academy, 1988.

Dr. R. Soma Reddy, Traveler's facilities in Medieval Andhra, <u>Itihaas,</u> vol. XIV, Hyderabad, 1988.

Dr. R. Soma Reddy, European Notices of Golconda-Hyderabad (some Social aspects) <u>Souvenir</u>, South Indian History Congress, Hyderabad, 1986.

Dr. R. Soma Reddy, The Worship of Female Deities and its impact on later Medieval Telugu Society <u>Osmania Journal of Social Sciences</u>, Hyderabad, 1982.

Dr. R. Soma Reddy, Cattle wealth of the Hindu Temple in Medieval Andhra, <u>Osmania Journal of Historical Research</u>, Hyderabad, 1982.

Dr. R. Soma Reddy, Rural Settlements, Migration and pattern of Castes composition in Medieval Andhra, <u>National Seminar on Migrations, Caste and Profession in Medieval South India</u>, Department of History & Archaeology, Vishakhapatnam, Andhra University, 1996.

Dr. R. Soma Reddy, Religion as an Integrating Factor in <u>Medieval Andhra Seminar on Religion as a Source of Integration in Indian Society</u>, Sociological Department, Osmania University, 1985.

Dr. R. Soma Reddy, Early History if Islam in Andhra Desa, <u>Indian History Congress</u>, Burdwan Session, 1983.

Dr. R. Soma Reddy, Role of Hindu Matha in the Social life of the Telugu Country during the 15th -16th Centuries, <u>National Seminar on Studies in the Socio Economic History, of Deccan- 15th -19th Century</u>, Department of History, Osmania University and Indian Council of Historical Research, New Delhi, 1977.

K. A. Nizami, Sufi Movement in the Deccan, <u>History of Medieval India</u>, ed. Sherwani & Joshi, Hyderabad, 1974.

K. S. S. Seshan, Hyderabad as seen by the French traveler, Count Modave, in Hyderabad -400, Saga of a city, <u>Association of British Council Scholars</u>, A.P. Chapter, Hyderabad, 1993.

Jagdish Mittal, Deccan paintings as a source of history in V.K.Bawa, Aspects of Deccan History, <u>Institute of Asian Studies</u>, Hyderabad.

J. Sarkar, Hyderabad and Golconda in 1750 as seen through French eyes, <u>Islamic culture</u>, vol.XX, 1936.

Henry Howard, The Golconda Diamond Mines, <u>The Philosophical Transaction of the Royal Society</u>, vol. XII, London, 1677.

I. P. Gupta, Mastulipatnam and the North Coromandel Region during the 18th century, in Indu Banga ed. <u>Ports and their Hinterlands in India, 1700-1950</u>, New Delhi, 1992.

Joseph J. Brenning, Textile Producers and Production in late 17th century, Sanjay Subramanyam ed. <u>Merchants, Markers and the State in Early Modern India.</u>

P. Swarnalatha & P. Sudhir, The Reluctant Weaver: Weaver Discontent in the Nortern Coromandel At The Turn of the 18th Century, <u>Proceedings of the Andhra Pradesh History Congress, vol.XII.</u>

Syed Basha Biyabani, Impact of Early Saints, Sufi of Khuttagulla, Kadiri Taluq, Anantpur District, 16th Century A.D., <u>Proceefings of the Andhra Pradesh History Congress,</u> vol. XV, Nellore, 1991.

Syed Masood Hassan Jafri, The Tradition of Social Amity in the Deccan, 1347-1911 A.D, <u>Itihaas,</u> 1983.

Sarojani Regani, The Shataka Literature, Source Material for A Study of the Social History of Andhra Pradesh, 15th -19th century, in <u>Itihaas,</u> vol. XVI, 1990.

T. Donappa, Vemana, Veerabrahman, <u>Andhra Jyoti</u>, 1973.

W. H. Campbell The One Great Poet Of The People, in V. R. Narla, ed., <u>Vemana through Western Wyes</u>, New Delhi, 1969.

Y. Vittal Rao, Religious Conditions in Andhra, <u>the Journal of the Andhra Historical Research Society</u>, vol.37, 1978.

Y. Vittal Rao, Gunupudi Bhimavaram Copper Plate Grant of Muhammad Kutub Shah of Golconda, 1612-1626, <u>Journal of Andhra Pradesh Historical Research Society</u>, vol.XXII.

C. Ramalakshmi, Literary conditions in Northern Circars under East India Company, <u>Proceedings of the Andhra Pradesh History Congress</u>, vol.I, 1976.

K. Jayashree, The Vipravinodin Community, <u>Itihaas,</u> vol. XVIII, 1992.

M. Kridhnamurty, Mackenzie Manuscript As a sourse of Comprenhensive Historiography, <u>Proceedings of the Andhra Pradesh History Congress</u>.

Mohammad Abdul Waheed Khan, Armenian Cemetry Discovered in the Old city, Hyderabad, in <u>Andhra Pradesh Historical Research Society</u>, vol. XXXIII, 1973-74, ed. Dr. R. Subrahmanyam.

Prema Nandakumar, Religious Movements in South India in South Indian Studies, <u>Dr. T. V. Mahalingam Commemoration Volume</u>, 1990.

Prof. J Tirumal Rao, A case Study of Dakkali, in Castes <u>Communities and Cultural in Andhra Desa, 17th & 18th century</u>, ed. Prof. R.Soma Reddy.

Rafat-e-Rizwana, Qutb Shahi Ahat ki Begamat, <u>A. P. Oriental Research Journal</u>, vol. VII, 1990. (Urdu).

Mulla Wajhi, <u>Sabras,</u> ed. Javed Vishist (Urdu).

Sarada Raju, Sefdom in South India during the Rule of East India Company, in <u>Itihaas,</u> 1973.

S. Dasarathi, Baghmati, Taramati and Premamathi in Deccani Miniatures of A. P. State Museum, <u>unpublished paper</u> Oriental Manuscript Library, Hyderabad.

Marie Delphine Roger, Cookery during the Qutb Shahi period, <u>unpublished paper,</u> Oriental Manuscript Library, Hyderabad.

P. M. Joshi and M. A. Nayeem, Studies in the Foreign Relation of India, from the earliest times to 1947, in <u>Prof. H.K. Sherwani Felicitation Volume</u>.

K. Aiyangar, Abul Hasan Qutb Shah and his Ministers, Madanna and Akkanna, <u>Journal of Indian History</u>, 1931.

P. A. Bhaunani, A Short History of the Foundation and Growth of Hyderabad, Journal <u>of the Hyderabad Archaeological Society</u>, 1917.

B. V. Rao, Telugu literature and Qutb Shahs, Triveni, April, 1942.

V. Narayana Rao, The Muhammadan Patron of Telugu literature, <u>India History Congress,</u> Hyderabad, 1946.

Ramachander Reddy, Fresh light on Qutb Shahi invasion of Tirupathi, <u>South Indian History Congress,</u> Hyderabad, 1986.

Jadunath Sarkar, The Old Hyderabad, <u>Islamic Culture</u>, 1937.

A M. Siddiqi, The Qutb Shahs, <u>Journal of Deccan History and Culture</u>, 1950.

V. V. K. Shastri, Mosques of the Qutb Shahi Period, <u>Salar Jung Museum Seminar</u>, 1983.

T. I. Poonen, Early History of the Dutch Factories of Masulipatnam and Petapoli, 1605-1636, Journal of Indian History, vol. 27, 1949.

<u>JOURNALS</u>

<u>Islamic Culture.</u>

<u>Indian Historical Quarterly.</u>

<u>Itihaas.</u>

<u>Journal of Andhra History and Culture.</u>

<u>Journal of Andhra Historical Research Society.</u>

<u>Journal of Hyderabad Archaeological Society.</u>

<u>Journal of Indian History.</u>

<u>Proceedings of Indian History Congress.</u>

<u>Proceedings of the South Indian History Congress.</u>

<u>Sabras (Urdu).</u>

GAZETTEERS AND MANUALS

W. Francis, Gazetteer of the Anantpur District, 1905.

C. F. Brackenbury, Cuddaaph District Gazetteers, Madras, 1915.

Edward Thornton, A Gazetter of the territories under the Government of the E.I.Co. and the Native states on the continent of India, vols. I-IV, London, 1854.

I. R. Hemingway, Madras District Gazetteers, Godavari, vol. I, Madras, 1907.

W. Francis, Madras District Gazetters, Vizagapatnam, 1907.

Gazeetter of the Nellore District, Madras, 1907.

Imperial Gazetter of Hyderabad state, Calcutta, 1909.

Imperial Gazetter of India, Oxford, 1908.

Gordon Mackenzie, A Manual of the Kistna District, Madras, 1883.

John A. C. Boswell, Manual of the Nellore District of the Presidency of Madras, Madras, 1873.

D. F. Carmichael, Manual of the District of Vizagapatnam, Madras, 1869.

Narahari Gopalakristnamah Chetty, <u>A Manual of the Kurnool District</u>, Madras, 1886.

Morris, <u>Manual of the Godavari district, Madras</u>, 1878.

T. J. Malidy, <u>Manual of the Ganjam District</u>, Madras, 1882.

J. D. B. Gribble, A Manual of the district of Cuddapah, Madras, 1872.

UNPUBLISHED THESES

Dr. R. Soma Reddy, <u>History of Religious Institution in Andhra Desa from A.D. 1300-1600, Ph. D. thesis,</u> Osmania University, 1980.

Karen B. Leonard, <u>The Kayasthas of Hyderabad city: Their Internal History, and their Role in Politics and Society from 1850 to 1900</u>, Ph D. thesis University of Wisconsin, 1609.

Syed Naimatullah, <u>Deeni Madarsas of Hyderabad</u>, M. Phil. Dissertation, Osmania University.

A Venkateswara Rao, <u>History of the Kalamkari Industry of Masulipatnam during the 17th and 18th centuries</u>, 1990, Ph.D. Thesis, Osmania University.

S. Krishna, <u>The Vastavai Family of Peddapuram, 1550-1850</u>, Ph. D. thesis, Andhra University, 1986.

Mohammad Ziauddin Ahmed, <u>The Relations of Golconda with Tran, 1518-1687</u>, Ph.D. thesis.

G. Bhadru, <u>Role of the Lambadas in Telangana Armed Struggle in Janagaon Taluk, 1945-1951,</u> M. Phil. Dissertation, Kakatiya University.